The Complete Guide to Critical Thinking, Stoicism & Emotional Intelligence

3 Books in 1

WINSTON MESKILL

The Complete Guide to Critical Thinking, Stoicism & Emotional Intelligence

3 Books in 1

---

111 Life-Changing Exercises to Build Discipline,
Sharpen Decisions & Master Emotions in Just 30 Minutes a Day

Table Of Contents

THE ART OF CRITICAL THINKING, LOGIC, & PROBLEM-SOLVING 311

Your Free Gift

As a special thank you for purchasing my book, I am thrilled to offer you four FREE exclusive downloads designed to enhance your emotional resilience and critical thinking skills.

1. **The Resilience Handbook**: Build your resilience with insights into key Stoic principles and the four main skills of emotional intelligence, equipping you to handle life's challenges with calm and confidence.

2. **How to Teach Kids Critical Thinking**: This guide provides engaging exercises tailored to develop critical thinking skills in children, helping them grow into thoughtful, analytical adults.

3. **Applying Critical Thinking Skills in Everyday Life**: Discover practical strategies to seamlessly integrate critical thinking into your daily routine, enhancing your decision-making and problem-solving abilities.

4. **History of Critical Thinking**: Dive into the fascinating evolution of critical thinking and understand its profound impact on modern society.

Inside These Bonuses, You'll Discover:

- **Resilience Strategies**: Techniques to enhance your emotional resilience and maintain inner peace, even in stressful situations.

- **Engaging Exercises for Kids**: Fun activities that make critical thinking accessible and enjoyable for children.

- **Daily Critical Thinking Tips**: Practical advice to improve your reasoning and analytical skills in everyday situations.

- **Historical Insights**: A comprehensive look at how critical thinking has shaped progress through the ages.

And much more...

To download your bonuses, simply scan the QR code below:

BOOK 1

Think Like a Stoic

A 4-Step Blueprint with 10 Powerful Exercises to Make Right Decisions, Identify What You Can't Control, and Master Emotions with Stoicism and Critical Thinking

Introduction

It is impossible for a man to learn what he thinks he already knows.

—EPICTETUS

You are commuting on your way to work, and someone pulls out in front of you. How do you respond?

Try writing down your answer. After you've read this book, I want you to answer these questions again, and see how different your answers are.

Your coworker blames you for a minor work mistake when it's actually their fault. Your boss gets to hear about it. What do you do?

Your romantic partner forgets an event that is important to you: An anniversary, a date night, or a birthday. What is your reaction?

A family member owes you money and has been avoiding you for months. How do you handle this situation?

When answering these questions, try to be honest with yourself. Don't think about what you should do, but what you think you *would* do. Think about how you come to your answers: What motivates the way you would act, and what acts as the impetus for your decisions?

When you come back to these questions after reading the book, you may be astonished by the transformation. Like much philosophy, stoicism can fundamentally change how you look at your life and the world. You will find that you are considering ethical and metaphysical principles in everyday life.

If you are reading this book, you are probably dissatisfied in some way with your life. You may have trouble mastering your emotions and are curious about different ways of regulating your behaviors in a more productive and ethical manner.

At the very least, this was how it was for me. For many years of my life, I worked a stressful job in finance, supplementing my income with prudent investments. To many, I would have been considered successful, but I remained unhappy and unfulfilled. I had trouble having emotional conversations with the people in my life and made a lot of bad decisions. Seeking ways to improve my life, I stumbled across the ancient philosophy of stoicism.

Now that I practice the stoic lifestyle, I am content and fulfilled. After many years of exploring stoicism, I have decided to write a book to share my knowledge and experience. I want others to find a better way of living that comes from stoic teachings.

Once you start living as a stoic, you will find that you are more dedicated to living well. By this, I don't simply mean that you will be making choices that make you happier—though you may well find that this indeed occurs. I mean that you will be making choices that make you a better person, and that gives you a more fulfilling and ethical life. This isn't to say that you are living an unethical life now, only that the ancient philosophy of stoicism gives you the tools for a whole new way of living.

But what is stoicism? Let's find out together.

PART 1:
THE THEORY OF STOICISM

Chapter 1:
Stoicism and You

It is not events that disturb people, it is their judgments concerning them.

—EPICTETUS

Stoicism identifies ethics with the study of how to live well. Rather than focusing on particular ethical quandaries, such as the trolley problem or ticking bomb scenarios, stoicism provides the tools for you to live well in your everyday life. It helps you to find what the ancient stoics called *eudaimonia*: contentment, or flourishing.

To understand the basics of stoicism, it's important to understand the philosophy of mind that underpins it. Stoicism holds that when something happens to you, your mind's first response is an impression: A sensory input. For example, when you are getting hungry, your first impression may be a pang of hunger.

Ancient stoics believed that what separates us from animals is the ability to assent or dissent from our impressions. A dog that has the impression of hunger will eat, if able. By contrast, a rational human being has a choice. We can assent or dissent from the impression of hunger.

By this, I don't simply mean that we can choose whether or not to eat—though that is part of it. Instead, I mean that we can apply our reason to evaluate our impressions. It is a physiological quirk of the human body that the impression of hunger can be the result of thirst or boredom. As rational beings, we can assess a hunger pang and decide whether or not to assent to it. If we have not eaten in some hours, we may assent to the impression and get something to eat. But, if we reason that we are simply thirsty, we may dissent from the impression, and drink some water instead.

You may be asking why this philosophy of mind is important. The answer is stoicism teaches that there is a gap between our impression of something and how we act. The decision of whether to assent or dissent is an exercise of reason. We don't simply act on animalistic instinct, to be driven blindly by our impressions. As rational beings, there is a process by which we can apply our reason.

For a stoic, morality is an extension of reason. In response to an impression, then, we can choose to act ethically.

According to the teachings of the ancient stoics, what is truly good is good in all contexts. If something can be bad for us in certain situations, then it is not the true good. It follows that the only true good is a virtue. By definition, being virtuous is never a bad thing. There is no circumstance in which it is bad to act virtuously.

To really bring this point home, consider one potential good: Wealth. Wealth is often a good thing because it can keep us fed, keep us clothed, and it puts a roof over our heads. However, it is not good in all contexts. Suppose that you were a desperate heroin addict. Wealth would not be a good thing for you then, because you would use that wealth to fund your addiction, leading to disaster.

It follows that wealth is not the *true* good: Even though it can be good to have!

As ethics is the study of living well, it follows that what is good is what allows you to live the best life. As virtue is the only true good, it follows that the best life must be lived virtuously.

Let's bring this thought back to the philosophy of mind, and the gap between our impressions and our actions. In response to an animalistic impression, we can choose whether to assent or dissent. When making this decision, we apply our human reason. In other words, we consider how to respond virtuously.

If something bad happens to you, there is no virtue in feeling sorry for yourself. This does not help you, nor does it help the world. To every impression, we have a choice. We can choose whether to assent or dissent, and that means we can choose whether to assent or dissent from negative feelings. This may sound superhuman—and, to some extent, the perfect stoic remains an aspirational ideal—but by practicing stoic habits and internalizing stoic thinking, you will be surprised by how resilient you will become.

Remember, virtue is the only good, and what is good is what allows you to live the best and most flourishing life. And you can always choose virtue. No matter what happens to you, you can respond with virtue. As such, it is always in your power to live the best life. It is always in your power to flourish and find your state of *eudaimonia*. You are in control.

The philosophy of stoicism is ancient, but it contains lessons that are as relevant today as they were in ancient Greece. Many famous figures, in both history and modern times, have cited stoicism as a philosophy that influenced and shaped them. Previous Secretary of Defense, James Mattis, carried Marcus Aurelius's *Meditations* with him when he was on deployment. Former President Bill Clinton reads *Meditations* every year, and Theodore Roosevelt brought the teachings of Epictetus and Marcus Aurelius on his famous "River of Doubt" expedition. Thomas Jefferson had books by Seneca on his nightstand when he died.

Stoic teaching has not only motivated politicians and leaders, however. Superstar quarterback Tom Brady cites stoicism as an inspiration, as well as Chicago Cubs manager Joe Maddon. Famous actors such as Anna Kendrick, Brie Larson, and Tom Hiddleston mention stoicism as a guiding force in their lives. Finally, stoicism has inspired successful authors like John Steinbeck and JK Rowling, and driven businessmen like Jack Dorsey, the co-founder of Twitter.

Now you can add your name to this illustrious list.

The key takeaway is this: Stoicism is wildly popular because it is maximally applicable, and enables you to be in control of your own life and happiness. It is a fundamentally empowering philosophy that challenges you to be the best and most virtuous version of yourself and to master those emotions that might otherwise lead you to make bad decisions.

Next, we'll look at the history of stoicism, and how it emerged from the most unfortunate of circumstances: a disastrous shipwreck.

Chapter 2:
The History of Stoicism

Misfortune is virtue's opportunity.

—Seneca

When sailing between Phoenicia and Piraeus, the wealthy merchant Zeno of Citium suffered an absolute disaster. A shipwreck sent all of his goods sinking to the bottom of the Mediterranean, along with much of Zeno's wealth. And yet, Zeno survived the shipwrecking and went on to create the ancient school of stoicism in 301 BC. He taught at the Stoa Poikile. The Stoa Poikile was the colonnade in the Agora of Athens and, later, the source of the word "stoic" for those that followed Zeno's philosophies.

When he later died, the following epitaph was given, comparing him to the legendary hero Cadmus who brought the alphabet to the Greeks (Laërtius, 2022/3rd century).

> And if thy native country was Phoenicia,
> What need to slight thee? Came not Cadmus thence,
> Who gave to Greece her books and art of writing?

Zeno did not write down his teachings, but his school survived through the works of his later adherents, such as Epictetus. Though Epictetus died a freeman, a teacher, and a philosopher, he was once a slave. From humble beginnings, Epictetus expanded on the philosophy of stoicism and forged his place in history.

Epictetus's life was not easy. Not only had he been a slave, but he was later banished from Rome with all other philosophers by the tyrant Emperor Domitian. Nonetheless, or perhaps *because* of his trials, Epictetus held fast to the teachings of stoicism and its power to overcome any challenge or difficulty. Epictetus taught that external events are ultimately beyond our control, but that we do have control over how we choose to react to those external events. And, as his life demonstrates, he did not simply talk the talk. Despite dying in great wealth and being admired by eminent figures such as the later Emperor Hadrian, Epictetus lived a life of simplicity with few possessions.

Epictetus's teachings were immortalized in his *Discourses* and *Enchiridion*, written by his student, Arrian. These texts had a profound impact on the Roman statesman and senator, Seneca, tutor to the Roman Emperor Nero. Like other stoics, Seneca believed that philosophy was more than theory, but something to be practiced and incorporated into a good life. And, like Epictetus before him, Seneca lived by his principles. In 65 AD, Seneca was compelled to take his own life by the Emperor Nero, having been (probably wrongly) implicated in a plot against Nero's rule. The consummate stoic to the end, Seneca took his life with calm fortitude, having prepared his estate and organized the disposal of his own body.

Fortunately for the world, Seneca wrote prolifically. His most famous philosophical work is *Letters From a Stoic* (2004/65), constituting one of the most important primary sources for ancient stoicism. In addition to his academic work, Seneca was a dramatist and playwright, famous for the tragedies *Medea*, *Thyestes*, and *Phaedra*.

The final great stoic of ancient history was Marcus Aurelius, Roman Emperor from 161 AD to 180 AD, and known as the last of the Five Good Emperors. Despite his great power and wealth—his official name was Imperator Caesar Marcus Aurelius Antoninus Augustus—Marcus Aurelius was deeply philosophical, writing his *Meditations* as a personal exercise to help him live a more ethical and productive life. Moreover, like all great stoics, Marcus Aurelius practiced what he preached. He did not want to be Emperor, only adopting the position out of a sense of duty. Even then, he refused the Senate's choice to confirm him alone, insisting that he would only take office if his adoptive brother, Lucius received equal powers. Also, Marcus Aurelius took his duties seriously, guiding his empire through the devastating Antonine Plague and the increasing dangers posed by the northern Germanic tribes.

Eminently quotable, his *Meditations* remain hugely influential and popular today. Most readers are struck by how humble and profoundly human Marcus Aurelius shows himself to be: Full of self-doubt, petty irritations, and constant self-exhortation to do better. Written as a personal journal rather than something to be published, Marcus Aurelius was clearly dedicated to becoming a better man, reminding himself to have patience for others and to practice virtuous action wherever possible. His example demonstrates that great stoics don't have to be perfect stoics all the time. The philosophy of stoicism is a skill that is improved upon with effort and time.

These remarkable and influential men came from a range of different backgrounds: From merchant to slave, to Roman Emperor. However, what they all had in common was a profound sense of integrity. Regardless of their varying backgrounds, wealth, and power, all were deeply concerned with how to live a virtuous life and put the philosophy of stoicism into practice. Now, all of them are remembered kindly by history, held up as paragons of their times. All of them were successful. All of them lived to a relatively old age. All of them strove for what they believed was humanity's natural state: A state of virtuous living that brought them *eudaimonia* and goodness.

These ancient examples of stoicism also go some way to demonstrate the core tenets of stoicism itself. All of them faced extreme hardship, in one way or another. Zeno was shipwrecked. Epictetus was enslaved and banished. Seneca was commanded to suicide. Even Marcus Aurelius, Roman Emperor, had to deal with immensely complex and difficult issues to keep his empire stable. However, none of them allowed themselves to despair. Think of what happened to them. We can imagine their first impressions: The profound grief of shipwrecking, the indignity of slavery, the horror of a compelled, violent death, and the heavy burden of a crown not wanted. Despite these impressions, all four of them chose to react according to stoic principles, choosing to act in a virtuous way. Zeno responded to his loss by pursuing wisdom and founding an entire school of philosophy. Epictetus chose temperance, not allowing himself to be defined either by his early slavery or late wealth. Seneca was courageous even in the face of death. And Marcus Aurelius accepted his burden and dedicated himself to justice and fair rule.

Not only did these figures of history endure, but they excelled. And, by following the principles of stoicism, you will be empowered to do the same. But what are those principles? In the next chapter, we'll find out.

Chapter 3:
Stoicism as a List of Principles, Not a List for Life

If at some point in your life, you should come across anything better than justice, wisdom, discipline, courage—it must be an extraordinary thing indeed.

—MARCUS AURELIUS

The main tenet of stoicism is that we choose how to react to external events. We might not be able to control what happens to us, but we can choose how we respond. To live a good life and achieve a state of *eudaimonia*, we should aim to respond in a virtuous manner.

The ancient stoics believed that there were four main virtues to live by: justice, wisdom, temperance, and courage. Modern stoicism has expanded on this list, but some argue that other virtues properly fall under combinations of the fundamental four. For example, kindness is a virtue, but arguably a combination of being patient (temperance), helping those in need (justice), and encouraging kindness in greater society (wisdom).

But what do these four fundamental virtues amount to?

To some extent, they are difficult to pin down with exact definitions. This is a feature of stoicism and virtue ethics, however, rather than a bug. Stoicism asks us to take responsibility for our moral reasoning and our choices. Sometimes it can be hard to see what is wise in a particular instance, or what would be just. However, as long as you are striving for virtue with integrity, and learn from your mistakes, you are living a good, rational life.

Much of modern ethics consists in positing hypothetical situations that test moral systems to breaking point. For example, the trolley problem asks whether we should redirect a train en route to kill five people so that it goes onto another track and kills only one person. Consequentialism—a type of ethics that focuses on the outcome of our actions, rather than why we made them—argues that we should redirect the train to minimize the loss of life. By contrast, deontological systems of ethics—those that focus on the rules by which you live, rather than the outcome of your actions—would say that it is wrong to take any action that would lead to someone's death: On such a theory, it would be wrong to redirect the train.

Of course, there are plenty of nuances and variations on the trolley problem. Questions abound: Is there a difference between action and inaction? Do the ages or occupations of the potential victims matter? But, from the perspective of the ancient stoics, these trolley problem dilemmas and others like it miss the point of ethics. For the ancient stoics, ethics was the science of good living and properly focused on everyday occurrences and principles that apply to general life. Focusing on implausible crisis situations, in this view, is just a distraction from what ethics should be doing.

In other words, stoicism asks us to apply virtuous thought not only to crises, but to our everyday life:

- **Justice:** Justice asks us to act in a way that promotes fairness, equitability, and what is deserved. It might mean sharing our resources or making sure that those who work hard are properly rewarded.

- **Wisdom:** If we are wise, then we do not act shortsightedly, or pursue short-term goods. We use reason to think through the nuances of a problem and weigh up the pros and cons of an action.

- **Temperance:** Temperance is the virtue of moderation. It means tempering your emotions so you don't act on your impressions out of anger or impatience or impetuousness. It also means avoiding excesses that convert pleasures into vices.

- **Courage:** If we are courageous, we are principled and show integrity. This might mean admitting that we are wrong when we make an error, or standing up to a bully to correct an injustice.

You can probably see how these four virtues don't give you a definitive answer to every one of life's problems. Some people have different notions of justice: Those who favor more conservative politics might focus on people being rewarded for hard work without excessive tax, whilst those who are more liberal might instead think in terms of equitability and the dismantling of unjust systems. Both individuals may be concerned with justice and yet have a fundamental ethical and political disagreement. This is fine. However, if both are stoics, they must be able to debate calmly, demonstrating both wisdom and temperance. They also must show courage, and defend their views honestly—and admit when they are wrong.

As such, stoicism is not a list of commandments, but instead an injunction to live in a more reasoned way. A great first step to a stoic life is to consider what justice, wisdom, temperance, and courage mean to you. What opportunities to embody these virtues do you encounter in the ordinary circumstances of your life?

You don't need to fight a war to be courageous, and you don't have to be a judge to uphold justice. Sometimes standing up for someone at work can be a profound act of courage, and makes your mark on the universe in a positive, virtuous way. Admitting your fault in an argument and making concessions can be a mark of great integrity and commitment to justice. Forcing yourself not to have another cookie demonstrates temperance, and is often very difficult!

As an exercise, then, for each virtue, think of one way you can incorporate it into your daily life. When you have determined these opportunities to embody virtue, put them into practice: This day, this week. Though you will learn more about stoicism throughout the rest of this book, it is never too early to commit yourself to a more virtuous and happy life.

Moreover, reflect on the power that is in your hands. Stoicism isn't telling you how to act. It's encouraging you to live your life in the way that you believe to be most virtuous. This book will not tell you how to vote, what job you should have, or whether or not to eat meat. Instead, all I will ask you is to apply your ethical reasoning and live according to your integrity and natural virtue. To sum up, you must think about your sense of justice, wisdom, temperance, and courage, and what they mean to you.

We now have a great sense of the theory and history behind stoicism. Now, let's start thinking about how to apply these philosophies to your life.

PART 2:
STOICISM AS AN INSTRUMENT FOR A MORE FULFILLING LIFE

Chapter 4:
How Stoicism Can Help With Finding a Goal in Your Life

As each day arises, welcome it as the very best day of all, and make it your own possession. We must seize what flees.

—Seneca

The ancient stoics believed that our natural state as humans is a rational state. This is what separates us from animals, who are guided by their impressions alone and cannot assent to or dissent from them.

When we choose to act virtuously, we are applying our rationality to the way we live our lives. The stoics believed that as rational beings, virtue was our natural state. This is why living without virtue leaves us feeling bereft and alone: We are acting contrary to our fundamental nature.

By contrast, when we act according to our nature and live virtuously, we flourish and find happiness.

What is your fundamental goal in life? By this, I don't mean your goal for the day, or even for the year. I don't mean your goal to secure a promotion or to find a romantic connection. I mean the fundamental goal that all other goals are working toward. The reason why you want the promotion or romantic partner.

Many people, when asked about their fundamental goal in life, give happiness as their answer. We want a promotion to advance in our career, bringing us a sense of achievement and increased monetary rewards for our labors. This, we hope, will bring us happiness. We forge romantic connections because we desire love and family, and the happiness that follows.

However, happiness can mean different things to different people. It is important to tease apart related notions, such as pleasure and contentment. In the parlance of stoicism, pleasure is an impression, and is often short-lived. It is the pleasure of a delicious bite of cake, or the feel of the sun against your face. Though undoubtedly a positive feeling, the feeling quickly passes: The cake is eaten, and the sun moves behind a cloud. By contrast, contentment, or fulfillment, is a more lasting good.

The stoics had their own notion of happiness: *Eudaimonia*. As with all ancient Greek, direct translation can be controversial, but it seems that *eudaimonia* is associated with a spiritual and profound sense of happiness. *Eudaimonia* is the result of living well in a spiritual sense, of finding inner contentment, and flourishing by virtuous principles.

Eudaimonia and Spirituality

I have said that *eudaimonia* gestures at spirituality. The "daimon" part of the word is a very early root for the word "demon" today: Though, in ancient Greek, it had no evil connotations.

However, we should not confuse spirituality with religiosity. Though spirituality and religion are clearly compatible, you can achieve *eudaimonia* regardless of what you believe about the origin of the universe and our species.

Once more, it comes down to your own personal understanding of the virtues. Deeply religious individuals may consider honoring God to be part of wisdom, whilst atheists may reach an entirely opposite conclusion. As we have discussed in earlier chapters, rational people can disagree on how best to embody the four, fundamental virtues. As long as you have integrity, and are temperate enough to disagree without hostility, disagreement is more than okay.

What Eudaimonia Is Not

Unlike pleasure or ecstasy, the state of *eudaimonia* is more lasting and consistent. Moreover, it is something that comes naturally with living a flourishing, virtuous life. In this sense, the pursuit of *eudaimonia* is synonymous with the pursuit of living a good life. As such, living a good, virtuous life becomes an end in itself, rather than a mere vehicle to your goals.

Dedicating yourself to living well also avoids the desperate pursuit of temporary pleasure known as the paradox of hedonism. The utilitarian philosopher, Henry Sidgwick (1874), wrote that "the impulse toward pleasure can be self-defeating. We fail to attain pleasures if we deliberately seek them." For example, striving for sexual gratification is unlikely to foster the deep, romantic connections that would ultimately satisfy. Similarly, pursuing drugs and alcohol can result in addiction and the breakdown of your entire life.

By contrast, to find *eudaimonia*, you need only commit yourself to living a good, virtuous life. This doesn't mean that you have to become a monk: Though the stoics teach that temperance is a virtue, temperance should not be equated with constant self-denial. It just means that you should apply your rationality to choose how you respond to the events of life and to take the path that is most virtuous according to your own, reasoned understanding of the four fundamental virtues.

Remember that even other, more wholesome goods may not be suitable ends in themselves. It is good—possibly even virtuous—to strive for wealth, health, and family. Nonetheless, you can be miserable and wealthy. Wealth will not bring you happiness in itself, especially if it is used to fund unwholesome activities that ultimately leave you cold. Relatedly, having your health cannot be an end in itself. Consider Seneca's example. He believed that justice demanded that he kill himself when compelled to by his emperor, and went to his fate with courage. Though you are unlikely to be compelled to suicide by a Roman emperor, you may still find that sometimes you must sacrifice your health to live a good, virtuous life. Even having a family is not a suitable end in itself. The most hurtful of disasters can be the result of actions taken by family members who were supposed to love you.

Stoicism teaches that if these goals are not good in all contexts, they cannot be the fundamental good. For stoics, there is a kind of contradiction in terms if we say that *the* good is sometimes bad. Though wealth, health, and family can definitely be elements of a good life, they are not the end in themselves. In this sense, then, stoicism helps you find a goal in life by stressing that the means and the ends of life are one and the same.

In summary, you don't need to be constantly working toward some ultimate destination. You can lower your gaze from the horizon and look around you. Though it is often virtuous to work toward long-term projects, ultimately, you will find happiness in the present. It sounds almost obvious when put this way, but there is wisdom in its simplicity: The purpose of life is to live it well.

To live well, though, we must remain positive. In the next chapter, we'll consider how you can use stoicism to transform negative events into positive opportunities.

Chapter 5:
Why Being Positive Is Important

He is a wise man who does not grieve for the things which he has not, but rejoices for those which he has.

—Epictetus

The stoic chooses how they react to external events that act upon them. When something bad happens, you have a choice of whether to assent or dissent from the negative impression you experience. This isn't to say that you can choose whether or not the bad thing will happen to you. However, you can choose how to respond. You can choose whether you act impulsively, or if you apply your human reason and act in a way that is virtuous.

When stoicism encourages us to remain positive, this is distinct from forcing a smile. Instead, stoics are asked to respond in a way that is virtuous and productive.

For example, suppose you did not get the promotion you had hoped for. Your first impression of this negative event may be disappointment or depression. You may feel inactive and unmotivated. However, you can choose whether or not to assent to these impressions.

Continuing the example, consider how you might react to this disappointing event in a virtuous way. If you are to embody courage, you will not allow this setback to defeat you. You will not allow yourself to collapse in on yourself. Meanwhile, to embody temperance, you will stop yourself from an impulsive or angry reaction. You will not give yourself over to jealousy and hate toward the individual who got the promotion you had hoped for. This decision will also allow you to embody justice because ultimately it is not the fault of the other person that you didn't get what you wanted. After all, the job was not owed to you. The other person did not steal from you or commit a moral crime, so it is unjust to be resentful toward them.

Most critically, however, you will want to embody wisdom. This means reflecting on the disappointment and understanding what went wrong. If you are wise, you will be able to identify areas where you can improve. Maybe you are lacking some crucial experience, or you did not put your best foot forward in the interview for the promotion. By being wise and identifying these weaknesses, you are granted an opportunity for growth. You can work on getting the experience you need or hone your interviewing skills. And, once you have used this event to grow, you will be in a great position to excel when the next opportunity comes along.

By reflecting on this example, you can see how remaining positive is about more than simply rejecting negative thoughts. Though the idealized stoic may be able to rise above even the natural disappointment of the event, in reality, humans are fallible and suffer disappointment in their lives. Stoicism doesn't ask you to pretend that nothing bad has happened to you: This is toxic positivity and can be as self-destructive as toxic negativity. It is fine to process your feelings honestly. Often, it is virtuous to do so, as it can take courage to face your feelings head-on. The key, though, is to use that disappointment as an opportunity for positive growth.

Another way of looking at things is that a negative, external event is an opportunity to be virtuous. As Epictetus (2008/2nd century) writes:

> What would have become of Hercules, do you think if there had been no lion, hydra, stag or boar— and no savage criminals to rid the world of? What would he have done in the absence of such challenges? Obviously, he would have just rolled over in bed and gone back to sleep. So by snoring his life away in luxury and comfort he never would have developed into the mighty Hercules.

Through adversity and setbacks, you are given the opportunity to grow into your own version of Hercules.

Relatedly, do not make the mistake of thinking that negative events must be met with aggression. Giving yourself over to rage, however righteous it might feel, is intemperate and therefore not virtuous. The only value of anger is as an impetus to necessary action. If you are committed to necessary action anyway, because you are committed to virtuous living, then anger serves no purpose for you.

Just because you do not abandon yourself to anger, however, does not mean that you have to be maximally forgiving, or a pushover. Justice often demands that you stand up for yourself, and you must have the courage to do so for the good of all. Depending on your own interpretation of justice, you may think that some people should be punished for certain actions, or that bullies or evildoers should be confronted—maybe even violently on occasion. On the other hand, such actions should not be motivated by anger. They should be motivated by virtue and reason. Otherwise, you are just a snarling dog, not a rational person.

More generally, try to keep hate out of your heart. Wisdom demands that you should attempt to understand different points of view, even if those differing views seem abhorrent at first glance. If you are talking to someone who is espousing horrible views, listen carefully and try to understand why they believe what they believe. This does not mean that you have to condone evil thoughts. But it does mean that you should try to learn. Once you have achieved empathy, you may be able to use that wisdom to persuade the other person to a better path. This is an effort that requires temperance and courage and aims at a more just world. By adopting stoicism and maintaining your integrity, you will have the resilience to withstand odious views and to correct them in a calm manner that might actually work to make the world a better place.

In this sense, stoicism can be a great help in your existing relationships. If you are committed to virtuous action, you are more likely to be empathetic and curious about your fellow humans. You will be more patient and temperate, less likely to get into arguments or to develop unhelpful grudges. And you will have a profound sense of integrity, preventing you from being taken advantage of, or being unmoored by the actions of unpleasant people. You will have self-respect and respect for others. People will respond positively to that, and your relationships will strengthen as a result.

The key takeaway is this, then: Every bad thing that happens is an opportunity for virtue.

In the next chapter, we'll think more about how we can keep our emotions in check so that we can remain in control in difficult situations.

Chapter 6:
How to Control Your Emotions and Make Right Decisions

Say to yourself first thing in the morning: Today I shall meet people who are meddling, ungrateful, aggressive, treacherous, malicious, unsocial [...] But I have seen that the nature of good is what is right, and the nature of evil is what is wrong; and I have reflected that the nature of the offender himself is akin to my own [...] the same fragment of divinity [...] We were born for cooperation.

—MARCUS AURELIUS

You are waiting in line, and someone cuts ahead of you. How do you respond?

Your first impression is probably something like anger. However, you have the choice of whether or not to assent to that impression. You have the choice to dissent, and not be ruled by intemperate emotions. You have the wisdom to choose another way to react than losing your temper.

This doesn't mean that you have to let the injustice continue. You may decide to speak to the person that cut in line, to remind them of the rules of good manners and polite society. This will take courage and may test your temperance to the limit. On the other hand, you will have acted as a rational human being, rather than an animal who is incapable of controlling their emotions.

Of course, none of us are perfect. Marcus Aurelius is held up as a paragon of stoicism, and his *Meditations* are full of petty complaints and minor irritations. We are human, and to be human is to be fallible. With this in mind, it's worth considering some stoic techniques for keeping your emotions in check.

One particular stoic technique is recontextualization. This involves examining events and breaking them down into their component parts. Recontextualization can be an effective way of removing emotionality from something that happens to you because it forces you to look at the event in a more analytical way. Furthermore, it can expose alternative explanations for events that foster empathy and patience.

Let's return to the example of someone cutting you in line. To recontextualize in the stoic tradition, we try to break down what happened into its component parts. For example:

1. You were standing in line. Analyze the size of the line, and how obvious it was to others.

2. The other person approached the front of the line. Referring back to point 1, consider whether they might have not noticed the line. Furthermore, evaluate their body language and facial expressions. Did they seem hassled, or upset?

3. The other person cut in. What is their body language now? Do they seem hostile and defensive, or relaxed and oblivious?

4. You felt an immediate impression. What was that impression: Is it anger, impatience, or something else? Are you still feeling it?

5. You now have the choice of whether to assent or dissent from those impressions. What would be virtuous?

By fully analyzing the event, you can foster your natural empathy for the other person. Maybe they did not see the line and didn't realize they were cutting in. Maybe they seem to be having a terrible day and are majorly stressed. This doesn't necessarily excuse their actions, but it allows you to approach the situation in a more empathetic, productive way. The more you try to empathize with the other individual, the less likely you are to lower yourself to angry or rude behavior.

Meanwhile, by analyzing your own impressions in a detached way, you allow yourself to face your emotions head-on without succumbing to them. By consciously reflecting on the choice to assent or dissent from the impression, you empower yourself to choose virtue over animal instinct.

Recontextualizing in the moment can be difficult. It is a skill, and like any skill, it is strengthened through habit and practice. You can practice recontextualization by applying it to what the stoics called "indifferents:" things that are neither the true good (virtue) nor the true bad (vice). Sometimes, recontextualizing indifferents can be a way of removing their allure. In one memorable passage of the *Meditations* (2006/170-180), Marcus Aurelius applies recontextualization techniques to sexual congress, presumably as a means of reducing the temptations he felt: "As for sexual intercourse, it is the friction of a membrane, and, following a sort of convulsion, the expulsion of some mucus."

You can see how recontextualization can make otherwise pleasurable things a little less seductive!

You can practice recontextualization to get yourself in the habit of doing so. Let's consider another example, and recontextualize bacon. We might recontextualize it as follows:

> A cut of fatty meat from a pig's belly, back, or sides, that is cured by being soaked in a solution of salt and nitrates, and then prepared for consumption by searing the meat in a hot pan.

Taking these two examples as your guide, try recontextualizing other indifferents in your daily life. Some possible indifferents for recontextualization practice might include:

- your radiator

- your clothing

- the rain

- your morning eggs

- walking

If you're not familiar with the exact breakdown of some of these examples, that's more than okay. Take this as your excuse to satisfy your curiosity about how radiators work and do a quick Google search to learn something new today.

Remember, however, that stoicism does not ask for us to be robots. Emotions are not something to be purged: They are part of what it is to be human. Instead of trying to remove your emotions, your focus should be on making sure that your emotions do not stand as an obstacle to making rational, virtuous choices. It's fine to be a little irritated, but do not surrender the power to dissent from that impression, and choose to act in a way that is not dictated by that feeling of irritation. In other words, your emotions are to be *tempered*, in accordance with the virtue of temperance—not annihilated.

As we've noted, recontextualization is a skill that needs habitual practice. Try to recontextualize one indifferent a day, until it becomes almost second nature. This will empower you to automatically recontextualize in situations where you might otherwise feel angry or emotional. Once this becomes an automatic, natural process in your thinking, you will be able to distance yourself from your emotions and make the right, virtuous choice.

However, not everything is a choice. Some events are out of our control, and it is important that we recognize and accept this. In the next chapter, we'll consider this challenge in more detail.

Chapter 7:
Recognizing What You Cannot Control

Grant me the serenity to accept the things I cannot change, courage to change the things I can, and wisdom to know the difference.

—THE SERENITY PRAYER

The world will throw you many curveballs in life. There are many things we cannot control, ranging from the mundane, like someone cutting you in line, to grander problems like crises in the Middle East. To live as a stoic, we must be able to recognize what we can control, and what we cannot.

Stoicism draws a clear distinction between the external and internal world. The internal world is your mind: Your opinions, your decisions, and your choices. By contrast, the external world is everything else. By the tenets of stoicism, you can always influence your internal world. No matter what happens in the external world, you can control how you react internally, assenting or dissenting to the impressions that the external world may produce. However, we cannot always exert an influence on the external world.

Most of the time, a simple reflection will be enough to know what you can control and what you cannot. Often, the mere acknowledgment of what you cannot control can be enough to grant you a sense of inner serenity and peace. Meanwhile, where you identify things that you can control, you can decide whether it is virtuous to try and do so. This prevents your energies from being wasted on what is beyond your power.

Let's return to a familiar example. You were competing for a promotion at work but did not get it. Reflect on what is within your control, and what is not. For example, the following aspects of the event are outside your control:

- The performance or prior experience of your competitors.

- The mood of your boss when you had the interview.

- The timing of the promotion opportunity.

Because these aspects are out of your control, it is wise and temperate to make your peace with them. However, this does not mean that you should passively accept the upsets of the world. There are aspects of the situation that you *did* control, such as:

- Your own performance in the interview.

- Your preparation for the interview.

- Your current levels of experience and performance.

As we have discussed in earlier chapters, by acknowledging the areas you can control, you can use this setback as an opportunity for growth. If you were underprepared for your interview, then have the wisdom to recognize this and learn from your mistake. If your performance levels are not competitive enough to secure promotion, you can work on your performance to give you a better chance in the future.

Sometimes you will be tempted to feel resentful about those things you cannot control. This is a natural first impression to have, but remember that you have a choice whether to assent or dissent from that impression. If your boss was in a terrible mood when you had your interview, this is deeply unfortunate and may have affected your prospects. However, it is not something you can predict or control. There is no way to use this information to find personal growth.

What you *do* have control over, of course, is your response to those things you can't control. You can choose to accept resentment into your heart, but this defeatism is unwise and intemperate. You may take your disappointment out on others, but this is not just. You may decide that, because you are not in control, you might as well not try, but this is not courageous. Instead, you should dissent from that impression of resentment, work on what you can control, and try to find acceptance of the rest.

The Serenity Prayer

The quotation at the start of this chapter is taken from the Serenity Prayer, used by Alcoholics Anonymous (AA). Though AA incorporates religious belief into its program to help its members, the aspirations contained within the Serenity Prayer are applicable to everyone regardless of belief.

Ultimately, the Serenity Prayer is fundamentally stoic in its inspiration. It even references fundamental virtues, such as wisdom and courage, revealing its philosophical underpinnings. Furthermore, as we have seen, the distinction between what we can control and what we can't is an inherently stoic idea. As Epictetus (2008/2nd century) said:

> The chief task in life is simply this: To identify and separate matters so that I can say clearly to myself which are externals not under my control, and which have to do with the choices I actually control.

Stoicism has an ancient pedigree, helping to influence millennia of philosophical and spiritual thought. The stoic underpinnings of the Serenity Prayer also demonstrate that its teachings are just as relevant today as they were in the second century.

Nuances in Control

On occasion, it may be difficult to determine what you can control. It is fine to limit yourself to what is practical: The exercise of separating what you can control from what you can't is eminently practical, because it allows you to expend your finite efforts in the most virtuous and productive way. When reflecting on what lies within your control, you need not only wisdom but temperance as well.

To illustrate what I mean, consider again the example of the unsuccessful interview for a promotion. In a very broad sense, perhaps you did have some control over your boss's mood. You might have recognized their bad temper and taken a variety of steps to cheer them up. You might have infiltrated their life and sent them anonymous presents. But this is too much. It is intemperate and unrealistic—not to mention intrusive.

Because you have finite energies, determining what is under your control and what isn't can admit of degrees. As our example demonstrates, there is some sense in which you might have had control over your boss's mood. However, you had much less control over your boss's mood than your own levels of interview preparation. As such, wisdom dictates that you focus on those aspects in which you have more power.

Being cognizant of what you can change is inherently humble, embodying the virtues of temperance and wisdom. However, it is not an excuse for inaction. When you do identify those things you can change, and it is just and wise to do so, you should have the courage to take action to make the world a better place.

In summary, then, always be thinking about what lies under your control, and what does not. Even when the situation is dire or in crisis, you must have the wisdom to recognize the limitations of your influence.

But how do we cope with disasters that we can't control? The next chapter thinks on this question in more detail.

Chapter 8:
How to Overcome Crisis

I judge you unfortunate because you have never lived through misfortune. You have passed through life without an opponent—no one can ever know what you are capable of, not even you.

—SENECA

You will experience tragedy in life. Perhaps you already have. The death of a loved one, a difficult break-up, stress at work, loneliness, guilt, anxiety, depression, and even suicidal ideation. The rich tapestry of human experience has its fair share of negative feelings and external disasters.

We have discussed how every crisis is an opportunity for virtue. In the face of awful events, you have an opportunity to demonstrate your integrity and goodness—not only to others but also to yourself. You may allow your feelings to be present, and come to terms with them with honesty and courage, but you can also choose to prevent these feelings from dictating your next move. You can take tragedy and find strength, not by denying that bad things happened to you, nor by pretending like they don't bother you, but by acknowledging what has happened and doing the next right thing.

Sometimes, however, tragedies can be so great that they are too much to handle. It is okay to accept your human fallibility, and not to pretend like you can overcome any challenge without help. Wisdom may dictate that you reach out to others, and it can be immensely courageous to accept help when you feel vulnerable. The main thing is to try: To maintain your integrity, and to try and be virtuous.

In addition, stoicism teaches us to prepare for some disasters, so that we are not completely thrown off when they occur. A particular stoic technique is to practice negative visualizations. Imagine what could go wrong, so that you have preparations in place if they do.

For example, suppose that you are about to go on a first date. You can use negative visualizations to prepare yourself for the date not going well. Maybe you will fail to hit it off with the other person, or you will find that your personalities are not as compatible as you had first hoped. Through negative visualizations, you will be in a position to mentally rehearse that disappointment, such that it does not break you if it comes. If applicable, you may also take steps to plan ahead for such disappointments. Maybe you'll have a backup plan for your evening, such as hanging out with friends, should the date not go well. Maybe you have a lovely dessert waiting for you at home, to be used as a celebration or commiseration.

On the other hand, do not take negative visualization too far. As Seneca (2004/65) teaches, "we suffer more in our imagination more often than in reality." If you are constantly rehearsing negative thoughts, you are subjecting yourself to unnecessary misery: Fueling your anxieties and potentially contributing to depressive symptoms. The trick is to find the right balance, using your wisdom and temperance. You can use negative visualizations to prepare yourself for setbacks, but do not adopt the technique as a crutch. Only do as much as is pragmatic to prepare you for virtuous action.

Another stoic technique that prepares you for crisis is to train yourself for hardship. Not only does this prepare you for disaster, but it also helps foster gratitude for the things you have. Despite the wealth he enjoyed later in life, Epictetus famously lived a humble life with few possessions. Many stoics practice voluntary discomfort, such as choosing to occasionally sleep a night on the floor, live a restricted diet for a limited time, or take a cold shower. This tests and builds your resolve, and reminds you of the many positive things you have in your life. It's also something you can do almost immediately. A great first step is taking a cold shower tomorrow morning. Try it. Test your resolve, and build on your resilience for when the external world throws a curveball your way.

The Man in the Arena

On April 23, 1910, the former president Theodore Roosevelt delivered a speech to thousands in the streets of Paris. This speech was later known as The Man in the Arena and contains much in the way of stoic wisdom. Roosevelt's words (World Future Fund) also offer great advice when it comes to how to handle critics—even when the critic is yourself.

It is not the critic who counts; not the man who points out how the strong man stumbles, or where the doer of deeds could have done them better. The credit belongs to the man who is actually in the arena, whose face is marred by dust and sweat and blood; who strives valiantly; who errs, who comes short again and again, because there is no effort without error and shortcoming; but who does actually strive to do the deeds; who knows great enthusiasms, the great devotions; who spends himself in a worthy cause; who at the best knows, in the end, the triumph of high achievement, and who at the worst, if he fails, at least fails while daring greatly, so that his place shall never be with those cold and timid souls who neither knows victory nor defeat.

Sometimes, you will face failures. You will feel the sting of disappointment when attempting great things. You will fall short of stoic ideals, struggling bravely against intemperate emotions that consume you in the moment of crisis. But you will have tried. You will still have your integrity, and self-dignity, even in those moments of failure, because you will have tried. As Roosevelt said, there is no effort without error.

As such, when you face a crisis, recognize that you are given an opportunity to prove to yourself your own resilience and virtue. Try to act with temperance and courage in your own ideals. If you fall short, then recognize that your efforts to be a better person are profoundly praiseworthy. Pat yourself on the back, dust yourself off and try again.

In summary, maintain your integrity, and try. In the next chapter, we'll see that your sense of integrity and the philosophy of stoicism are inherently linked.

Chapter 9:
Integrity

Just that you do the right thing. The rest doesn't matter. Cold or warm. Tired or well-rested. Despised or honored.

—Marcus Aurelius

Stoicism is fundamentally linked to integrity. It asks you to choose a virtuous path, even when external events threaten to destabilize your life, or you face crisis and disaster. The stoic doesn't abandon their principles when they become inconvenient. Remember Seneca's example. When compelled to suicide by Emperor Nero, he did not abandon his principles. He got his affairs in order and took his life.

Ultimately, by cleaving true to your morals, you will live a happier and more flourishing life. Rather than pursuing short-term advantage, you will find the longer-lasting, inner peace that comes from having self-respect, and knowing that your nature is inherently good. You will know that you have been tested and that you have done the right thing. You will have lived according to your nature as a virtuous, rational being.

Maintaining your sense of integrity will take discipline and a strong sense of self. All of us are tempted at some time in our life to do something unvirtuous. Sometimes these situations will be mundane. Maybe your boss praises you for work that you know another person was responsible for, or someone else is blamed for a mistake that you made. If you are just and courageous, you will be honest—even if that denies you some short-term advantage in your work.

Remember that virtue is the only true good. All those other short-term advantages are ephemeral and, in certain contexts, not even desirable. Your boss doesn't blame you for a small mistake: Is this worth your integrity, and the resentment of your colleagues?

Nonetheless, we are human, and vice can be seductive. It is therefore prudent to take steps to strengthen your resolve and integrity.

A big part of integrity is having a strong sense of self. If you know who you are, and what matters to you, it will be easier to see the bigger picture when you are tempted by short-term vices.

Take the time to understand your principles. What is important to you? Get a pad of paper and write them down. If your mind goes blank, then use the list below as a jumping-off point:

- honoring your elders

- being self-sufficient

- working to protect animals and the environment

- helping those in need

- honoring your faith

- being open to learning new things

- forgiving others and giving them another chance

- standing up to bullies

- engaging in charitable works

- being an active member of your democracy

- honoring the traditions of your culture

It doesn't matter if some of these principles don't resonate with you. What's important is that they get you thinking about what matters to you.

By making explicit those things that matter to you, you will be less tempted by actions that would compromise those principles. For example, if you are cognizant that standing up to bullies is deeply important to you, then it will be easier to find your courage to stand up to someone who is bullying someone else. After all, these principles are meant to be what matters to you most. If you choose not to act, you are sacrificing what matters most to you for the sake of avoiding a confrontation. That seems like a bad trade!

In addition to understanding your principles, understand your strengths. Again, as an exercise, take the time to write down some of your strengths. If your mind goes blank at these kinds of things, pick and choose from the (non-exhaustive) list below:

- being hard-working

- reliability

- honesty

- kindness

- trustingness

- lovingness

- intelligence

- tolerance

- friendliness

- perseverance

- generosity

- curiosity

- loyalty

- open-mindedness

- politeness

- creativity

Understanding your strengths is part of building a stronger sense of self. The more you know what you're about, the more likely you are to maintain that sense of self and not sacrifice your integrity for petty advantage.

Finally, consider your weaknesses. This isn't about beating yourself up, but about humility and prudence. It is important to understand where you might be tempted to commit vice. Remember that everyone has their flaws. On your pad of paper, write down your own. Once more, you can refer to the following list to get you thinking about your own foibles:

- distractibility

- shyness

- fear of confrontation

- laziness

- gullibility

- greediness

- enviousness

- short-tempered

- arrogance

- resentfulness

There is no virtue in pretending you don't have the weaknesses that you have. Understanding your nature is an important part of improving yourself. If you are cognizant that you are often short-tempered, then this represents something you can actively work on. By contrast, if you do not face your shortcomings, you will never have the opportunity to correct them and grow into your best self.

Meanwhile, by understanding where you are more likely to err, you can commit yourself to extra resolve in just those kinds of situations. As you feel more confident in your sense of self and virtue, you may even begin testing yourself to strengthen your resolve further. For example, if you know that you are shy, you may take steps to put yourself out there in social situations, building on your resilience. Just don't rush things. Slowly expand your comfort zone, so that your personal growth is manageable and realistic.

Alternatively, when you understand your weaknesses, you might take steps to avoid the kinds of situations that would tempt you. If you know that you are greedy, then maybe you should avoid the local food court during your lunch hour. It is often easier to resist temptation when it is not directly in front of you. Just don't rely too much on avoidance. Sometimes, it may be wiser and more courageous to take active steps to work on yourself.

In summary, by understanding your principles, your strengths, and your weaknesses, you will have a strong sense of self. This fosters your integrity. Understanding your own nature is itself an act of integrity because it involves appraising yourself honestly and courageously. Meanwhile, the stronger your sense of self, the more resilient you will be to the challenges the world may throw at you. You will find it easier to maintain your integrity and resist those temptations that would compromise your principles.

In other words, you will be able to find your balance. In the next chapter, we consider a few additional ways of tempering your emotions and finding inner peace.

Chapter 10:
Finding Your Balance

Nothing satisfies greed, but even a little satisfies nature.

—Seneca

If you believe that happiness is your life's goal, then it makes sense that you would want to maximize it. When you find something that makes you happy, you will want more of it. When you lose that thing which made you happy, you will feel sad.

However, it is important to understand what we mean by happiness. In Chapter 4, we considered a distinction between pleasure and contentment, linking the latter notion to the stoic concept of *eudaimonia*, or flourishing.

Because *eudaimonia* is the consequence of living virtuously, it does not make sense to think of it in terms of a unit that can be maximized. By contrast, we might think of pleasure in terms of hedonic units. This makes pleasure particularly unstable. If something is more easily quantified, even vaguely, then it is more susceptible to peaks and troughs. This instability can lead to a disordered life.

This is one of the reasons that you should seek *eudaimonia*, rather than mere pleasure. Because the state of *eudaimonia* is a natural byproduct of living well, you can't be tempted by vice or morally unhealthy behavior as a way of getting more of it.

With this in mind, the ideal stoic simply busies themselves with living virtuously and does not worry about the rest. However, you can't become an ideal stoic in a day. Moreover, there is nothing incompatible between stoicism and pursuing lesser pleasures in moderation. As such, it is important to talk about these lesser pleasures and how you can find your emotional balance.

The stoics were not unemotional—a quick read of Marcus Aurelius's *Meditations* will prove that—but they did believe that extremes of emotion can be unhealthy. This is because extreme emotions can cloud your reason. For example, excessive lust can cause you to take leave of your senses and distract you from behaving virtuously. As such, it is best to defend yourself against such strong impulses.

One strategy for doing this is through our recontextualizations. Perhaps you remember Marcus Aurelius's recontextualization of sex from Chapter 6, comparing it to the friction of genitals and the expulsion of mucus-like material. Through recontextualization and breaking pleasurable acts into their mechanical form, you can temper their appeal.

Another applicable strategy is voluntary hardship. In Chapter 8, we talked about occasionally sleeping on the floor, restricting your diet, or taking a cold shower. This can protect you from extreme emotionality because you will know that you are resilient enough to go without. You will be less obsessive about gathering money if you know that you can live well without the trappings of wealth. You will be less fearful and therefore less likely to be led by fear.

More generally, the stoic will be suspicious of extreme states. It can be pleasurable to lose yourself to the moment, but if those moments make you incapable of reasoning, then you are experiencing pleasure as a beast experiences pleasure. Again, the solution isn't to become a robot. There is nothing wrong with pleasure itself. It just shouldn't be achieved through vice, and it shouldn't prevent you from virtuous reasoning.

If you feel like an emotion is reducing your capacity for reason, start by analyzing the triggers for that emotion. The stoics believed that the primary passions are appetite and fear. We have an appetite for what appears to be good, and fear for what appears to be bad. The first step, then, is to discover whether your extreme impulse is the result of appetite or fear.

From there, consider using recontextualization. Breaking things down to their mechanical parts can reduce your appetite or fear of them. If the extreme impulse persists, or you still feel its force to an extent, consider strategies for reducing its power. For the time being, you might avoid situations that expose you to the full extreme of those passions.

Afterward, you can start building your resilience toward that extreme impulse. This might take the form of voluntary hardship. As you build resilience, you can test yourself with previous triggers, taking care to pay close attention to your own thoughts and behaviors.

Let's consider an example. Suppose that, whenever you visit the local food court, you always come away with a donut. Even though you're trying to watch your weight, you find it impossible to resist as soon as you can smell the glazing.

The triggers for your extreme impulse are fairly easy to identify. It's the surroundings of the food court and the smell of the glazing. Moreover, it is straightforward to identify this as an appetite—literally! This gives you a good starting point of understanding from which you can start to temper your impulses.

To reduce your extreme appetite, we can start with the recontextualization of the donut. By breaking down the donut and eating it into its mechanical parts, your appetite for the donut may well decrease:

> It is a deep-fried cake batter, high in carbohydrates and fat, topped with a high-sugar glazing and shaped in a ring. It is mashed into uneven parts by the action of your teeth and transported to your gastrointestinal tract by the contraction of muscles in your throat. As these uneven parts pass through the gastrointestinal tract, they are mixed with digestive juices that break the parts into smaller parts. Waste products pass through the large intestine and are excreted from the body; the rest is absorbed through the walls of the small intestine into the bloodstream, where they are transported across the body.

Train yourself to think of this recontextualization whenever you think of a donut. Hopefully, this will reduce the extremity of your appetite for it. However, if you still think you will be strongly tempted, you can avoid the food court for the time being. To strengthen your resolve, you may use voluntary hardship and adopt a restricted diet to reduce your sugar intake. When you have built up your resolve, you can return to the food court and test your resilience, paying close attention to your thoughts and behaviors.

You can use similar strategies for excessive fears. Though the stoic use of "fear" is broader than simply phobia, we can take claustrophobia (the fear of enclosed spaces) as an example. Clinical treatments of claustrophobia use exposure therapy: This works by building up your resilience by exposing you to gradually stronger triggers for your phobia. You might start by just thinking about tight spaces. Next, you might put yourself in a tight space that you can easily leave, and so on. This idea is analogous to voluntary hardship as a way of building resilience. Recontextualization can also be useful in bringing your awareness to what your body is feeling and how it is responding.

Note, however, that there is wisdom in asking for professional help when tackling symptoms of a mental disorder like extreme claustrophobia.

The key takeaway is that, once you start freeing yourself from extreme impulses, you will be immune to the vagaries of fate. When you lose or gain something pleasurable, it will not cause you to abandon the principles of living well. You will achieve a lasting state of *eudaimonia*, rather than suffering the rollercoaster instability of chasing pleasure. With recontextualization and voluntary hardship, you will achieve mastery over your emotions.

Sometimes, though, you will fall short. Sometimes, your mastery over your emotions will slip and you'll make a bad decision. The ancient stoics knew this, and thus stressed the importance of self-reflection. In the next chapter, we'll look at self-reflection in more detail.

Chapter 11:
Why Self-Reflection Is Important

I will keep constant watch over myself and—most usefully—put each day up for review. For this is what makes us evil—that none of us looks back upon our own lives. We reflect upon only that which we are about to do. And yet our plans for the future descend from the past.

—SENECA

As a stoic, you must be committed to approaching life in a reasoned and rational way. The ideal stoic always responds with virtue, but the fact is that being a stoic is a skill that you need to practice to improve. You will often fall short of the stoic ideal. However, if you apply self-reflection, you will be able to learn from your shortcomings and grow as a person.

Self-reflection serves as a positive practice for a variety of reasons. As noted, it can be used to learn from your mistakes. However, it can also be used to recognize virtuous behaviors and cultivate them. Honest self-reflection is an act of integrity. Finally, self-reflection can involve gratitude exercises that strengthen your emotional resilience. Let's consider each in turn.

Learning From Your Mistakes

Reflecting on your mistakes allows you to learn from them. It is a straightforward enough idea, but there are a few techniques that can help you self-reflect in a more targeted and productive way.

Albert Ellis, the pioneer of cognitive behavioral therapy (CBT), was explicitly influenced by the works of Epictetus and Seneca. He wanted a form of therapy that worked on restructuring our thoughts and behaviors, protecting us from the vagaries of life. In addition, he understood the importance of the stoic practices of self-reflection. With this in mind, it's worth a quick explanation of CBT to help demonstrate how you might approach your self-reflection.

The fundamental principle of CBT is the cognitive cycle. There are four elements to the cycle: emotions, thoughts, behaviors, and physical sensations. The idea is that all of these elements are interconnected and influence one another. For example, if you have the physical sensation of being hot or out of breath, this can contribute to feelings of panic, which in turn can influence the kind of thoughts we have and behaviors we exhibit. Meanwhile, by using breathing exercises as an explicit behavior, we can rescue feelings of panic, which in turn can help with the physical sensation of being out of breath. Ultimately, all four elements contribute to each other and have a causal influence over each other.

From there, CBT works by focusing on elements of the cognitive cycle that are more tractable. It is easier to change your behaviors than your emotions: If you have ever been told to "just stop worrying," you will appreciate this idea! As such, many CBT treatments work on identifying negative patterns of behavior and replacing them with more positive habits. Similarly, because thoughts are also a bit more tractable than emotions and physical sensations, other treatments involve identifying negative patterns of thought and amending them accordingly.

These treatments, of course, depend heavily on self-reflection. They involve reflecting on negative patterns of behavior or thought so that they can be amended in the future. With this in mind, try to think about the cognitive cycle when you apply stoic self-reflection to yourself. Think about triggers for certain thoughts and behaviors, identify the emotions and physical sensations that they tend to correspond to, and think about what patterns of thought and behavior they can lead to.

For example, suppose that you lost your temper with someone today. Self-reflection will identify this as something to be amended: Depending on the circumstances, you will not have acted in a just, wise, or temperate manner. However, instead of simply acknowledging this and feeling guilty, you should reflect on what led to your imperfect behavior. Identify the trigger for your impatience. What physical sensations were you experiencing? Maybe you were hot, or hungry: You'll be surprised how these sensations can affect our emotions and our thoughts. Think about what chain of behaviors or thoughts led you to act in an impatient way.

Once you fully understand the issue, you will then be in a position to start modifying that behavior and living a more virtuous life.

Learning From Your Successes

Learning from your successes is just as important as learning from your mistakes. With this in mind, you should apply the same levels of self-reflection to your virtuous actions.

The reason is much the same. Identifying positive patterns of thought and behavior is the first step to fostering those patterns as deliberate habits. For example, if you know that you are your best self when you are well-rested, you can start really thinking about your sleep hygiene to ensure that you can live well.

As with reflecting on your mistakes, you can use modern CBT techniques to great effect. Think about your thoughts, behaviors, emotions, and physical sensations, and try to understand how they all fit together to result in positive, virtuous action. It may be that some of these positive triggers are easily repeatable or can be deliberately fostered. By deliberately forming good habits, you will be in a better place to make virtuous choices, regardless of what life throws at you.

Integrity and Self-Reflection

If you are genuinely self-reflecting, and applying modern CBT techniques to that reflection, you may discover traits or patterns of behavior that are unflattering. For example, though it's very common, you might find it a little embarrassing that you get a bit grouchy when you're hungry. Sometimes, it will take courage to look at yourself objectively. You will find faults and foibles that may not be particularly gratifying.

This is where integrity comes in. Genuine self-reflection requires honesty and integrity, so practicing self-reflection is a great way of strengthening your sense of self.

If you are getting stuck in the weeds of self-reflection, you may find it helpful to journal. Writing down your self-reflections like Marcus Aurelius can give you a more objective record of your thoughts and behaviors, and allow you to see long-term patterns more easily. After all, it is difficult to see a pattern of behavior from one instance: If your self-reflections are written down, you can reflect on those self-reflections and identify the patterns.

Gratitude Exercises

Finally, let's discuss the role that self-reflection can have in practicing gratitude.

Though they may sound a little twee, gratitude exercises are experimentally proven to have a positive impact on your mental health (Wong et al, 2018). Humans innately have a negative bias due to our evolutionary history: After all, people who thought a rustling bush was a sabertooth tiger were less likely to be eaten when a sabertooth tiger *was* actually there! However, we don't have to worry about physical threats in the same way we used to, and our negative bias can result in negative feelings about ourselves, the world, and the future. This, in turn, can result in symptoms of depression.

We can combat this negative bias, however, by practicing gratitude exercises. These can be very straightforward. A simple gratitude exercise is to write down one thing you're grateful for at the end of each day. By deliberately bringing our attention to positive things, we can help our brain overcome its evolutionary history and see the world in a more objective light.

This connects to stoicism because combating our negative bias can help us look at ourselves and the world more rationally and objectively. It can help reduce general feelings of resentment that may distract us from making virtuous choices in response to negative events. If you are cognitively aware of positive things that happen in your life, you will find the negative events easier to bear.

As Marcus Aurelius wrote, "when you arise in the morning think of what a privilege it is to be alive, to think, to enjoy, to love."

To summarize: Constantly be reflecting on your day and your actions. You will learn much, and discover many opportunities for growth.

Chapter 12:
Stoicism and Religion

Live a good life. If there are gods and they are just, then they will not care how devout you have been, but will welcome you based on the virtues you have lived by. If there are gods, but unjust, then you should not want to worship them. If there are no gods, then you will be gone, but will have lived a noble life that will live on in the memories of your loved ones.

—MARCUS AURELIUS

In Chapter 4, we briefly touched on the idea that *eudaimonia*, though relating to a kind of spiritual happiness, is compatible but not reliant on religiosity. More generally, stoicism is a philosophy that can be adopted by theists, agnostics, and atheists alike. The key tenets of stoicism—that we have control over how we react to external events, and should choose virtue as a rational method for living a good life—do not rely on belief in a god or external power.

That said, stoic thought has had a profound influence on religious thought, especially Christian theology. Stoic philosophy influenced Aristotle, who in turn influenced Christian thought with his moral philosophy. In addition, Aristotle's cosmological argument for the existence of god is still argued by theists today. This argument holds that every natural event has a cause and that there must be a first cause that is therefore separate from the natural order. Many people think of this as God.

Putting aside the historical relevance of ancient Greek philosophy to Christian thought, we can consider parallels between stoic philosophy and many major religions. For example, stoics like Epictetus believed that we should live simply and humbly, to avoid forming a dependence on material wealth and possessions. Such an idea is mirrored in Matthew 19:24 of the Bible (2017/1769): "It is easier for a camel to go through the eye of a needle than for a rich person to enter the Kingdom of God." Meanwhile, Gautama Buddha (1894) said that "a kind man who makes good use of wealth is rightly said to possess a great treasure; but the miser who hoards up his riches will have no profit." In many religious traditions, wealth can be a distraction from living a virtuous life.

Relatedly, as a philosophy of how to live well, stoicism's focus on individual virtue can be compared with many of the world's religions. Much of Christian thought focuses on this idea of virtue and vice, most famously represented by the seven cardinal virtues, and their corresponding deadly sins:

Cardinal Virtue	Deadly Sin
Chastity	Lust
Temperance	Gluttony
Charity	Greed
Diligence	Sloth
Kindness	Envy
Patience	Wrath
Humility	Pride

Finally, we can compare stoic thoughts about hardship with the teachings of many major religions. Stoicism teaches us to be stoic in response to suffering, focusing on how we can find inner peace and *eudaimonia* by responding virtuously to negative events. The ancient stoics teach that hardship is an opportunity for virtue. Meanwhile, in James 1:2-4, the Bible (2017/1769) says that

> Count it all joy, my brothers, when you meet trials of various kinds, for you know that the testing of your faith produces steadfastness. And let steadfastness have its full effect, that you may be perfect and complete, lacking in nothing.

These ideas are also found in the Islamic tradition. Al-Fadl Ibn Saleh said that

> There is a blessing in calamity that the wise man should not ignore, for it erases sins, gives one the opportunity to attain the reward for patience, dispels negligence, reminds one of blessings at the time of health, calls one to repent and encourages one to give charity.

Given the compatibility of religious thought with stoicism, you may find that your stoic convictions are strengthened through your relationship with faith. If your faith inspires you to live virtuously and to avoid intemperate emotions that would distract you from living well, then you will find that your religion helps you live according to the principles of stoicism.

On the other hand, stoicism is a philosophy, not a religion. As it happens, the first stoics were largely pantheists, believing in the ancient Greek or Roman pantheon of gods. Though early stoics were no doubt influenced by their religious beliefs; however, stoicism stands on its own two feet and is independent of any particular faith.

Ultimately, the most religious element of stoicism is the belief that the cosmos corresponds to a profound order. The stoics believed that this order was put in place by the gods, and this underpins the idea that humanity has a natural state: To live rationally and virtuously. However, the tenets of stoicism can be followed without a belief in this particular premise. Regardless of whether we believe that our natural state is a virtue, we can still hold that the best life is lived virtuously, both for ethical and psychological reasons. We can believe that intemperate emotions and impulses can lead us to act poorly, and that inner contentment comes from living a good life, rather than from the pursuit of hedonistic pleasures. We can choose to live moderately out of a desire to live a good life, whether or not we believe that our virtue will be rewarded in an afterlife, and whether or not virtue stems from a god.

To summarize, then, stoicism is compatible with, but not reliant on, many of the world religions that exist today. The focus on individual virtue, stoicism through suffering, and moderate living are found in many theological traditions, demonstrating a commonality of wisdom in human moral philosophies all across the world. On the other hand, this kind of wisdom is not the sole preservation of religion. The desire to be virtuous is part of what it is to be a moral person, regardless of our particular beliefs. We all want to be capable of facing adversity with integrity and courage. And—though we all occasionally fall short—we all want to be able to resist the excesses of self-destructive impulses.

Chapter 13:
The Reality of Death

This is our big mistake: to think we look forward to death. Most of death is already gone. Whatever time has passed is owned by death.

—SENECA

Many of us find the idea of our own mortality to be frightening. However, death is a natural part of life. The stoic should be capable of coming to terms with their own mortality and be able to use the finiteness of life as a prompt to virtuous action.

If you do fear death, then you are not alone. It makes good evolutionary sense that the human being would be programmed to fear death. This fear helps us avoid threats to our life that would prevent us from reproducing. However, we can overcome this evolutionary instinct through reason. You do not have to be a slave to this fear.

Like with many fears, we can try using recontextualization to reduce our terror of death and dying:

> The physical processes of the body start to operate more slowly. The heart beats more slowly, resulting in blood being transported across the body more slowly. This results in a deficit of oxygen to key organs such as the brain, resulting in reduced function. Because the brain has reduced function, the function of the lungs becomes more erratic, and other organs are impacted by the abnormal hormone production from the brain. In time, the heart muscle stops entirely. The brain stops functioning altogether and the lungs cease functioning.

Stoicism treats death like any other (potentially negative) external event that we cannot control. Because we can't avoid the reality of death, what is important is how we react to its approach. We can choose whether to assent or dissent from our impression of fear and decide how to respond in a way that is virtuous.

As such, let's examine how the virtues might apply to our response to death or dying. First of all, we must be wise and accept that death is not something we can thwart. Though medical science is a wonder, it is unlikely—at least in our lifetimes—that it will do away with death forever. Moreover, it is not clear whether this would even be a good thing. Without death, we would have an increasingly aging population putting an excessive burden on younger generations. In some sense, death is a way of passing the torch to our children and grandchildren.

Once we have used our wisdom to accept the reality (and potential societal benefits) of death, we can consider other virtues. We should try to be temperate and avoid our fear from overwhelming our reason. Epictetus (2008/2nd century) says it best: "I cannot escape death, but at least I can escape the fear of it."

Of course, tempering our fear of death may be easier said than done. We have already talked about how recontextualization may help, but the stoics had other strategies for helping us find our courage.

One such strategy is *memento mori*: The contemplation of death. A Latin phrase, *memento mori* translates to "remember that you have to die." When a conquering hero returned to ancient Rome, he would receive a parade to celebrate his victory. However, it was customary for a slave to follow the general close behind, reminding him of his mortality. This was considered an exercise in humility, to remind the general that despite his victories, he was still a man.

As well as an exercise in humility, the practice of *memento mori* prepares us for the reality of death. Epictetus told his followers that they should contemplate the death of their children when kissing them goodnight. This may seem macabre, but the result is a newfound appreciation of life, rather than a paralyzing terror. In this sense, contemplating death is about *carpe diem*, or "seizing the day." Contemplating death brings into sharp relief those parts of life that matter and are important to you.

Additionally, the contemplation of death is a form of negative visualization. In Chapter 8, we talked about how negative visualizations can act as a kind of rehearsal for negative events, helping us to prepare ourselves emotionally for when they occur. By contemplating your own mortality, you are practicing facing death with honesty and courage. This is much better than pretending it won't happen to you and being terrified when the moment comes.

Finally, consider the quotation at the start of this chapter. Seneca compares death with the past. The idea is that the past is just as inaccessible to us in the present as the future is after we die. We only have what we have in the present. If you can truly take this to heart, this will reduce your fear of death: After all, you are not afraid of the past as a concept.

With these thoughts in mind, we can try to temper our fear of death, and find the courage to respond to the reality of death in a virtuous way: By seizing life. As Marcus Aurelius (2006/170-180) wrote, "death hangs over you. While you live, while it is in your power, be good. Now."

When it comes down to it, death is the ultimate opportunity for virtue. When compelled by Emperor Nero to kill himself, Seneca faced his death with temperance and courage, judging that it was just and wise for him to follow the commands of the state, even though he was probably innocent. Though our deaths are unlikely to be as dramatic, we will still have the opportunity to face death with courage, wisdom, and temperance. And, in the meantime, the reality of death is a fantastic motivator to seize the present and live well now.

Stoic Death and Faith

Of course, if you have religious faith, you may not believe that death is the end.

The ancient stoics believed in an afterlife, though Hades's underworld was not considered as pleasant as the Christian or Islamic heaven. Ancient Greeks did not anticipate a final judgment of souls that would sort them into heaven or hell—though some myths did allow for particularly evil souls to face some kind of punishment, this was the exception rather than the rule. Instead, the underworld was a bland place occupied by shades: weak souls that no longer felt joy or terror, or indeed much of anything at all.

If you have faith, you may be able to depend on your faith to find courage in the face of death. This is entirely compatible with stoicism: Your faith and the stoic philosophy are mutually supportive. Though the ancient stoics thought the finitude of life was an injunction to live well now, this is compatible with the idea that we should live well because death brings judgment.

Either way, the key takeaway is this: Death should be faced with calmness and courage, and that death should motivate us to live virtuously in the present.

We have considered the tenets of stoicism and thought about a few ways you can try to incorporate stoic thinking into your life. Now, we focus on exercises that encourage and foster stoic thought.

PART 3:
PRACTICAL EXERCISES FOR A STOIC LIFE

Next, we look at stoic exercises that will help you to internalize stoic principles and become a stoic yourself.

It is worth noting that not all of these exercises will be for everyone. You are encouraged to experiment with what works for you, and to implement those practices that are more effective for your particular personality. That said, try to try every exercise at least once, and approach them with honesty and courage.

Exercise 1:
Start Analyzing Your Life

Whenever you are about to find fault with someone, ask yourself the following question: What fault of mine most nearly resembles the one I am about to criticize?

—Marcus Aurelius

In Chapter 11, we talked about the importance of self-reflection in living a good stoic life. We also talked about modern cognitive behavioral therapy (CBT), and how it focuses on analyzing triggers, physical sensations, and patterns of thought and behavior. These exercises expand on these ideas.

For all of these exercises, it's worth having a pen and paper, or a journal for you to write your answers in. Writing down your self-reflections can help you focus on the exercise and give it your full attention.

Analyzing What Makes You Happy

By understanding what makes you happy, you can start formulating potential patterns of behavior that can help you when you're feeling upset. For example, if you know that petting your dog always cheers you up, being cognizant of this can codify that behavior as a strategy. You can commit to petting your dog whenever you feel down. Not only will this help you regulate your own emotions in a positive way, but your dog will no doubt love the attention too!

The first step, though, is to discover those patterns and habits that make you happy. Writing down your answers, consider the following questions:

- What made you feel happy today?

- What made you feel happy this week?

- What always makes you feel happy?

- What is your happiest memory?

When you have answered these questions, try analyzing patterns between those answers. Do they all have something in common? Are there some points of contrast? Try to really understand what is underpinning these happy-making events.

For example, let's suppose you answered as follows:

- It made me happy to pet the dog today.

- It made me happy to go for a long walk with my dog and partner this week.

- It always makes me happy to come home and see my partner and dog.

- My happiest memory is marrying my partner.

In these answers, there is an obvious trend in what makes you happy: Your family and relationships with your partner and dog. This might demonstrate that you are motivated by your family and that one of your fundamental priorities is to have a positive family life. The fact that your happiest memory is marrying your partner demonstrates that ultimately your partner comes before your dog—no doubt your partner will be pleased!

Now that you know this about yourself, you can start formulating strategies for regulating your emotions. You now know explicitly that your happy-making strategies should center around your family. Maybe a good strategy for cheering yourself up is to give your partner a big hug.

This all might seem obvious, but you'd be surprised by what we gloss over by not taking the time to do explicit analysis. If asked directly, you'd probably be able to say that your dog makes you happy, but that doesn't mean you have fostered patterns of behavior involving your dog as a strategy for regulating your mood. Make use of what you have learned, and put it into practice.

Analyzing What Makes You Sad

We can use a mirrored exercise to analyze what makes you sad in life. Write down your answers to the following questions:

- What made you feel sad today?

- What made you feel sad this week?

- What always makes you feel sad?

- What is your saddest memory?

Potentially, you will want to replace the word "sad" with other negative emotions, such as "dissatisfied" or "angry." You can tailor the exercise to a particular negative emotion that you know has an impact on your life.

Like with the previous exercise, you should now examine your answers and try to identify trends and patterns. If all your answers center on work, then this should be your prompt to really think about your job and whether you are in the right career. By contrast, if your answers suggest that you are miserable in your relationship, then it may be time to think about that in more detail.

Of course, some events make us sad but are a part of life. Your saddest memory might involve the death of a loved one: This is not necessarily something to exorcize from your psyche. Relatedly, if work often leaves you dispirited, this doesn't mean you should immediately quit your job. Remember that wisdom and temperance are virtues. Your own situation might make it difficult to find another job, at least in the short term. As such, this exercise should be used as a prompt for you to think more about negative aspects in your life, rather than as a prompt to immediate action.

It may also be worth returning to this exercise every month or so. You can also do this with the previous exercise. Keeping track of how your priorities are changing is an important part of understanding yourself and your personal journey.

Analyzing Other People

Past behaviors are a predictor of future action. As such, taking the time to analyze other people can help you predict their actions in the future.

Once again, it's a good idea to have something to write down your answers in. This is because your analysis will benefit from the ability to look back at your answers over time so that you can identify trends of behavior.

Get in the habit of thinking about interactions you have in the day. Write down the salient points, asking yourself the standard journalistic questions:

- **Who?** Who were you talking to, and what relationship do you have with them? Are they family, a co-worker, a stranger, or a friend?

- **What?** What were you talking about? What happened in the interaction? Try to think about their body language, and their paralanguage: Those ways we communicate in addition to the literal meaning of our words, such as tone, inflection, and speaking rate.

- **Where?** Where did you have the interaction? Was it in a public place, or a more intimate setting? Were you at work or at a social event?

- **When?** When did your interaction take place? Was it at lunch, or just before? Were you tired or fresh? Try to think about the full context of the interaction as a clue to existing patterns of behavior.

- **How?** If things went well, or poorly, how did that come about? Were there signs that your interaction was going a certain way? If it was a negative interaction, were you discussing a potentially difficult or controversial topic between you?

Again, you'll want to review your answers over time and try to find patterns in the data. If you find that a conversation with your co-worker about politics always turns unpleasant, then you will be able to avoid such conversations in the future or try to amend the way you're approaching the topic. By analyzing these patterns, you'll be able to modify your own behavior if it is wise to do so and to predict likely ways the other person will behave in different contexts.

Remember, though, that this is not about power or manipulation. Throughout, always have the virtues in mind: How you can use this information to be fairer to other people or to control your temper and remain temperate.

Analyzing Yourself

A final exercise in the analysis is applying reflection to your own behaviors.

We have talked in Chapter 8 about understanding your triggers and patterns of thought and behavior. Instead of repeating ourselves, let's instead think about analyzing those times when we fall short: Where we did not act wisely, temperately, courageously, or justly.

Just as the first two exercises were mirrors of each other, this exercise mirrors the analysis of other people. Ask yourself the journalistic questions of who, what, where, when, and how: This time, however, really apply the scrutiny to yourself.

You can also incorporate insights from CBT in your answers. When considering what happened, try to think about your own physical sensations and the emotions you were feeling. Consider how they might have influenced your thoughts and behaviors, and how these different aspects are interconnected. Relatedly, try to understand the contexts in which those physical sensations or emotions arise. For example, if you are always hungry before lunch, and being hungry makes you a little irritable, a temperate and wise response might be to have lunch a little earlier each day.

When analyzing your actions, try to avoid being judgmental. Being excessively hard on yourself can distract you from virtuous action as readily as jealousy or anger. Excessive guilt is intemperate and is often demotivating, preventing you from making wise changes to how you go about things.

Indeed, in all of these analysis exercises, try to avoid judgment, and exercise your honesty and integrity. These exercises are about gathering the information you can use to live a better life—not about formulating opinions or judgments.

In addition to analysis, we can also consider evaluation. The next exercise looks at how we might do this.

Exercise 2:
Start Asking Yourself Why

The soul becomes dyed with the color of its thoughts.

—MARCUS AURELIUS

In Exercise 1, we considered using analysis exercises as a way of identifying patterns of thoughts and behavior in ourselves and others. The idea was to gather the information that could be wisely applied to living a better life.

These exercises build on the analysis exercises. Some of this will be familiar: We should examine our analyses in a meta-analysis, to identify trends and patterns. For example, I asked you to look for patterns between those things that make you happy, so you could truly understand what was at the core of these happy things.

However, these exercises go a bit further, because it asks you to ask why even in mundane situations. The thought is to get into the habit of self-reflection and understanding so that it becomes second nature.

Causal Explanation

There are two approaches we can take when asking why we are behaving or feeling a certain way. The first kind of "why" focuses on the causal explanation of your current state. We have focused on this in the previous exercises and in Chapter 8. We considered how your physical sensations could be contributing to your current thoughts and behavior, or how the context of an interaction could affect the tenor of the conversation. Asking about this kind of "why" is effective in giving you strategies, because it highlights parts of the causal picture that you can control.

The following exercise helps you practice asking yourself the why associated with a causal explanation.

1. Set an alarm for a time tomorrow when you are able to practice a stoic exercise.

2. When that time comes around, reflect and write down

    a. your current mood

    b. your physical sensations

    c. what you are thinking

    d. how you are behaving

3. For each of your answers, now think about why they have come about. Think about the full context that you're in: Such as where you are, and what time it is. Try to be as detailed as you can.

4. Repeat this exercise over a few days or weeks.

5. Reflect on your answers. Try to identify any patterns so you have a better understanding of your own nature.

Let's consider an example of stages 1-3. You set an alarm for 5.30 p.m. tomorrow because you will be home from work and able to conduct a stoic exercise. When the alarm comes around, you reflect on the questions included in stage 2. Suppose your answers are as follows:

•   I am feeling demotivated and fed-up.

•   I am tired. There is tension in my shoulders and in my jaw.

•   I am thinking that I'm glad to be home, but that I can't be bothered to do anything.

•   Before doing this exercise, I was sitting on the couch watching television.

Now we can think about the causal explanation behind these answers. Don't be discouraged if some of your answers are causal explanations for the other answers: This simply reflects the truth of the CBT cognitive cycle.

- I am feeling demotivated because I'm tired from a long day of work. I have a lot of pent-up frustration because I had to deal with lots of small issues that should have been sorted out in advance. My boss is on my back and I'm feeling worn down by it. The tension in my shoulders and jaw is making me feel fed up and on edge.

- I'm tired because I've had a stressful, long day at work. The tension in my shoulders and jaw probably relates to that stress as well, as well as irritation and frustration that my workday involved.

- I'm glad to be home because my workday was so stressful. I can't be bothered to do anything, because when I sat down to watch television, all the motivation just seemed to flow out of me. This lack of motivation might also stem from poor morale after work, as well as a general tiredness.

- I'm sitting on the couch watching television because I can't be bothered to do anything else. I just want to relax and not worry about work for a while. I'm tired.

Understanding the causal "why" identifies some points that you can think about more deeply. Clearly, you have had a bad day at work. This has resulted in some negative impressions, but this is the time to apply virtuous reasoning to your situation.

Part of this involves the wisdom of identifying those aspects of the current situation that you can change, and which parts you cannot. You can't change how the workday went, but you can control what you do next. The most tractable aspect of the situation is probably your behavior, so wisdom dictates that you should try to get up from the television and do something else. You have identified that television is contributing to your lack of motivation. Of course, this is easier said than done: It takes courage and temperance to force yourself off the couch when you don't feel like it. Maybe you should go for a walk, or make contact with a friend.

Understanding the "why" also identifies that there is some problem at work. You can't change the day you've just had, but you can influence how the next day goes. Again, the most tractable aspect of the situation is your behavior. You've identified an issue with tiredness: Consider if this relates to a lack of sleep, or whether it stems entirely from stress. If it's partly the former, then you can set yourself up for a better day tomorrow by going to bed earlier. When it comes to the problem at work itself, consider owning up to your mistakes with your boss. This act of justice and courage will demonstrate virtue and may mollify your boss, who will know that you are taking responsibility and steps to correct the situation. It will also help you to feel better about yourself. You will have demonstrated your integrity, and the problem will become something to work through and learn from, rather than something to dread or avoid.

Purpose

The second kind of "why" you can ask is about the purpose of things.

To demonstrate the difference between this kind of "why" and causal explanation, consider someone asking you why you are working. You may give two different answers:

- I am working because the lunch hour has finished.

- I am working to support my family.

The first answer is a causal explanation. The second is about purpose.

By thinking about this second kind of "why," you can get a better understanding of what is important to you, and build meaning and gratitude into your life. At the end of the day, pick one thing that you did that you found challenging or unpleasant. You can be as specific or general as you like. It could be your work, or it could be a particular project, taking out the bins, whatever you like. Now think about the purpose of you doing those things. Again, you can tailor your answer to how short or long-term you want it to be. Taking the three examples mentioned, some sample answers might be:

- I work to support my family and to give my child the best start in life.

- I'm working on this project because it's part of a company strategy to make the most of an existing niche in the market.

- I took out the bins because it really upsets my partner when I forget to put them out the night before collection.

These answers demonstrate different scopes. The first is very long-term and profound, speaking to your fundamental motivations. This kind of scope helps you understand your principles, and reminds you of your virtues and the things in life you are grateful for. The second answer is much more limited in scope but is still helpful in motivating yourself: You are part of a team effort, and you play your part in that large group project. This can be motivating. The third answer is also relatively limited in scope, but it has a profundity in its simplicity. You are taking out the bins because it makes your partner happy.

By understanding the purpose of your actions, you build your resilience. It is harder to weather negative events if they feel pointless. By reflecting on their purpose, you can be resilient to those negative impressions and empower yourself to act in a rational and virtuous manner.

To summarize, get into the habit of understanding the "why" behind your behavior, both in the sense of casually explaining why it happened, and finding the deeper purpose behind it. Through understanding, you will find resolve and wisdom.

Exercise 3:
Create Your Virtual Friend

If anyone can refute me—show me I'm making a mistake or looking at things from the wrong perspective—I'll gladly change. It's the truth I'm after, and the truth never harmed anyone.

—MARCUS AURELIUS

There is a long philosophical tradition of using dialogues to communicate complex points. The most famous example is probably Socrates. Plato and Xenophon presented Socrates's teachings in the form of a dialogue between Socrates and various other individuals.

There are great advantages to this presentation. Because it is presented as a dialogue, complex ideas can be broken down into natural steps. The writer must think from the perspective of the individual receiving these new ideas, and have that individual ask questions on behalf of the reader. Better still, the writer is forced to consider arguments against their position. As it is a dialogue, the writer's position is naturally challenged by the other, imaginary individual, such that the writer has to meet those challenges with reasoned arguments.

More generally, it is always good practice to imagine challenges to your beliefs. If your beliefs are incorrect, then considering arguments against them is the first step to discovering the truth. Alternatively, if your beliefs are defensible, then considering contrary arguments will give you a better, more reasoned understanding of your position. You will understand the arguments against your position and have counterarguments that support your belief. This is how things are meant to be: to be open to argument and rational dispute.

As an exercise, then, think about a position you hold that is controversial or complex. This may be an overtly philosophical or ethical issue, or something that is more mundane, such as the right way to load the dishwasher. Write down your position, and then write from the perspective of a virtual friend that might disagree with you. Test your own thoughts by explicitly challenging them, and see where the dialogue goes. This will lead you to a more considered and thoughtful position. Again, it is best to write down this dialogue—either with pen and paper or on a laptop. This will help you dedicate yourself to the exercise, and will also give a record of how your reasoning skills are improving.

Suppose that we are considering the right and wrong of challenging someone who has been rude to us. Let's say they have made an off-color remark that is vaguely insulting. Our dialogue might start as follows:

> **Winston:** If I do not challenge this behavior, the other individual might reach the opinion that it is okay to act in this way. This is unjust both to myself and them and perpetuates bad behavior.

> **Friend:** The better course of action is to be temperate. The other individual may not realize that they have been rude. Making a big thing out of it may lead to them responding defensively, rather than correcting their behavior. Wisdom, therefore, dictates that you should let this go, at least until it becomes a pattern of negative behavior.

> **Winston:** I do not know if that is courageous, or fair. I would rather treat the other individual as a rational human being, who will respond to me in a calm and reasoned manner. I should not assume that they will react negatively. This doesn't do them any credit and speaks to contempt toward them.

Try to follow the dialogue to a natural conclusion. This exercise will foster your natural reason and help you to see things from various perspectives. It will also force you to think more deeply about what is virtuous, and the best way to live your life.

Using this exercise also fosters humility in your positions, which will aid you in being temperate and wise. We should always assume that we have something to learn. There is a danger of being too stubborn in our positions. The first quotation I gave in this book speaks to this very issue: "It is impossible for a man to learn what he thinks he already knows" (Epictetus, 2008/2nd century). If we are too fixed in our beliefs, we become incapable of learning.

Let's consider another, more mundane example: The correct way to load a dishwasher. Your dialogue might go as follows:

Winston: The cutlery should be face up in the dishwasher so that the part of the utensil that has touched food is not covered. This allows for the dirtiest parts to be washed more effectively.

Friend: There is a safety risk in loading the cutlery face up because this means the blades of knives are face up. If you slip or reach for the utensils without thinking, you risk cutting your hand on those blades. Even a fork can leave a nasty injury if you were to break your fall on the prongs.

Winston: I acknowledge a slight safety risk, but I've never slipped or fallen over while unloading the dishwasher. Additionally, emptying the dishwasher is my responsibility, and I am cognizant of the fact that the blades are facing up. There is little chance of me forgetting. As such, the safety risks are very minimal. The benefits of clean cutlery outweigh these minimal risks.

Friend: If the cutlery is not clean when the dishwasher is finished, you could simply put the dishwasher on again, or manually wash the utensils. You are exaggerating the supposed benefits of loading the cutlery face up.

Winston: Putting the dishwasher on again would be wasteful, and washing knives manually likely involves safety risks on a par with loading those knives face up in the dishwasher.

In this dialogue, there is no great matter being discussed. However, by taking the time to think of it like a dialogue, you practice the art of rationally debating a topic. Not only does this exercise help you challenge and understand your own beliefs, but it also helps foster a habit of healthy questioning and openness to other points of view. This will help you avoid clinging to false beliefs, as well as expose you to other interesting ways of viewing the world.

The key takeaway is this: Through dialogue with your virtual friend, you commit yourself to a path of curiosity and wisdom. You begin seeing things from a different point of view. In the next exercise, we'll take this thought further and consider how adopting a third-person perspective can be virtuous.

Exercise 4:
Adopt the Third-Person Perspective

It never ceases to amaze me: We all love ourselves more than other people, but care more about their opinion than our own.

—MARCUS AURELIUS

Many self-compassion exercises involve imagining the perspective of a patient, loving friend. For example, when we are tempted to have persistent, negative thoughts about ourselves, we are enjoined to consider the perspective of a friend that might have a more compassionate take on the situation. From there, we can compare the perspective of this imaginary friend with our own perspective, and mark the differences between the two. Through this, we understand where our self-compassion is falling short, and can more easily identify disordered, negative thoughts.

We can adapt something like this to create a stoic exercise. However, if you are struggling with extreme, negative thoughts, you might try practicing self-compassion as a method for tempering your disordered thinking.

In the stoic tradition, we reframe the maximally kind friend as someone who is maximally virtuous: Someone who typifies the virtues of justice, temperance, wisdom, and courage. We consider how they might have acted and compare those actions to our own.

You might think that creating a virtual person for this task is unnecessary, but you'll be surprised by the insights you can achieve just by simulating a third-person perspective. By consciously removing the first-person perspective from our reflections, we can achieve a more objective, fairer perspective on what has happened.

The exercise, then, is as follows. Think about a recent event that left you feeling guilty, upset, or some other negative emotion. Describe the incident in detail, giving the full context, and being honest with yourself about how you behaved. As always, it is best to write this down, to make it a more deliberate exercise, and for ease of comparing it to another perspective later in the exercise.

Now, present the same situation to your maximally virtuous person. Imagine how they might have acted. Again, be as detailed as you can be. The more you think about the situation, the better.

You can now compare your virtual person's behavior with your own. Almost by definition, your maximally virtuous, virtual person would have acted better than you, but this is not an exercise in berating yourself. Take note of how you might have acted more virtuously, but take care to understand *why* you did not act in this maximally virtuous way. Try to understand what led you to fall short, and think of strategies to prepare yourself for similar circumstances in the future.

Let's consider this exercise in the form of an example. Suppose that someone cut you in line at a coffee shop. Giving a full description of the events, you might write something like the following:

> It was my lunch break and the line was long. Someone just cut in front of me and I didn't do anything—not really. I just tutted really loudly and clenched my jaw. I remember feeling really irritated, and, if I'm honest, I was a bit short with the barista when I reached the front of the line. It ruined my lunch.

Now think about how a maximally virtuous person might have acted. Your own description will depend on your own understanding of the four virtues, but here is one sample answer:

> My maximally virtuous friend was cut in line at the coffee shop. They calmly explained to the person who cut in line that they were being discourteous, but the other person was probably rude to them in return. Nonetheless, my friend displayed courage and justice by challenging their behavior. When treated rudely, my friend reflected on the fact that the other person's intemperate behavior was unnatural, and probably the result of some unhappiness or disordered life. This helped them feel empathy and compassion for the other person, without condoning their behavior. Reflecting on the wisdom of a well-lived life, my friend reached the front of the line and was courteous to the barista. Throughout, they were calm, contemplative, and temperate.

We can now compare the two scenarios. There are some obvious contrasts: In the first description, we showed intemperance by allowing our irritation to ruin our lunch, and we were unjust by passing on that rudeness to the barista. We also lacked courage, because we didn't calmly challenge the discourteous behavior of the person who cut in line.

However, we can go deeper with our comparisons and think about *why* there was a difference between the two scenarios. Maybe we have an issue with confrontation, and this forms a more general pattern of not standing up for what we think is right. If so, this is something to attend to and work on. Though you may not feel courageous now, there is courage and wisdom in admitting to your weaknesses and resolving to improve.

As an added exercise, you can also try to adopt the perspective of the person who upset you, in this case, the person who cut you in line. If you are honest with yourself, you have probably done something similar to them in the past: Maybe you've never cut in line at a coffee shop, but maybe you've taken a parking spot that someone else was waiting for, or pulled out in front of someone while driving. Unless you are a saint, you have probably done something in the last year that was discourteous or selfish. With this in mind, you should be able to extend your empathy toward the other person. Try to think about what might have caused them to act in such a discourteous way. Consider whether they might not have seen the line, or been somehow ignorant of their actions. If it is not plausible that their rudeness was accidental, consider how they might have been feeling. Try to be maximally empathetic and nonjudgmental. Write down a possible scenario that can explain their behavior in a temperate manner. For example:

> They are running very late, and they have had an awful day. Someone has been rude to them and they want to take it out on other people. Rudeness can be contagious like that. Out of frustration with their day and the world, they decided to cut in line. It wasn't good behavior, but it was the result of intemperate emotions and a negative state of mind.

Recognize in this description that you don't have to pretend that the other person's behavior was prosocial. What is important is that you try to genuinely understand and empathize with their actions. By deliberately fostering empathy, you will find yourself more temperate in your own emotions: By reflecting on their likely unpleasant circumstances, you are less likely to be consumed with anger or irritation. Furthermore, by trying to understand the nature and causes of vice, you will be demonstrating wisdom and curiosity about the world and other people.

Exercise 5:
Implementing Stoic Principles in Your Life

First say to yourself what you would be, and then do what you have to do.

—Epictetus

Living according to stoic principles is a skill that is improved by practice and habit. As such, you should be looking for opportunities for virtue in your life, to demonstrate your reason and stoic ideals.

Previous chapters have discussed various ways in which you can foster a habit of stoic thinking. We have talked about the importance of self-reflection, as well as voluntary discomfort and negative visualizations. For this exercise, however, we will talk about how stoic principles can be incorporated into your normal, daily life.

The first thing you need to learn is to take a deep breath. Most of us are in the habit of acting on impulse. If something negative happens to us, we automatically have a negative impulse, which becomes a negative thought or manifests in counterproductive or useless behavior. For example, our favorite sports team loses a crucial game. We immediately feel disappointed and upset, think angry thoughts, and let out a frustrated sigh. In this, you have not done anything excessively problematic. You have not upset or hurt anyone else. However, you *have* missed an opportunity for virtue. You have surrendered your reason to animal impulses, and ceded the ability to assent or dissent from the negative impressions caused by external events.

Even when you don't think it matters, never squander an opportunity for virtuous, reasoned action. Because living according to stoic principles relies on forming a habit, every opportunity to practice virtue will make it easier to practice stoic living in the future. So, take a deep breath when something happens, and deliberately reflect on the fact that you can choose whether to assent or dissent from your immediate emotions.

This will not always be easy. You are probably used to letting your immediate impressions drive your actions. In danger of being repetitive, I want to really stress the point: Living according to stoic principles is a skill that improves over time with continuous practice.

Because the implementation of stoic principles relies on practice, the best way to live a stoic life is to foster stoic habits. Meanwhile, a good habit has five aspects: It is specific, planned, flexible, feels positive, and is supported by others. If your new habit has these five aspects, you are much more likely to stick to it. With this in mind, let's look at each aspect in turn.

- **Your habit is specific.** Primarily, this means that your habit has specific goals. Try to avoid goals that are vague or too general. For example, the goal of living according to stoic principles is laudable, but it is too vague to be the basis of a good habit. Instead, think specifically about how you aim to live according to stoic principles. Maybe this means committing to completing a self-reflection exercise each day. It's okay to start small and build up over time. If you try to do everything at once, you will inevitably fall short and may become demotivated. In contrast, by being specific, you will be able to hold yourself to account and measure your progress in exact terms.

- **Your habit is planned.** If you want to keep to your new habit, then it's helpful to be exact with your planning. For example, if your goal is to complete a self-reflection exercise each day, you are more likely to keep to your habit if you fix a particular time in the day to complete your exercise. Incorporating routine into your habit makes it easier to keep up. In addition, planning ahead can identify potential obstacles and put in place a strategy for overcoming those complications. Rather than beginning your habit and realizing on the first day that you don't have a journal to write down your self-reflections, it is better to plan ahead and acquire everything you need before getting started.

- **Your habit is flexible.** The more that a new habit interferes with your daily routine, the more likely you are to abandon it. As such, it is okay to build in some flexibility to your planning. Continuing the example of committing to daily self-reflection exercises, it is worth acknowledging from the outset that sometimes your chosen time will not work. For example, suppose you have chosen 5.30 p.m. as your time to complete a self-reflection exercise. Sometimes you will have to work late or have a social event immediately after work. Rather than beating yourself up or abandoning your self-reflection exercise that day, accept flexibility into your habit and resolve to do your exercise at another time.

- **Your habit feels positive.** The most successful habits are those that feel rewarding. Hopefully, living a more stoic life will naturally provide this aspect, because you will start to feel calmer and more regulated in your emotions. However, you can take additional steps to get your habit started in the right way. Consider gamifying your habit, building in rewards. For example, every time you complete a self-reflection exercise, you might reward yourself with a piece of chocolate. Associating your habit with positive feelings helps keep you motivated.

- **Your habit is supported.** You are more likely to stick to your habit if someone else knows about it, and offer encouragement. We feel more accountable to others than ourselves, so making a semi-public commitment to your new habit can be an effective way of keeping you motivated. This might take the form of a small announcement to your friends on social media, or simply telling a few friends, family, or your partner. In addition, if you can persuade others to join you in your new habit, you will be able to keep each other motivated and accountable and talk through any difficulties you are having with your new routine.

I understand if you are anxious to start doing everything at once. However, it is important not to overwhelm yourself. Asking yourself to be the ideal stoic overnight is like entering a BMX race as a way to learn how to ride a bike, or performing a concerto to thousands of people as a way to learn how to play the violin. Such an approach is unwise and intemperate.

On the other hand, it is also okay to foster a few explicit habits, while more generally trying to live more virtuously. The main thing is that you don't overextend yourself, or start beating yourself up when you fall short. Striving to live a better, more virtuous life is to be celebrated, but it is not always easy. Acknowledge now that you will not always be your best self, and resolve to be fair to yourself. Hold yourself to account with empathy and kindness, and focus on improvement rather than self-beratement.

Just remember the key aspects of a good habit: specificity, planning, flexibility, positivity, and support.

Next, we'll consider additional ways to ground yourself and find your inner peace when you feel overwhelmed.

Exercise 6:
Achieving Inner Peace and Balance

It's ruinous for the soul to be anxious about the future and miserable in advance of misery, engulfed by anxiety that the things it desires might remain its own until the very end. For such a soul will never be at rest—by longing for things to come it will lose the ability to enjoy present things.

—SENECA

The ancient stoics taught that we should display caution when thinking about the future. Though there is nothing wrong with having projects and goals and using negative visualization to prepare you for the crisis, this should be balanced with temperance. If we are consumed by the future and what we don't currently have, then we will feel its loss a thousand times: Every time we reflect on not having it, we suffer for it again.

As such, it is important to learn how to stay present to help you avoid intemperate obsessions about the future. With this in mind, we can use mindfulness exercises to help you achieve inner peace, and maintain your emotional balance.

A straightforward mindfulness exercise you can try is the body scan. The idea behind the body scan is to direct your attention to different parts of your body in sequence. The exercise helps you focus your attention on the present, and is a relaxing way of finding your inner calm.

The steps to a body scan are as follows:

1. **Adopt a comfortable position.** You can sit or lie down for this exercise.

2. **Pay attention to your breathing.** Take a few deep breaths, breathing in through your nose and out through your mouth. Pay attention to how your chest rises and falls with each breath and the temperature of the air as it passes through your body.

3. **Redirect your attention to your body.** We are now in the body scan. Starting with the top of your head, gradually scan your entire body. For each body part, try to be cognizant of how it feels: Any aches or pains, the temperature, and any pressure against a surface it may be touching. Take as much time as you like over each body part.

Mindfulness, like stoic living, is a skill. You can improve at it with practice, and, at first, you may find intrusive thoughts distracting you from the exercise. If this happens, don't worry or berate yourself. This will make the thought more intrusive, or invite other thoughts that undermine your body scan. Instead, simply take note of that thought, and gently redirect your attention back to your body.

Another mindfulness exercise you might try is progressive muscle relaxation (PMR). Like a body scan, the exercise involves you redirecting your attention to different parts of your body in sequence. However, at each body part, you are asked to tense the relevant muscles tightly for five seconds, and then to deliberately relax those muscles for the subsequent fifteen seconds. Throughout, pay attention to how those muscles feel, and mark the difference between how they feel when they are tense and when they are relaxed.

The steps are as follows.

1. **Adopt a comfortable position.** As with a body scan, you can be sitting or lying down for this exercise. You can keep your eyes open or closed.

2. **Pay attention to your breathing.** To get yourself in the zone, think about the inhalation and exhalation of your breath, the temperature of the air, and how your chest rises and falls.

3. **Redirect your attention to your body.** It's time to begin the PMR.

4. We start with the **forehead.** Raise your eyebrows as far as you can and keep that tension in your forehead for five seconds. Then, relax your eyebrows for fifteen seconds.

5. Next, your **mouth and jaw.** Squeeze your lips together and scrunch your eyes closed for five seconds. Then, relax the muscles for fifteen seconds.

6. Redirect your attention to your **neck and shoulders.** Bring your shoulders up and keep them tense for five seconds. Then, relax them for fifteen seconds.

7. Next, your **chest.** Bring your shoulders back toward the middle of your back, creating a butter-fly shape. Keep the muscles tense for five seconds, then relax them for fifteen seconds.

8. Redirect your attention to your **arms.** Reach out with your arm and tense them for five seconds, before relaxing them for fifteen seconds. Then repeat for your other arm.

9. Focusing on the **upper arm,** pretend that you are showing off your biceps to someone by bending your arm and tensing the muscle group. Hold the pose for five seconds, then relax for fifteen seconds. Then repeat for your other arm.

10. Moving to the **lower arm,** clench your fist and tense your tricep muscle group for five seconds, before relaxing for fifteen seconds. Repeat for your other arm.

11. Now move on to the **buttocks.** Trying to isolate the muscle group in your buttocks, tense them for five seconds, and relax them for fifteen seconds.

12. Next are the **legs.** Stretch out your leg and tense it for five seconds, then relax the muscles for fifteen seconds. Repeat for the other leg.

13. Redirect your attention to your **calves.** Curl your toes up toward your knees to tense your calves, holding the position for five seconds, and then relaxing the muscles for fifteen seconds. Then repeat for your other leg.

14. Finally, focus on your **feet.** Curl your toes downwards to tense the muscles in your soles. Hold the foot tense for five seconds, and then relax it for fifteen seconds. Repeat for the other foot.

15. **To finish**, bring your attention back to your breathing. When you are ready, gently end the exercise.

Throughout this exercise, it's important not to extend the length of time you are tensing your muscles beyond five seconds. If you tense your muscles for too long, you risk straining them. In addition, if you ever feel pain in a muscle group, you should stop tensing them to prevent further damage.

These two exercises should get you started with mindfulness. If you are interested in other exercises, a quick search on YouTube should find a variety of guided mindfulness exercises for you to use, including breathing exercises, relaxing visualization exercises, and other versions of the body scan and PMR. The key lesson is that mindfulness exercises can redirect your attention to the present, and assist you in tempering an undue focus on the future.

Now, we'll think more about your emotional resilience and how you can strengthen it through your lifestyle choices.

Exercise 7:
Practicing Emotional Resilience

A blazing fire makes flame and brightness out of everything that is thrown into it.

—Marcus Aurelius

Stoicism, in a word, is about resilience. The philosophy asks you to remain stoic in the face of negative, external events, tempering your immediate impressions and exercising virtue where others would be overwhelmed.

Many of the exercises and practices outlined in this book will build on your emotional resilience. We have talked about voluntary hardship and negative visualizations, both of which prepare you for more difficult circumstances and remind you to be grateful for what you have. Similarly, mindfulness exercises designed to help you regulate your emotions will strengthen your resilience, as well as self-reflection practices that allow you to identify harmful patterns of thought and behavior.

However, here, we will focus on your emotional resilience and consider how it might be strengthened further.

The main thing to know is that emotional resilience is connected to other forms of resilience. It is harder to regulate our emotions if we are physically or psychologically unwell, or if our social life is limited. Consequently, let's look at each of these other forms of resilience.

Physical Resilience

Physical resilience is your health and fitness. If you look after your health, you will be more capable and independent and will find it easier to regulate your emotions.

We will focus on three ways you can boost your physical resilience: Your diet, exercise, and sleep hygiene.

Your Diet

Everyone knows the basics of a balanced diet, but sometimes it is difficult to stick to a healthy lifestyle. Most of us could stand to reduce our intake of carbohydrates, such as those found in bread, sugary foods, and non-diet soft drinks. High-sugar foods cause our insulin levels to spike—insulin being the hormone primarily responsible for breaking down sugar into energy for the body. Constant, high levels of insulin in our body cause our cells to grow resistant to the hormone, resulting in insulin dysregulation and, in extreme cases, diabetes. In turn, diabetes is associated with strokes, heart attacks, and a variety of other, unpleasant medical conditions.

If you don't have a healthy diet, you can practice stoic living by resolving to change what you eat. Improving your diet will test your temperance and wisdom, and is a healthy way of practicing voluntary hardship. Furthermore, it is good for your health.

Improving your diet involves fostering a new, healthy habit. Refer to Exercise 5 to remind yourself of the fundamentals of a good habit. First and foremost, don't be afraid to start by taking small, but meaningful steps that you gradually expand upon. You don't need to completely revolutionize your diet overnight. Focus on a specific way you can improve your diet, and start there.

Exercise

Like with our diet, most of us know that we should be getting daily exercise. The Centers for Disease Control (CDC, n.d.) advises that we should do 150 minutes of physical exercise each week, which breaks down to 30 minutes over five days.

Once more, doing more exercise is an opportunity to practice virtue. There is courage in forcing yourself to do a bit of exercise when you don't feel like it. In some sense, it is a voluntary hardship, especially if you do not naturally enjoy it.

On the other hand, as per the aspects of a good habit, try to find something you enjoy. Try a new sport or activity to discover a kind of exercise that is at least tolerable. The more fun you find it, the more likely you are to stick to your goal of doing more exercise and building your physical resilience.

Sleep Hygiene

Many of us forgo sleep hygiene as a necessary cost of an ordinary, busy life. However, this is a false choice. Good sleep hygiene is compatible with almost any lifestyle and can improve the quality of your sleep and reduce fatigue the next day.

The fundamental principle of sleep hygiene is routine. Try to stick to going to bed at the same time each night, and getting up at the same time each morning. If you can, continue this routine into the weekend. There is no scientific reason to try and "catch up on sleep" on the weekend: This is simply not how our bodies work. Instead, stick to routine, so that your body learns to feel tired and awake at the same times each day. This will help you wake up more refreshed, and make it easier to fall asleep.

In addition, an excellent first step in sleep hygiene is to leave your mobile phone outside the bedroom. Ideally, your bed should be used only for sleep and sex. If you are disciplined in this way, your brain will immediately associate the bedroom as a place for sleeping, psychologically aiding you in getting to sleep. Browsing your phone before going to bed busies your mind, making it more difficult for the brain to shut off when you try to sleep. Furthermore, the blue light from your phone mimics daylight, which signals your brain to keep the body awake and active.

More generally, try to avoid screens or high-attention activities for an hour before bedtime.

Psychological Resilience

Psychological resilience is closely related to emotional resilience. If you have symptoms of depression, generalized anxiety disorder (GAD), or another psychological disorder, then you may find it harder to regulate your emotions and keep yourself on an even keel. It is hard to be temperate or to dissent from negative impressions if you have an underlying health condition undermining your efforts.

On the other hand, taking your psychological health seriously can be a fantastic way of improving your emotional resilience. If you are suffering symptoms of a psychological disorder, accepting treatment to help you manage those symptoms will aid you in living according to the principles of stoicism.

As such, it is important to talk to your doctor if you may be suffering from the symptoms of a psychological disorder. This is an injunction to take your health seriously and to reach out for help if you need it. Reaching out is an act of wisdom and courage, not weakness.

Social Resilience

Humans are social creatures. We have naturally organized ourselves into groups, and our emotional resilience is closely tied to the health of those communities. If you feel like an active participant in your society, you will feel more confident and have a stronger sense of self. In turn, this will strengthen your emotional resilience. In addition, having a good support network is highly effective for supporting your emotional resilience when it would otherwise be difficult to do so.

Take this moment to reflect on your social life. Try to be honest with yourself, but be nonjudgmental: Many people, especially when they get a little older, find it difficult to maintain friendships and balance their social life with busy routines. If you do find room for improvement, it is worth reflecting on the wisdom of prioritizing your social life a little more. Fostering a good support network is an act of prudence.

How you foster your social life will depend on your personality, situation, and interests. If you have friends but you've fallen out of touch, you might consider reaching out to them and inviting them to hang out with you. By contrast, if you've been neglecting your social life for a while, it might be time to get out there and make some new friends. A great first step is to join a club for an activity you find interesting, from dance to board games.

You may find that your social life is particularly difficult to balance with family responsibilities. The first thing to note is that your dedication to your family is admirable. However, by taking a bit more time for yourself, you may find that you are in a better position to help your family. Taking the time to socialize can improve your mood and well-being, which in turn can make you better at regulating your emotions and making good decisions for your family. You may also find that you are more productive in the time that you are not socializing because you are happier and more motivated.

In summary, then, to work on your emotional resilience, consider other aspects of your life. Your physical and psychological health, as well as the health of your social life, can have a profound impact on your emotional well-being. Most of all, remember that taking a bit of time for your own health isn't selfish: It is responsible and puts you in a better position to act virtuously toward others. When you're healthy, everybody wins.

Of course, all these aspects of life require perseverance and discipline. The next exercise focuses on strengthening your discipline, helping you to remain committed to living as a stoic.

Exercise 8:
Practicing Discipline

We should discipline ourselves in small things, and from these progress to things of greater value.

—Marcus Aurelius

Discipline is a fundamental part of the stoic ideal. Having the emotional control to assent or dissent from negative impressions, and not be led by intemperate emotions, is at the core of living according to stoic principles. So, how can we strengthen our discipline in the face of a world that often throws us curveballs?

An excellent way of practicing discipline is voluntary hardship. In Chapter 8, we talked about a few exercises in voluntary hardship you could undertake. To remind you, these included occasionally:

- sleeping on the floor

- taking a cold shower

- restricting your diet

These are little tests of your discipline, helping you to improve and foster your resolve. They are a small way of proving to yourself that you can weather discomfort. In addition, these exercises are great ways to help you feel grateful for the things that you have. You may find yourself appreciating your bed more after a night spent on the floor.

Discipline is also strengthened by a sense of purpose. In Exercise 2, we talked about how it's important to self-reflect on the purpose of the activities you undertake. You will also find these exercises will strengthen your discipline because it is easier to commit to a course of action if you understand why it is important to you.

However, let's consider other ways we can strengthen our discipline. One insight from the ancient stoics is that you can't be disciplined about the big things unless you are also disciplined about the smaller things in life. With this in mind, let's talk about getting up in the morning, and making your bed.

Marcus Aurelius was not a morning person. In his *Meditations* (2006/170-180), he urges himself to be better at getting up promptly and without complaint:

> At dawn, when you have trouble getting out of bed, tell yourself: "I have to go to work—as a human being. What do I have to complain of, if I'm going to do what I was born for—the things I was brought into the world to do? Or is this what I was created for? To huddle under the blankets and stay warm?

Here, we see Marcus Aurelius appealing to his sense of purpose. He is also urging himself to have more self-respect.

Of course, a sense of purpose and self-respect are connected. Nonetheless, it is worth thinking about what you have to offer the world. As a human being, you are capable of rational, virtuous action and making the world a better place. But you can't do any of that from under the covers of your bed.

A more contemporary injunction to starting your day well comes from Admiral William H. McRaven, in his 2014 Commencement Address to the University of Texas. A decorated navy seal, McRaven urges us to make our bed in the morning. As he puts it:

> If you make your bed every morning, you will have accomplished the first task of the day. It will give you a small sense of pride and it will encourage you to do another task and another and another. By the end of the day, that one task completed will have turned into many tasks completed. Making your bed will also reinforce the fact that little things in life matter. If you can't do the little things right, you will never do the big things right. And, if by chance you have a miserable day, you will come home to a bed that is made—that you made—and a made bed gives you encouragement that tomorrow will be better. If you want to change the world, start off by making your bed.

This advice is fundamentally stoic in tone. By practicing discipline in making your bed, you set a positive tone for the rest of the day, and you foster discipline for those pursuits that are a little grander.

As an exercise then, commit to getting up at a certain time each morning, and not hitting the snooze button. When you get up, make your bed and go about your day promptly, and with determination. This small act of discipline will foster the self-respect and purpose that will help you remain disciplined in other areas of life. You will also find that this discipline and routine will improve your sleep hygiene, which can have a number of positive effects on your physical health and mood.

If you can combine this exercise in discipline with exercises in voluntary hardship and self-reflecting on your purpose, you will be well-equipped to deal with those events that test your discipline more severely. Sometimes, you will be tempted by intemperate emotions. You will feel angry and go to act accordingly, or you may be tempted to break your diet by the smell of chocolate cake. When you feel this temptation, reflect on your accomplishments. Reflect on the fact that you have already proven to yourself that you can go without and that you can remain focused and disciplined. Allow the impression of temptation to be an opportunity for virtue: To demonstrate the improved temperance that you have worked so hard for. In this way, you will remind yourself of your own accomplishments, building further on your self-worth and sense of purpose. This forms a virtuous cycle.

In summary, remain disciplined in the small aspects of life, and the rest will follow. The more you work on your discipline, the greater your sense of self-worth, and the easier it will be for you to remain disciplined.

Exercise 9:
How to Identify Things You Can and Cannot Control

No person has the power to have everything they want, but it is in their power not to want what they don't have, and to cheerfully put to good use what they do have.

—Seneca

Stoicism asks us to clearly separate things that we can control, and things that we cannot. The stoics taught that we always have control over how we respond to external events, but that we often don't have control of those external events themselves. For example, we can't control whether or not someone cuts us off in traffic, but we can choose whether or not we respond with fury.

To live according to stoic principles, it is important to get into the habit of separating those things you can control and those you cannot. However, it's also worth recognizing that control admits degrees. There are events you cannot control at all, some you can completely control, but also many events which you have imperfect influence over. For example, as noted in Chapter 7, if your boss is in a terrible mood, you might have some influence over the situation.

The following exercise encourages you to reflect on different events and sort them according to these three categories. The more you practice sorting events in this way, the more effective you will be in sorting events that you have not come across before. Like many stoic practices, this is a skill that improves with use.

Start by drawing three concentric circles, such that the second circle encompasses the first, and the third encompasses both the first and the second. Make the circles large so that you have room to write inside their areas. The first circle represents those events you can control, the second circle represents those events that you can only influence, and the third circle represents those events that you have no control over.

Next, write down a list of around twenty everyday occurrences that tend to negatively affect your quality of life on a daily basis. If your mind immediately goes blank, you can use the list below as a prompt to get you going, all based on negative events that could happen before your lunch hour.

- you are very tired when your alarm goes off in the morning

- you run late in the morning

- the shower takes ages to warm up

- the traffic on your commute to work is awful

- someone cuts you off in traffic

- you are irritated by the time you get to work

- your colleague chides you for running late

- the coffee machine is on the fritz again

- your boss criticizes you for little mistakes

When you've written down your negative events, now sort each one of them into a circle. Taking the examples above, we might sort them as follows:

- First circle (events you can control):

  - you run late in the morning

  - you are irritated by the time you get to work

- Second circle (events you can influence):

  - you are very tired when your alarm goes off in the morning

  - your colleague chides you for running late

  - your boss criticizes you for little mistakes

- Third circle (events you cannot control):

    o the shower takes ages to warm up

    o the traffic on your commute to work is awful

    o someone cuts you off in traffic

    o the coffee machine is on the fritz again

Depending on your point of view, you might disagree with how I have categorized some of these events. This is because control admits of degrees, and the boundaries between each circle may be down to personal perspective. For example, you might think that the shower taking ages to warm up actually belongs in the second circle because you could take steps to fix the shower or hire someone who can fix it. It's okay to disagree with my categorization. The important thing is to be cognizant of which parts of the situation fall into your influence, and which parts do not.

It might help to break down an event into separate parts so that you can sort them more precisely. Continuing the example of the shower taking ages to warm up, we might break down this situation into the following two parts:

- when you first moved into your apartment, the shower already took ages to warm up.

- the shower needs to be fixed.

The first part is something that falls properly outside your control, assuming some common sense about what practically falls under your influence. Technically, you could have broken into the apartment before you moved in and fixed the shower after taking a plumbing course, but it's okay to sort events on the basis of what's sensible. The second part, meanwhile, might actually belong in the first circle as something you can directly control.

How you sort events based on these nuances is not critical. The important thing is that you are reflecting on those nuances and thinking about the limits of your control. By thinking deeply and deliberately about these issues, you'll get better at them. This will prevent you from trying to change things you can't control, as well as preventing you from denying responsibility for those areas of your life that you can change.

Meanwhile, always remember that you have control over how you respond to something happening to you—regardless of whether or not you had control of the thing that happened. A good exercise for internalizing this wisdom is to practice drawing a line between the event and your response.

Start by writing down an account of something that happened to you in your day that left you feeling negatively affected. Outline what happened, and how it made you feel. An example might be something like this:

> I made a small mistake at work. Because it was a formula in an excel worksheet, the small error cascaded into a bigger error, and my boss soon noticed. They acted like I was stupid and made me feel small. I feel angry toward them because it's unfair: It was clearly just a small mistake, and we got it fixed pretty quickly. I had to take a walk after to calm myself down.

Next, look back through your account and highlight those passages that are about how you responded to what happened. Draw a distinction between what initially happened and your response. For example:

> I made a small mistake at work. Because it was a formula in an excel worksheet, the small error cascaded into a bigger error, and my boss soon noticed. They acted like I was stupid and **made me feel small**. **I feel angry toward them because it's unfair**: It was clearly just a small mistake, and we got it fixed pretty quickly. **I had to take a walk after to calm myself down.**

The bolded phrases correspond to your response. Now, think about how you ultimately had control over your response, and how you might have reacted differently in a more virtuous manner. It may help to adopt the position of a maximally virtuous person, as outlined in Exercise 4. Remember that this is not an exercise in berating yourself, but instead about gently reminding yourself what you can control and what you cannot.

In this exercise, we are simply separating the initial event from your reaction. Don't worry about whether aspects of the initial event also fell under your influence. This is not the purpose of this particular exercise. Instead, this exercise is about internalizing the thought that you control how you respond to the events that happen to you. By internalizing this idea, you will be empowered to respond more temperately in the future and to choose a rational, virtuous reaction rather than being led by your emotions. In turn, this will help you live a stabler, more contented life.

The key takeaway is that learning to identify the limits of your influence is something that needs practice. Get used to deliberately reflecting on the matter. If you keep practicing, it will become your natural way of thinking.

Next, we'll expand on another aspect of Part 2, and consider exercises for practicing negative visualization.

Exercise 10:
Practicing Your Negative Visualizations

How ridiculous and how strange to be surprised at anything which happens in life.

—MARCUS AURELIUS

In Chapter 8, we discussed the art of negative visualization: The practice of mentally rehearsing unpleasant events so that you are emotionally prepared for them when they come. In this exercise, we look more closely at negative visualizations and how they can be used to live according to stoic principles.

As an exercise, think about an ongoing project or goal you are working toward, or just something you care about that is ongoing or about to happen. This might be a work or DIY project, or perhaps a romantic date tomorrow evening. Now, imagine it ending in failure. In your journal, or on a piece of paper, write out in detail what this failure might look like. Try to be realistic rather than fanciful about what might happen. For example, if you are thinking about an upcoming romantic date, you might outline failure as follows:

> The conversation is stilted and awkward. We don't really hit it off, and they keep checking their phone. There are long silences and, when I talk about myself, they seem entirely uninterested.

This is a realistic outcome, as opposed to:

> My date immediately stabs me with a fork. I fall back, bringing the table on top of me, and then the restaurant bursts into flames.

Undoubtedly, the second scenario would also represent a failed date, but it is not particularly realistic!

Now that you have outlined a realistic failure scenario, try to anticipate how you would react. Consider this an exercise in radical honesty. Instead of thinking about how you would like to respond, think about how you probably *would*. Later in the exercise, you will have the opportunity to consider a more virtuous path. For now, write down how you would likely feel, what physical sensations you might have, what kind of thing you would be thinking, and how you would behave. An example answer might be:

I feel uncomfortable with the silence. There's tension in my shoulders and jaw. I want to leave the restaurant. I feel a bit like a failure. I keep trying to catch the waiter's attention so we can get the check and end this date.

Really try to imagine yourself inhabiting this scenario. You may even find that you start to feel some of the physical sensations now. You may find this uncomfortable, but try to stay with it. Remember that you get to choose how to respond to negative impressions you feel. Ride through the emotions and recognize that you are capable of withstanding them without any great disaster occurring.

Next, try to write out how you would *want* to act in this kind of scenario. Again, you can refer to physical sensations, emotions, thoughts, and behaviors when considering your answer. Furthermore, you can consider stoic virtues and how you might best demonstrate wisdom, temperance, justice, and courage. For example:

The silence is initially uncomfortable, but I reason that my date must be feeling the same. I purposefully relax my shoulders to ease tension and reflect on the fact that not every pair of people is a good romantic match. In a week or so, this won't matter to me, and there's no reason for it to hurt me now.

Given that I know there's not going to be a second date, I relax. If they continue to seem uncomfortable, I'll suggest that we bring the date to an early close: I don't want them to have a bad time. Otherwise, I'll make light conversation to help them feel less tense, and to practice my conversational skills.

In this answer, all four of the main virtues are demonstrated. You demonstrate wisdom by recognizing that one bad date is not going to be something that's going to affect you in the long run. You demonstrate temperance by easing your shoulders and calmly changing tack from having a romantic date to a light conversation. You show justice by considering your date's needs, and ending the date early if they continue to feel uncomfortable. And—perhaps most of all—you show courage by confronting your thoughts and feelings with honesty and virtue.

As an extra step to this exercise, you might consider how you will likely feel about the negative scenario one month or year in the future. This will often help you to put the situation into perspective. You're not going to think about a bad date you had last year. You may have had dozens of dates since then, or even entered into a relationship. A lot can happen in a year. You may not even be able to remember your date's name.

Another use for negative visualization is to anticipate disasters so they can be avoided. For example, suppose you are about to begin a large work project. Before you start, you might imagine all the ways that the project could be a disaster. You may discover that some of those disasters are preventable. By using negative visualization, you have identified potential problems and can take steps to pre-empt them.

We can practice using negative visualization in this way with the following exercise. As with the last exercise, think about an ongoing or upcoming event and outline how it might go badly.

Next, reflect on *why* this might happen, rather than focusing on your likely reaction. For example, when visualizing a work project going badly, you might think about how you fall behind schedule in a way that stresses you out and causes you to make a variety of different mistakes.

Now, you can think about why you might fall behind schedule. Maybe it's because you don't have a schedule at all, and haven't taken the time to plan out the different stages of the project and assign time to complete those stages.

This highlights a way you can forestall a negative scenario: You can put together a schedule for your project to make sure it is organized, and to make sure that appropriate time is parceled out for each stage. By using negative visualization, you have anticipated potential flaws with your current plan and can take steps to account for such problems.

To summarize: By using negative visualizations, then, you will not only be better prepared for things going wrong—they are also less likely to go wrong in the first place.

PART 4:
LAST, BUT NOT LEAST

Chapter 14:
How to Explain Your New Stoic Life to Others

What if someone despises me? Let them see to it. But I will see to it that I won't be found doing or saying anything contemptible. What if someone hates me? Let them see to that. But I will see to it that I'm kind and good-natured to all, and prepared to show even the hater where they went wrong. Not in a critical way, or to show off my patience, but genuinely and usefully.

—Marcus Aurelius

You have read the earlier chapters in this book, tried out a few of the exercises, and are on your way to living according to the principles of stoicism. However, how do you tell other people about your new lifestyle? Even more fundamentally, should you?

Reasons and Reasons Not to Tell Others

When deciding whether to tell other people about your new lifestyle, it is worth reflecting on why you want to. Some reasons will be virtuous, whilst others will be intemperate. For example, we learned in Exercise 5 that a good habit is one that is supported by the people in your life. As such, there may be wisdom in telling others about the stoic habits you are trying to foster, to hold you in some sense accountable to them to remain disciplined.

Another good reason to tell people about stoicism is if you genuinely feel it will help them. Stoicism has a lot to offer people who feel that their lives are out of control, and are feeling overwhelmed. However, if this is your motivation, make sure you take a deep breath and don't come across too strong. Stoicism is not a religion, and it is certainly not a cult: So, remember the virtue of temperance and avoid coming across too insistent or needy. Remember the wisdom of understanding what you can control, and what you cannot control. Though you are in a position to bring other people's attention to the philosophy of stoicism, you are ultimately not in control of the decisions other people make about how to live their lives. As such, be prepared to rein it back if the person you're trying to help seems irritated or put off. Otherwise, you risk turning them off stoicism for life, and your actions have been counterproductive.

Finally, you might want to tell others about your stoic lifestyle simply because it is important to you. It is natural to want to share your principles with close friends and family members. Just make sure that you don't come across too strong or preachy, to avoid being off-putting. Instead, focus on your own personal experiences of stoicism and share as much as you would like to share about your journey.

On the other hand, there are bad reasons to share your newfound stoic way of living. Definitely resist telling others about your stoic lifestyle if your desire is to show off. Being boastful is not acting in accordance with stoic principles. It is better to be temperate and to have the courage of your conviction without requiring the approval of others. As Marcus Aurelius wrote (2006/170-180), "settle on the type of person you want to be and stick to it, whether alone or in company."

Moreover, showing off about stoicism is just plain annoying!

Telling Others

On the assumption that you have a practical, virtuous reason to tell others about your stoic lifestyle, how best to do it?

Again, it somewhat depends on your motivation. If you are just sharing an important part of your life, then you can focus on your own personal experience of stoicism, rather than attempting to persuade the person you're talking to of stoicism's benefits. Furthermore, how you tell someone about stoicism will depend on who they are to you, and the given context. If the context and your relationship with the other person is more casual, then you should not overload them with a lengthy lecture about the tenets of stoicism. On the other hand, if you are talking to a close friend and they seem to have an interest, you can go into a bit more detail about what stoicism is.

Regardless of your motivation, your relationship with the other person or the context, one good piece of general advice is to scaffold. Start small, and build from there if the other person seems interested in what you're saying.

By starting small, I mean this in terms of your enthusiasm and the level of detail you give. To demonstrate this in action, consider the following situation. Suppose you are in a conversation with a friend. The dialogue might go as follows:

Friend: I've been experimenting with cold showers. They're meant to be good for reducing inflammation.

You: Oh, I've also been doing that, but for a different reason. It's this thing I've been trying called voluntary hardship. It's supposed to build your resolve and help you feel more grateful for the things you have. It's actually been really fulfilling!

Friend: Voluntary hardship? I've never heard of that. Where did you get that from?

You: I've been looking into the philosophy of stoicism, it's a part of that. The basic idea behind stoicism is that you can control how you respond to negative events, even if you can't control the negative events themselves. I'm finding it really empowering, and a great way of feeling less overwhelmed by things.

Friend: Sounds cool!

You: Yeah! I can tell you more about it, if you'd like!

Here we see scaffolding in action. You start with a throwaway comment about voluntary hardship, which is an extraneous aspect of stoicism, rather than the core of the philosophy. When your friend showed an interest, you gave more detail and introduced more theoretical ideas by outlining the basic tenet of stoicism. Now that your friend continues to show interest, you can build on this further and really get into the theoretical weeds of what you've learned from the philosophy.

This dialogue also demonstrates two further positive aspects when talking about philosophy. First, you didn't force your beliefs on the other person, and only continued when you were prompted to do so by their level of enthusiasm. We can imagine the conversation going a different route:

Friend: I've been experimenting with cold showers. They're meant to be good for reducing inflammation.

You: Oh, I've also been doing that, but for a different reason. It's this thing I've been trying called voluntary hardship. It's supposed to build your resolve and help you feel more grateful for the things you have. It's actually been really fulfilling!

Friend: Oh, cool. Yeah, it's also meant to be good for reducing muscle soreness. Have you found that?

Here, your friend has returned the subject of the conversation to the health benefits of cold showers. That's okay. Follow the natural flow of the conversation, and don't insist on talking more about stoicism if your friend isn't into it. Otherwise, you'll just put them off.

The second positive aspect is that you've opened up by talking about your own personal experiences. Again, this prevents you from forcing your beliefs on your friend. You haven't talked about how *they* would benefit from practicing voluntary hardship; instead, you've mentioned how it personally helped *you*. This prevents your friend from feeling pressured, or like you are trying to proselytize.

The key takeaway is this: Stoicism is a philosophy, not an article of faith. It shouldn't really matter if other people live according to their own, distinct set of principles, as long as they seem to be flourishing and happy. Though the stoics believed in their philosophy as a way of living well, there is no need to insist on it being the one and only way to do so. As such, you can be temperate and relaxed when telling others about it. Nothing great should be at stake.

Chapter 15:
Eat Sleep Stoic Repeat

Waste no more time arguing about what a good man should be. Be one.

—MARCUS AURELIUS

You now have the fundamentals of stoicism in hand, along with a variety of exercises designed to help you start living according to stoic principles. But at what point do you become a stoic?

The truth is, there is unlikely to be a moment you can pinpoint as the moment you became a stoic. Remember again that living according to stoic principles is a skill. You will get better at it the more you practice. At some point in time, you will reflect on your day and realize that your automatic way of thinking is now stoic. You will realize that you are no longer being led by your impressions and emotions, but are exercising your ability to assent or dissent from them in the way that you act. You will start to feel more temperate and in control of your feelings, and begin to feel the happiness that the ancient stoics called the state of *eudaimonia*.

However, this will not be the end of your journey. Sometimes you will fall short of the ideals you hope to live by. On occasion, your temper will get the better of you, or you will be tempted to some vice. But you will self-reflect on what happened, and carry on. Though you may stumble, you will continue on your path. You are in good company: Marcus Aurelius, one of the most famous stoics in history, often fell short, candidly writing about it in his *Meditations* (2006/170-180). Living according to stoic principles is a lifelong project, but the rewards are great. By living your best life, you will feel your best self.

Along your journey, remember that this book is just a guide. It is not a set of laws or a religious text. This book is to be used as you see fit: To remind you of some tenet, to offer some helpful exercises, or to give you a little push of motivation. Feel free to pick and choose exercises that gel better with your nature. Equally, feel free to re-read individual chapters out of order. As long as you are committed to living according to stoic principles, there is no wrong way to return this book. It is your resource.

I have repeated throughout this book that living according to stoic principles is a skill. This means that know-how can only achieve so much. You can understand the tenets of stoicism inside and out, but there is no substitute for habit and practice. Think of it this way: Learning all the physical and anatomical details of riding a bike is not the same as learning how to ride a bike. Similarly, learning about the tenets of stoicism is not the same as learning how to be a stoic. If you want to be a stoic, you must commit yourself to daily practices, using the exercises in this book as your guide.

At the start, it may not be easy to live according to stoic principles. You have picked up this book because you are dissatisfied in some way with how you manage your emotions. It will take time and effort to overcome these bad habits that have led you to seek an alternative way of living. If you have struggled with your anger in the past, a couple of exercises will not magically fix your temper. On the other hand, if you persist, continue to think about stoicism, and practice stoic exercises, you will gradually see an improvement. You will reflect on your anger, determine triggers to better understand your own nature, and apply wisdom and courage to guide yourself to a more temperate way of feeling. Over time, you will start to occasionally catch yourself before you let your temper get the better of you, and if you keep practicing, this will become more and more common. Though you may always have to keep an eye on your anger, eventually you will get to the point where you can reliably rein your temper back.

To really bring the point home: Living according to stoic principles is a process. Try not to be impatient, and maintain your discipline and resolve. As Marcus Aurelius wrote (2006/170-180):

> If something is difficult for you to accomplish, do not then think it impossible for any human being; rather, if it is humanly possible and corresponds to human nature, know that it is attainable by you as well.

The frustrations and process of learning to live stoically are themselves opportunities for virtue. Demonstrate courage by being honest about your shortcomings, and responding to small failures with perseverance and effort. Demonstrate wisdom by understanding that this is a process, and that, even when you suffer setbacks, you are progressing in your ability to live according to stoic principles. Demonstrate justice by making amends for those setbacks that negatively affect other people, so that you can transform a moment of anger into an opportunity for growth. And, perhaps most of all, demonstrate temperance by not allowing a small setback to throw you entirely off track. Don't be consumed with guilt or self-recriminations beyond what is useful for your self-improvement. Don't assent to negative emotions that only seek to demotivate you.

Through these virtues, and living with honesty and integrity, you will have the power to compensate for your foibles, and find a state of *eudaimonia* even before you are the perfect stoic. You will feel proud of your efforts to live a better life and will have a better sense of self and self-respect.

In other words: Persevere. The journey itself is the reward.

Conclusion

Putting things off is the biggest waste of life: it snatches away each day as it comes, and denies us the present by promising the future. The greatest obstacle to living is expectancy, which hangs upon tomorrow and loses today. You are arranging what lies in Fortune's control, and abandoning what lies in yours. What are you looking at? To what goal are you straining? The whole future lies in uncertainty: Live immediately.

—SENECA

We arrive at the end of the book. Let's recap the key takeaways.

Stoicism is an ancient philosophy that teaches we can always control how we respond to external events, regardless of whether we can control those events themselves. For the ancient stoics, philosophy was the study of how to live well. Given this, and that we control how we react to events, the thought is that we should apply philosophical thinking to how we respond to life's curveballs. The stoics believed that we should always act in a way that demonstrates four key virtues: courage, justice, temperance, and wisdom. By choosing to control our emotions and react in a virtuous manner, we live according to what is good, and achieve the state of flourishing, or *eudaimonia*, that living well brings.

Of course, living according to stoic virtues is easier said than done. To this end, the stoics taught that we should be constantly reflecting on our actions. In doing so, we can apply reason to our actions, learn from our mistakes, and build on our successes. In addition to this self-reflection, stoicism teaches that we should constantly test ourselves, and build on our innate resilience. We can practice voluntary hardship, to teach ourselves that we are able to cope with discomfort and to remind ourselves to be grateful for the good things that we have. Moreover, we can use negative visualizations, to prepare ourselves for negative events, and to forestall those events with deliberate forethought.

In this book, we have built on these practices and included techniques from modern psychology. I have noted the throughline from ancient stoicism to psychiatric treatments like cognitive behavioral therapy (CBT) and applied principles of CBT to enhance our stoic self-reflections. For example, we have thought about the cognitive cycle, and how our thoughts, behaviors, feelings, and physical sensations are all causally interconnected. We have applied this insight to our self-reflections so that we can more effectively learn from our past experiences and identify triggers that tempt us to counterproductive action. We have also adapted exercises from the psychology of self-compassion to help guide our reflections and applied mindfulness techniques to help ground us in the present and find inner temperance and calm. Throughout, I have stressed how living a stoic life requires perseverance and practice, and that, like any other skill, you will get better at it the more you try.

All of us can take steps to live in accordance with stoic principles. All of us can take steps to master our emotions. As Seneca wrote (2004/65), "begin at once to live, and count each separate day as a separate life." Do not be afraid to strive for great things by the promise of setbacks or occasional failure. By embracing stoicism, even those failures are opportunities for virtue and to live a better life. Remember Epictetus's words (2008/2nd century): "If you want to improve, be content to be thought foolish and stupid." As long as you are trying, you will have your integrity and sense of self and will be able to flourish in the busy business that is life.

The best of luck in your journey.

Your Free Gift

As a special thank you for purchasing my book, I am thrilled to offer you four FREE exclusive downloads designed to enhance your emotional resilience and critical thinking skills.

1. **The Resilience Handbook**: Build your resilience with insights into key Stoic principles and the four main skills of emotional intelligence, equipping you to handle life's challenges with calm and confidence.

2. **How to Teach Kids Critical Thinking**: This guide provides engaging exercises tailored to develop critical thinking skills in children, helping them grow into thoughtful, analytical adults.

3. **Applying Critical Thinking Skills in Everyday Life**: Discover practical strategies to seamlessly integrate critical thinking into your daily routine, enhancing your decision-making and problem-solving abilities.

4. **History of Critical Thinking**: Dive into the fascinating evolution of critical thinking and understand its profound impact on modern society.

Inside These Bonuses, You'll Discover:

- **Resilience Strategies**: Techniques to enhance your emotional resilience and maintain inner peace, even in stressful situations.

- **Engaging Exercises for Kids**: Fun activities that make critical thinking accessible and enjoyable for children.

- **Daily Critical Thinking Tips**: Practical advice to improve your reasoning and analytical skills in everyday situations.

- **Historical Insights**: A comprehensive look at how critical thinking has shaped progress through the ages.

And much more...

To download your bonuses, simply scan the QR code below:

BOOK 2

Unlocking Emotional Intelligence

Practical Guide and Exercises
for Personal Transformation Journey

Introduction

There is no separation of mind and emotions; emotions, thinking, and learning are all linked.

    –ERIC JENSEN

Have you found yourself feeling confused and lost in a sea of emotions, unsure of how to manage their intensity? Are you curious to discover how certain individuals effortlessly manage difficulties while others struggle? Well, imagine being armed with knowledge that allows you to decipher intricate emotional states and harness their power to foster closer links with those dearest to you. My objective lies in empowering you to recognize and regulate the complexities associated with human emotional experience while promoting growth as well as your overall happiness level.

Being emotionally intelligent (EQ) can lead to greater happiness and fulfillment in life compared to just having a high IQ. It has been proven that people with higher emotional intelligence tend to enjoy better personal as well as professional lives (Cherry, 2022). Developing your emotional intelligence can reduce stress chemicals in your body—like having your very own mini-anti-stressor inside you! By growing your EQ, you learn to better regulate and lower your body's stress responses. You end up experiencing less anxiety and improved health and mood.

Sometimes, life feels overwhelming because of all the different emotions we experience. Some days, everything might feel great; other times, we may struggle just to get out of bed. No matter what, though, it seems like too often, our emotions take charge instead of us taking charge of them! Maybe you want better ways to understand and handle them so they don't mess up plans at work or your social life with friends and family. Perhaps even more importantly, would you love guidance toward living overall with less worry and fear? In case these lines describe you too, well, I am writing today to tell you—it won't remain so! Understanding the hidden triggers beneath the surface of your mind leads directly into the pathway of peaceful living experiences! Taking care of yourself is now easier than ever!

Unlocking your emotional intelligence has huge potential for positive changes in your private universe. This book will be your trusted companion throughout this voyage. Its content offers useful tips and lots of exercises showing ways in which better managing your feelings helps tackle difficulties and strengthen bonds. When you finish reading it, you may even treat tricky predicaments with poise and make choices that match who you really wish to become! Enjoying the guidance might even open chances to enhance important ties and live an extra meaningful life!

Gaining skills to manage your emotions means improving your inner life while strengthening close ties. Better communication equals better bonding all around! Developing emotional competencies lets you turn bad things into good new possibilities, helping you learn more about yourself. A win for you and other treasured contacts—at home and work! Reading this book would truly benefit many aspects of your private and professional interactions.

It's the right moment to take full control over how your emotions affect you! Ahead lies a demanding yet worthwhile adventure guaranteed to develop self-control abilities. Throughout these chapters, you'll find ideas echoing your reality, along with exercises designed to build your emotional prowess, helping you progress toward the capability to utilize emotions as resources to reach happiness goals. This book is divided into parts, and there is a fully dedicated part solely to working on various exercises that should benefit most people. You get to decide what works best for you personally since exercises helpful to one individual might not fit another!

As the author of this book, I bring a deeply personal and relatable perspective on emotional intelligence because my path to getting here wasn't easy either. I also experience all kinds of emotions and face obstacles throughout my life, similar to everyone else. And just like you guys, I desire contentment within myself. You will see my experience scattered across the chapters, making each section relatable to most readers' individual lives and helping you connect to its contents better.

I once put forth a lot of effort in a job where I frequently felt weighed down and smothered. Many people constantly asked, "How are you?" but I was unable to adequately relate to or discuss serious subjects, so I acted impulsively rather than thoughtfully. Despite the fact that life is meant to be enjoyable, this kind of existence continued, making me depressed and lonely.

To break free from such agony, I began searching for answers elsewhere. A particular belief system called Stoicism captured my attention later on. These ideas helped shape my current perspectives and beliefs, which helped me handle things differently. Its preaching gave me instruments to take on tougher spots headfirst while remaining calm and collected during life's storms. Applying some of the stoics' ideas even aided in forming bonds to share the joys of simple pleasures and find tranquility during difficulties that arise unexpectedly.

One fine day, I thought to pen down whatever insights worked for me after learning how to manage troublesome occurrences. It occurred to me that sharing my own experience might help other seekers, too. Since then, I've started jotting down various happenings that altered my perception of life and the corresponding lessons learned. This book intends to leave encouragement and inspiration wherever possible for those willing to read between the lines.

Are you ready to join me on this exciting adventure, exploring new skills and ideas for dealing with your emotions? All you need is a willingness in your spirit and eagerness in your brain since the knowledge gathered in this awesome collection of notes will certainly guide you along each twisty turn in the process. Don't forget that perfect results aren't expected here; instead, small steps forward mean a lot!

Let's get started!

PART 1:
THE THEORY OF EMOTIONAL INTELLIGENCE

Chapter 1:
What Is Emotional Intelligence— Understanding the Four Skills

Until you make the unconscious conscious, it will direct your life, and you will call it fate.
    –C.G JUNG

In today's society, where wealth, power, and appearances are highly valued, it can be easy to forget about the importance of managing our emotions. After all, emotions matter, too! They influence not only our happiness but also our overall satisfaction with ourselves, the relationships around us, and even our work performance. At times, we might have faced situations where some negative feelings took over us completely, leaving us clueless about our next move, whereas there will always be a few people who look composed under any circumstances, just like water lilies, taking those tough moments head-on without giving up easily. That is exactly what I mean when we discuss emotional intelligence. Take the first step toward understanding yourself better by understanding these four skills.

Take a moment to relax and get ready for what lies ahead. In this chapter, I share insights that set a strong foundation for growing emotionally. We'll look at four main abilities related to these emotions: knowing ourselves well (self-awareness); regulating our emotions and actions (self-management); being aware of other people's feelings (social awareness); and managing close relationships (relationship management)—all vital to overall emotional growth. This initial stage helps build a sturdy foundation.

Self-Awareness

Being self-aware means taking a close look at yourself from the inside. It involves thinking seriously about how your actions match up with what's important to you personally, like morals and values that make sense in your own life. When there's conflict or mismatch between what you do and those personal standards of yours, it can leave you feeling upset, discouraged, or even downright saddened. On the flip side, when everything lines up right and properly for you personally, the positives really start rolling in—inner harmony and a boost in confidence! This introspective focus includes considering how others perceive our choices, too, which makes us more open, accepting, and willing to work together constructively! So, all told, developing strong self-awareness skills leads to a happier and healthier existence overall.

Exploring your inner self could evoke conflicting emotions, either new or old. But all of these different feelings and ideas blend together to create your unique personality. Being receptive to varied emotional aspects provides insightful knowledge about yourself. Exploring self-awareness can also lead to personal growth and fulfillment. It demands patience and compassion since the goal is to accept our flawed selves rather than achieve perfection. The path ahead might reveal strengths and areas needing improvement. By discovering our true abilities and being genuine, we enhance our lives. Inner reflection opens doors to new opportunities.

Gaining self-awareness isn't simply knowing things; it involves receiving them with an open heart— like having a supportive friend listen non-judgmentally, allowing you to freely share emotions. This caring presence encourages you to understand yourself better. Through its guidance, learn to appreciate your reactions without shame. It results in being more at peace with who you really are. The moment you cultivate self-awareness, you automatically give birth to emotional intelligence. You become better equipped to comprehend and take charge of the sentiments that surface within you, thereby creating stronger connections in both professional and personal circles by sharing your emotions with others. Emotional intelligence helps us form stronger bonds because it allows us to relate to each other emotionally and build trust and cooperation. With the added capability to identify and acknowledge others' feelings intuitively, we learn to navigate social situations while handling stressors so we're able to collaborate effectively; everyone feels respected, heard, and valued!

Self-awareness helps you handle difficult situations with poise and resilience. Recognizing personal preferences and biases allows for breaking out repetitive behavior cycles. In times of struggle, self-understanding directs you toward making mindful decisions. Embracing your aptitudes lets you utilize them purposefully while acknowledging flaws gives room for further development. Awareness fosters confidence by inviting suggestions instead of feeling ashamed or helpless. Personal insight leads to successful careers and contentment over time.

Self-Management

Self-management means being aware of our actions and reactions in various scenarios. It allows us to deal with unforeseen incidents like angry outbursts or getting sidetracked during work. Individuals skilled in this trait know exactly what must be done to reach specific objectives, such as reaching health targets or disciplining kids fairly when needed. We all have duties we should tend to; self-managed people take action on them instead of making excuses or blaming others. It's essential to regulate our mindset, conduct, and responses since nobody else will do it for us.

Taking charge of yourself requires effort, just like tending a garden. This includes caring for qualities such as discipline and patience, so they blossom into rugged traits like resilience. The idea is to train yourself to withstand difficult times caused by strain or obstacles. While we are unable to change the exterior environment, attentiveness toward internal equilibrium brings peace to the chaos around us. As such, becoming proficient at managing reactions makes you a steadier person.

People who possess good self-awareness are better equipped to understand and handle their thoughts, impulses, and sentiments effectively. They know ways to regulate such inner experiences without over-reacting or bottling up everything. Once individuals gain awareness of those thoughts or feelings, they next figure out how to convey or respond accordingly in particular circumstances—a skill often known as self-control. By developing sound capabilities here, people can successfully lead themselves in their private lives and careers. So, self-awareness and self-control assist you in your self-management journey.

Adopting self-management doesn't mean stuffing down your feelings altogether—quite the opposite, actually! Rather than disregarding your emotions, it emphasizes respectful acknowledgment of your sentiments, followed by recognizing your command over deciding your subsequent reaction or course of action. You see, emotions happen, yet they don't automatically dictate what happens following the emotional event. That said, choosing right afterward creates a positive space between emotional stimulus and resultant reactions, permitting people to selectively proceed based on their own higher principles and long-term vision. To put it another way, just as skilled dancers gracefully execute complex dance steps, effective emotion management enables us to skillfully navigate interpersonal relationships through intentional behaviors that are directed by our ambitions and ideals.

When focusing on effective self-management practices, it centers on comprehending our limitations. Since human resources are limited (energy and schedules), being intentional and balanced allows wiser utilization, leading to successful self-maintenance without shame or apologies. Remember that embracing self-management implies setting appropriate boundaries and saying yes only when fitting or enjoyable. Allocate time for vitalizing activities that match unique interests to sustain both physical and spiritual health.

Social Awareness

Social awareness is a crucial skill that allows you to properly comprehend and interact with people. It entails being aware of various points of view, sensing emotions, engaging in effective communication, and adapting to social settings. This calls for attentive listening during interactions, observing others' emotional cues, correctly adjusting your conduct, and taking cultural variations into account. Building lasting relationships and carrying out productive conversations is made simpler by having social awareness.

Essentially, having social awareness means putting into action the old saying, "Walk a mile in someone else's shoes." It involves expanding your point of view by stepping into the feelings of someone else. Through this capability, we establish deeper relationships built upon authentic comprehension and true empathy. Developing this talent enriches our lives through stronger human bonds founded on sincerity and compassionate understanding.

Pursuing a life guided by social awareness brings many benefits, like becoming an empathetic listener who hears beyond what is being said. Instead of just hearing words, you become conscious of hidden thoughts and emotions, too. In doing so, you create an environment where individuals experience warmth, validation, dignity, and closeness in their personal associations. A caring approach fosters deep interpersonal bonds fueled by mutual trust and respect.

Cultivating social awareness pushes us toward connecting better with those near us while simultaneously examining ourselves introspectively. To achieve true inner perception and strengthen our connection with others, we must mix the colors of our emotions, just as a gifted artist paints a stunning work of art by combining hues to reveal something beautiful. Self-awareness and observing the feelings of others harmoniously come together through social awareness. The final composition unveils itself when our outward expression matches our internal emotions, which, similar to any fine painting, leaves a profound impact on all who witness it. This self-social awareness duet develops over time as we practice mindfulness and empathic interaction with others.

Empathy is a precious diamond in the treasure chest of social awareness. It entails sensing somebody else's emotions along with them, mirroring their happy or sad times. By strengthening shared ties across diverse groups of people, this skill connects them and fosters a connection that transcends language barriers. Despite no verbal exchange required, empathy produces powerful interpersonal ties imbued with kindheartedness that reach the core of an individual's spirit, and ultimately, it graces our existence with rare poignancy. Strive toward making this delicate yet strong quality an integral part of your interactions with others. Remember, it may remain latent until you choose to bring forth its resplendent presence intentionally.

Exploring the realms of social awareness reaches beyond physical encounters. Digital interfaces have created a vast universe for communication, and it is of equal importance to handle these networks with care. Every electronic word has weight behind it because it can shape people's perceptions and trigger reactions. Respond thoughtfully to messages and posts online while keeping empathy top of mind. Treat every individual using technology equally, without judgment or prejudice. With such consideration given during virtual conversations, construct a supportive online atmosphere where everyone feels connected in positive ways.

Relationship Management

Relationship management skills depend on having worked through the previous traits of EQ: social awareness, self-management, and self-awareness well enough. Like building blocks stacking neatly upon each other, they all link together seamlessly to aid relationship navigation skills. Conflicts can erupt in homes and workplaces from the failed navigation of relationships due to weak relational know-how! When conflicts appear, there's not always an escape button available to patch things up. Thus, developing solid relationship management skills helps prevent relationship breakdowns in the future.

Effective relationship management involves creating meaningful connections with individuals, not necessarily forming friendships. Focusing on mutual benefit indicates an awareness of how working collaboratively with coworkers, classmates, or acquaintances adds value to personal and professional lives. People who are good at managing relationships understand the value of getting along with people they might initially disagree with while also appreciating that certain people are best kept at a distance due to inherent personality differences. Given the variety of environments encountered daily, such scenarios commonly arise unless one works in isolation from society.

At its foundation, effective relational management relies greatly on the harmonious interaction between the parties involved. The give-and-take process entails adaptable dialogues driven by authentic care that deeply comprehend situations viewed from multiple perspectives. This leads to a productive discussion where minor issues are resolved promptly rather than festering ill will. When disagreements emerge, addressing concerns openly eases stress while strengthening relationships as clear understanding replaces doubts.

Active listening is a fundamental skill in relationship management. Pay attention to what the other individual shares during conversations—not just listening to their words but tuning into their underlying feelings, too—actively focusing signals our deep appreciation. Empathy grows when you truly listen without interrupting or dismissing others. Such a mindset shows a keenness to delve further and form stronger bonds. Giving undivided focus to friends or acquaintances conveys true respect and care.

Conflict is an unavoidable thread in the fabric of relationships. Fortunately, acquiring conflict-resolving techniques lets you react calmly under pressure and better appreciate both sides through reasonable points of view. Address conflicts creatively, without using force, by harmonizing opposing viewpoints so that individuals are pleasantly dedicated to effective collaboration. Embracing problem-solving wisdom smooths turbulent relationships, thus benefiting shared experiences significantly over time.

Sometimes, relationship management calls for the fortitude to set up healthy boundaries; safeguarding ourselves equally safeguards our fellow companions. Just like a carefully grown plant needs space to prosper or room for roots to expand in the soil to absorb vital nutrients, humans require similar considerations, too. Maintaining kinship ties requires regular care so that they grow and flourish just like plants. This requires that both parties respect each other's autonomy and acknowledge each other's unique essence. Over time, this encourages more fruitful outcomes because it draws on both parties' respect and admiration for one another.

Despite a few hiccups or stumbles along the road, strive to establish trustworthiness while forming bonds because ideal interactions aren't always possible. Focus on honest rather than perfect communication because, when handled properly, vulnerability creates solid foundations. Learn communication skills that encourage warmth among participants, encouraging people to fully participate or be open through kind treatment and inclusion. As jigsaw pieces connected together with common goals despite their inherent differences, people can grow closer in harmony by acknowledging flaws and differences. When interacting with different cultured people, cherish their individual characteristics since that is how genuine alliances are formed: tolerating differences and seeing similarities that eventually result in a collaborative whole that is advantageous to each member individually and collectively.

Key Takeaways

- Emotional intelligence plays a vital role in both personal development and fruitful communication.

- Emotional intelligence consists of four key abilities working together: self-awareness, self-management, social awareness, and relationship management.

- Knowledge about your own emotions, responses, and behaviors can help unlock opportunities for improvement and evolution within yourself. This allows you to start exploring thoughts and experiences that bring you closer to becoming your best self.

- Self-management means learning to channel and express your feelings thoughtfully to promote better results in life's circumstances. You will discover ways to remain steady in times of adversity and build stronger networks through honest expression.

- Apprehension of others' sentiments promotes a higher degree of connection and shared understanding between individuals. By developing this talent, stronger bonds form through active engagement and increased levels of sympathy.

- Relationship management requires effective conversation techniques as well as assertively communicating individual needs without causing discomfort to those around us. These talents allow us to establish balanced and mutually advantageous affiliations.

Now that you understand the basic building block of emotional intelligence let's find out why EQ is important in the following chapter with some examples.

Chapter 2:
Why Emotional Intelligence Is Important?

All learning has an emotional base.

−Plato

According to research, nearly three-quarters of professionals encounter setbacks linked to deficiencies in emotional abilities, specifically struggling with managing conflicts between colleagues, poor direction over teams during stressful conditions, and struggles with adjusting to alterations or inspiring confidence in oneself among peers (Kazemitabar et al., 2022). These factors significantly contribute to career disruptions. Therefore, cultivating proficiency in handling emotional dilemmas is indispensable for long-term success.

Having advanced emotional intelligence lets you relate better to others and handle challenging circumstances with kindness. It helps you understand and manage yourself while connecting smoothly with those around you. Your mindset affects everyone close to you at home or at work. Everyone has varying backgrounds, which must be acknowledged daily due to unforeseen happenings and shifting scenarios. Heightened EQ helps us react aptly during adversities such as arguments, adjustments, and hindrances. Compassion plays a crucial role here; maintaining appropriate consideration for our inner emotions empowers mindful reactions under pressure. To sum up, mastering higher levels of emotional intelligence benefits every aspect of our existence.

In this chapter, we will see real-life examples of the benefits of emotional intelligence, the impact of emotional intelligence on personal and professional success, and a few case studies showcasing the consequences of low emotional intelligence.

Real-Life Examples of the Benefits of Emotional Intelligence

We often go about our days facing numerous feelings that prompt us to act or react in particular ways. We sense something before processing information rationally. This instinct was intended to aid quick responses to external triggers. Nonetheless, our brains developed further so that we could analyze and govern our moods instead of letting transitory emotions dominate our choices. For instance, a short hesitation before impulsively saying or acting aggressively when upset or taking a pause before blaming someone based solely on current feelings are little steps to isolate sentiments from logic and actions. Essentially, separating rational thought from immediate sensations makes sure we don't give in to momentary upsurges. This is one real-life example of emotional intelligence.

Improved Communication and Conflict Resolution

Imagine working in a workplace full of people who communicate with empathy and handle conflicts diplomatically rather than aggressively. This pleasant atmosphere results directly from employees' enhanced emotional intelligence. People with strong emotional intelligence excel at completely hearing and understanding sentiments and then communicating their own perspectives in an assertive yet sympathetic manner. Such communication strategies transform heated disagreements into fruitful opportunities for collaborative advancement. The icing on the cake is that among these people, a culture highlighting real concern for other professionals naturally flourishes, ultimately raising general happiness. Having emotional intelligence that promotes real communication rooted in humanity is what it all comes down to in the end.

Resilience in the Face of Challenges

Life presents many difficulties, requiring us to draw upon strengths like resilience to overcome setbacks. Think of individuals tackling hurdles in their jobs or private lives. Emotional wisdom affords them the tools essential to journey past barriers while remaining optimistic about future possibilities. People adept in understanding and managing emotions are quick to examine what went wrong and gain knowledge about themselves through those incidents. These same people then make the most of their newly acquired information by applying it to new situations by being more inventive and flexible.

Having copious amounts of emotional savvy supplies the courage needed to meet life head-on, even after falling short occasionally.

Enhanced Leadership Abilities

Top bosses who possess high levels of emotional insight energize employees and cultivate flourishing workspaces. Managers endowed with strong EQ intuitively recognize staff requirements, effectively explain targets, and encourage the development of skills. These kinds of leaders welcome input and bolster a collaborative mindset where workers happily assist each other. When in charge, such managers create environments propitious for exploring novelty and sharing assistance among coworkers. Essentially, directors gifted with refined EQ construct positive atmospheres by leveraging proficiencies tailored toward interpersonal interactions.

Authentic and Fulfilling Relationships

Healthy connections rely heavily on emotional knowledge. Romantic unions flourish when both individuals acknowledge one another's emotions by being sensitive and caring toward each other. In such scenarios, conflict resolution transpires peacefully because both parties are willing to discuss concerns honestly without getting defensive. Effective communication is integral, too, since speaking and listening attentively have become second nature. Such fulfilling affiliations blossom thanks to solid emotional foundations that promote genuineness and shared growth simultaneously.

Effective Stress Management

Navigating life can be taxing; however, emotional smarts aid our handling of stress in a useful way. People in possession of emotional insight can pinpoint indicators of stress, devise techniques to cope with burdens and shield emotional equilibrium. That's not all; emotional astuteness makes sure people can manage responsibilities in a way that does not jeopardize psychological or emotional states. Since stress is something we must deal with on a regular basis, developing our emotional intelligence is essential to maintaining our emotional well-being and making sure our responsibilities are met.

Empathy and Connection in Customer Service

The capacity to interact effectively and sensitively with clients is an essential aspect of any occupation requiring client contact. For example, consider a customer service representative who excels at addressing problems promptly but is also tender and understanding. Possessing emotional intelligence enables them to connect better with customers by perceiving the range of emotions experienced by each individual. As a result, these employees might craft tailor-made answers and build affinities capable of fortifying customer reliance and commitment.

Conflict Transformation in Family Dynamics

Family dynamics benefit from members possessing decent amounts of emotional intuition. Parents keen on tuning into their children's emotional states and truly hearing them out help develop stronger relationships built on deeper comprehension. They display patience throughout conversations and show sensitivity toward little ones under stress. As a result, loving and affectionate attachments occur between parents and offspring through ample opportunities to bond through open dialogues centered around emotional matters.

Inspiring Teamwork and Collaboration

Working teams whose participants exude high emotional acumen enjoy success derived from efficient collaboration. Team tasks where associates actively exchange opinions while valuing contrasting viewpoints generate better outcomes once differences get settled through diplomatic methods. It's also worth mentioning that these teams form friendly atmospheres wherein every member experiences being accepted and recognized for their unique talents. Teams enriched by robust emotional intelligence foster assorted situations of cooperation and camaraderie as teammates feel included and appreciated.

Observe how these daily incidents reflect the potency of emotional intelligence. Exhibiting abilities related to self-awareness, self-management, social awareness, and relationship management can heighten our personal interactions, which formerly seemed plain and dull, to more purposeful and contented affairs devoid of inner turbulence. By mastering emotional intelligence like a pro, we convert chaotic scenarios into tranquil encounters and unsatisfying moments into gratifying occurrences.

The Impact of Emotional Intelligence on Personal and Professional Success

Personal Success

Personal progress necessitates emotional intelligence since effective interpersonal relationships rely on this set of skills. As discussed earlier, people with a higher EQ have a propensity to engage with others more successfully due to their improved ability to control their own emotions, which leads to more fruitful conversations. Their skill in recognizing and responding to other viewpoints opens doors for mutual progress through the unrestricted exchange of ideas. This emotional capacity enables the development of long-lasting and genuine relationships because it keeps close relationships afloat during trying times via open communication and cogent action.

- The art of self-mastery: Emotional intelligence gives us the power to handle adversity using inner strength. We know how to manage our emotions properly when trouble strikes, gain knowledge from these experiences, and come out even stronger as a result. By doing this, difficulties are transformed into chances to advance personally and boost our confidence and autonomy. Every challenge we overcome makes us stronger on the inside as much as on the outside.

- Building meaningful connections: When you have high levels of emotional intelligence, resolving arguments within relationships becomes simple. Your empathetic communication helps you understand everyone's point of view and work toward solutions harmoniously. Mutual affection develops since each person feels seen and understood, and respect and admiration bloom between companions who share genuinely deep bonds. The end result? Personal fulfillment and lasting connections grounded in truthfulness and sensitivity to individual needs.

- Better decision-making: People who are emotionally intelligent tend to be better decision-makers. They make intelligent choices that will help them achieve their objectives by taking into account both facts and emotional responses. Since they are aware of how emotions might influence decision-making, they make decisions that are in line with valued ideals and crucial goals. Their well-considered decisions demonstrate responsible maturity rather than hasty impulsivity.

- Enhanced communication: People who are emotionally astute excel at developing communication with others. They sense and interpret other people's emotional signals, fine-tune speech styles, and connect sincerely with friends through honesty and openness. Understanding the needs of individuals who pay attention enables them to constructively interact. Their clarity when sharing thoughts encourages amenable exchanges.

Professional Success

Having high levels of emotional intelligence at work boosts job effectiveness. Team members cooperate more effectively because messages are communicated more clearly as a result of increased comprehension abilities when emotions are recognized and managed. Complex initiatives are better understood by problem-solvers than by those lacking these perceptive abilities. Since they are more sensitive to emotions, they foster happier environments where activities are completed without difficulty.

- A blueprint for leadership: In corporate scenarios, top executives boasting high emotional quotients set new standards for effective teamwork. By setting an example of dependability and fortitude under pressure, leaders who are adept at managing their emotions increase their employees' trustworthiness and motivation. These captains lead their teams admirably and with confidence while being adept at navigating challenging situations.

- Adaptability and growth mindset: People accept life's minor setbacks as opportunities to grow more intelligent when they are equipped with a healthy dose of emotional awareness. You bloom in that "I wonder if I can" frame of mind as you embrace innovations with excitement rather than anxiety. You keep growing while overcoming obstacles with cool resourcefulness if you can adjust to changes with ease.

- Strategic decision-making: A professional who has emotional intelligence knows how to handle challenges without getting overwhelmed. They are able to weigh all aspects—both logical and emotional—before making judicious judgments. By staying level-headed while processing both types of information, they arrive at well-thought-out conclusions that help them achieve their larger objectives.

- Increased job satisfaction: An emotionally smart individual tends to have a higher degree of job satisfaction because of their capability to cope with difficult scenarios at work. Their positive mental state helps them stay committed to their tasks. Due to their strength of character and optimism, they feel content in their roles. These employees possess the aptitude to control their feelings properly, so dealing with distress becomes simpler.

Case Studies Showcasing the Consequences of Low Emotional Intelligence

Building and maintaining good relationships can be difficult for those with poor emotional intelligence. They lack crucial interpersonal skills and have problems emotionally connecting with others. The absence of adequate understanding could hinder their capacity to appreciate and respond to emotions in themselves and those around them. Furthermore, managing and directing their emotions productively prove problematic, impeding their capacity to take suitable action promptly. These shortcomings prevent the formation of meaningful relationships.

Case Study 1: Workplace Communication Breakdown

Let's say there is a skilled professional named Amy whose talents significantly exceed those of the average person. Nevertheless, despite her skills, she encounters difficulties at work because of a lack of emotional intelligence. Her failure to understand her coworkers' emotions leads to misunderstandings or a lack of interest in their opinions. Collaboration is hampered by this poor relationship with her team members. She risks not just her own personal growth but also the success of her team by ignoring the value of emotional sensitivity in relating to others. Going forward, if one wants to perform at their best in a professional setting, one should pay attention to developing an acceptable level of emotional intelligence.

Case Study 2: Strained Personal Relationships

Let me tell you about a man named Dan who, due to a lack of emotional intelligence, experiences difficulty in his personal life. He has frequent arguments with his girlfriend since he has a natural tendency to react violently whenever strong emotions surface. Lack of effective emotion management and communication leads to resentment and estrangement, which slowly erodes their relationship. The situation involving Dan provides a reminder of EQ's potent effects on one's love life.

Case Study 3: Leadership Challenges

Allow me to share with you a story about a CEO named Harry. When he tries to lead his team, difficulties arise from his low degree of emotional intelligence. Harry has a propensity to disregard or discard people's reactions because he lacks the ability to perceive other people's inner emotions. Such apathy eliminates his chances of sparking strong excitement, leaving the group with deflated spirits and low productivity. Harry's circumstance highlights the detrimental consequences that poor emotional competence has on leading people and creating a healthy work environment.

Case Study 4: Missed Opportunities in Conflict Resolution

Meet Emily, who struggles to tackle disagreements due to her lack of emotional intelligence. She deals with disputes by becoming argumentative and explosive. At work, such reactions result in heightened tensions, stalling resolutions, and impaired teamwork. This highlights the impact of weak emotional intelligence on handling disagreements diplomatically and obtaining agreeable solutions for everyone involved. The example of Emily shows the consequences of insufficient emotional intelligence in resolving strife peacefully and productively.

Case Study 5: Undermined Decision-Making

Michael, like many others, is struggling to make smart decisions due to his limited emotional intelligence. When confronted with emotionally charged situations, he tends to cave into spontaneous decisions influenced by temporary sentiments instead of reason-based considerations. Consequently, the results often deviate from what'll benefit him in the long term or improve his business as a whole. As Michael's case illustrates, if one lacks emotional intelligence, the capability to critically assess difficult options decreases, thus blocking individual and professional development.

These examples show just how significant the effects of insufficient emotional intelligence can be. From our private lives and careers to broader social and business dealings, deficiencies like limited self-awareness, weak interpersonal rapport, poor coping mechanisms, and so forth can have noticeable repercussions. With enough knowledge about the impacts, you will better recognize the significance of cultivating stronger emotional abilities.

Key Takeaways

- Emotional intelligence serves as a road map for developing oneself and fostering interpersonal connections.

- Building EQ leads to better coping methods when faced with challenges and crises.

- Richer relationships based on caring, trust, and efficient problem-solving under pressure are directly influenced by increased emotional intelligence.

- High-emotional intelligence leaders tend to inspire more team loyalty and collaboration among their teams in the commercial and corporate arenas.

- Making balanced judgments based on good thinking and adequate sensitivity to others' feelings or situations is eventually aided by developing emotional intelligence.

- Improving emotional intelligence offers a means to finding satisfaction.

We learned the importance of emotional intelligence with some examples in this chapter. But what exactly are emotions? And how do they work in our brains with hormones? Let's find out in the next chapter.

Chapter 3:
What Emotions Are?
How Do They Work?

I don't want to be at the mercy of my emotions. I want to use them, to enjoy them, and to dominate them.

　　　　–OSCAR WILDE

As we continue exploring emotional intelligence further, comprehending emotions is like mastering a secret tongue unique to each person: Sometimes spoken boldly, sometimes whispered subtly, and sometimes felt deeply. We must understand the chemistry behind it and how it shapes our perspectives and moods, even influencing thoughts and memories. Exploring our emotions offers invaluable insight into who we are while assisting in navigating our complicated inner world. Within our emotional realm, the fusion of subjectivity and science creates a rhythmic beauty of its own.

In this chapter, we will delve into the close links between emotions and hormones. Learn about how our thoughts evoke feelings, which subsequently trigger hormone releases that shape our internal stability and overall well-being.

How Emotions Are Connected to Hormones

Emotions are our physical or mental reactions to diverse scenarios or occurrences. They encompass all those distinct positive and negative feelings familiar to humans. From contentment to agony, every emotion acts as a notification about someone's current state of mind and necessities. So, understanding emotions means getting clearer signals about yourself and making wiser choices in daily life.

Everywhere you look at human beings, you see emotions tied tightly to bodily processes! Specifically, our hormone-balancing system, called the endocrine system, does most of the work here. These glands collaborate closely inside your body so that experiencing emotions results in appropriate levels of hormones being released that increase or lessen the intensity of these emotions.

Take, for example, the sensation of fear. When you sense some potential trouble looming ahead, your brain then activates a chain reaction: It instructs two tiny glands (the adrenals) to release adrenaline, popularized as the fight-or-flight hormone, causing sensory hyperawareness, an increased pulse, and blood redirection, helping you move faster. On other occasions, like positive social connections or joyful news, a special substance called oxytocin gets unleashed, often dubbed the love hormone, leading to improved rapport via higher trust levels in yourself and others while also boosting empathetic skills.

Serotonin, another crucial neurotransmitter, impacts our moods significantly; lesser amounts of this substance might leave us feeling downhearted, maybe even depressed. On the flip side, dopamine gets discharged whenever we accomplish something or get excited about anything amusing. All these neuromediators work together harmoniously, much like musical instruments within an ensemble. Each serves its own unique function in generating our inner world of emotional experiences.

Understanding the complex relationship between emotions and hormones helps us better understand who we are. Once we grow accustomed, we gain the capacity to react to our everyday encounters more deliberately and sympathetically, ultimately helping us to develop into wiser, more competent people capable of establishing friendly connections and succeeding. We unleash the potential within our deepest selves via conscious awareness of and control over our biological effects. In the end, developing emotional intelligence can be facilitated by understanding how emotions and hormones interact.

Thoughts Provoke Emotions, Emotions Provoke Hormones, Hormones Influence Our Inner Peace and Health

Thinking patterns have a significant impact on our attitude and perspective on everyday happenings. The thoughts that race through our minds evoke emotions that might be either positive or negative. Consider this example: Imagine waking up each morning with a sense of eager optimism and anticipation for what is ahead. That mental approach influences feelings like hopefulness and happiness. The opposite is also true: focusing on pessimism results in anxiety or disappointment. Your everyday emotional ups and downs are influenced by the way you think.

When you experience an emotion, it triggers signals from your brain, which prompt certain glands in your body to release specific hormones, as we learned earlier. These hormones play a vital role by serving as communication channels between different body parts, such as the nervous system, immune system, and cardiovascular systems, among others. They help regulate our physical responses, too. One great example of how this works is that when you are feeling content or satisfied (happy), there's a rise in the production of dopamine in your nervous system, leading to not just feelings of elation but also enhanced motivational learning capacities.

Hormone releases cause a variety of physical changes throughout the body through processes such as increasing heart rate, changing blood pressure, and so on. You could occasionally notice some typical physical symptoms going along with various moods. For example, in stressful situations, adrenaline may cause symptoms like a racing heartbeat, stiff muscles, or shallow breathing, yet on other occasions, intimacy and affection are brought on by high amounts of oxytocin, which produces a pleasant warmth.

Negative thinking habits may start a never-ending loop where upsetting emotions cause stress hormones, similar to cortisol, to be released into your body. This can lead to higher amounts of stress, damaged immunity, and psychological discomfort. On the flip side, nurturing optimistic perspectives has the ability to spark feelings of enjoyment, serenity, and connectedness by stimulating happy hormones to materialize in your entire being, thus contributing positively toward your total well-being both physically and mentally!

Key Takeaways

- Emotions manifest as bodily or mental responses triggered by varying situations.

- Our thoughts provoke emotions.

- Emotions cause hormones to be released.

- Our body experiences a number of physical changes as a result of hormone release, including alterations in blood pressure and heart rate.

- Thus, hormones influence our inner peace and physical health.

In this first part, we learned the theory of emotional intelligence. In the following part, we are going to learn to use emotional intelligence as a solution (or as an instrument) for a better and more quality life.

PART 2:

EQ AS A SOLUTION FOR A BETTER AND MORE QUALITY LIFE

Chapter 4:
How and Why Not to Care

Care about people's approval, and you will always be their prisoner.

−Lao Tzu

Caring excessively about what others think can have a negative impact on your health and happiness. Worry and stress can accumulate, leading to low confidence and a sense of unworthiness. Over time, this pattern may cause you to put on an act, living lives that fit others' criteria instead of fulfilling your own wants and aspirations. As a result, you drift further away from internal calmness and fulfillment. Paying too much heed to external views can push us toward discord and unease.

This chapter will examine how we shouldn't base our decisions on what other people think in order to improve our well-being. We'll learn practical ways to stop depending on acceptance from others and start fostering our own inner delight. We'll learn methods for setting appropriate boundaries, breaking free from perfectionism's grip, and adopting self-compassion. We can reclaim peace and tranquility inside ourselves by taking these actions and adopting a new attitude.

Practical Strategies to Overcome Caring Too Much About Others' Opinions

Living in a connected culture involves frequently seeking input and validation from those around us. However, our ongoing need for validation might cause us to place a greater emphasis on external approval than on fulfillment within. To avoid this trap, let's examine some useful techniques that strengthen our inner worth and give us the courage to be sincere, honest, and genuinely ourselves. These methods will assist us in achieving emotional independence and internal self-confidence.

Self-Reflection

Start by acknowledging the factors contributing to your dependence on others' acceptance. Give thought to whether you're searching for validation due to feelings of emptiness or apprehension about disapproval. Realizing the underlying reasons permits you to tackle them head-on, ultimately moving toward psychological restoration and improved mental well-being.

Define Your Values

Define the core values and principles that help create your own identity. It is easier to reduce the impact of outside opinions when you have a realistic image of yourself. Your convictions are strengthened, and you can resist external evaluations by concentrating on your real qualities. You can build authenticity on a firm foundation by tying your actions to your basic principles.

Practice Self-Validation

Cultivate a routine whereby you validate yourself. Recognize your successes, work hard, and pay attention to your personal development. Learn to appreciate what makes you special and understand that your self-value doesn't originate from externals. Developing such behavior creates a pool of internally derived self-respect. Start developing this daily habit and watch your confidence thrive over time!

Set Boundaries

Maintaining wholesome boundaries is vital to preserving your emotional equilibrium. Reject unwanted suggestions or commentary detrimental to your advancement. Setting proper limitations indicates your self-determination, thereby creating a space ruled by your independent choice. Act on these measures with courtesy and become more autonomous!

Embrace Constructive Feedback

Distinguish between constructive criticism that spurs good development and damaging remarks centered on negativity as part of lessening dependence on other people's viewpoints. Negative evaluations that don't further your cause should be ignored. Accept constructive criticism that is in line with your qualities and use it to develop yourself personally. Create this mentality right away and put it to good use.

Focus on Self-Growth

Instead of concentrating on obtaining approval from others, concentrate on enhancing yourself. Establish targets, chase goals, and put effort into betterment. The moment your attention revolves around your personal progress, the views of those around you matter less. Apply these steps and begin working toward becoming stronger inside.

Practice Mindfulness

Devote some time each day to practicing mindfulness techniques like meditation or deep breathing exercises. Being present in the moment liberates you from longing for validation from others. Harboring a non-biased perspective promotes inner tranquility. Incorporate mindfulness rituals into your daily life as a method to distance yourself from undue obligations and get external confirmation. Practice conscious living habits to achieve serenity.

Celebrate Small Wins

Take note of even small victories and enjoy them. By valuing your accomplishments, you can boost your self-assurance and reduce the influence of outside evaluations. Adopt this mindset right away and celebrate your everyday accomplishments to create a solid foundation for your confidence.

Setting Healthy Boundaries

Taking care of yourself by setting healthy boundaries is like creating your own personal safe zone. It means being clear about what makes you feel good or bad and respecting those feelings so that everyone feels happy and comfortable, including you! We need these safe zones because they help us stay in control and keep our important things inside them, just like how we all have our special place at home!

Self-Awareness as the Foundation

To be honest, if I don't know who I am and what matters most to me, it will be difficult to communicate my limits clearly, let alone even set any boundaries! The first step would be getting to really understand myself and taking notes when something upsets or bothers me. Self-awareness + reflection = the foundation needed before we talk more!

Communicate Clearly

When talking to others about our needs, it helps to do so calmly but firmly so that everyone listens and takes notice! If we explain ourselves gently as well, then it shows we want a fair solution for all involved, and ultimately, we hope it all works out in harmony. Just remember, sometimes people will still say *no*. That's okay, too because no one should forget their worth simply because they hear *no*. Boundaries mean we take care of ourselves, and there are many other great people waiting around, willing to show us love!

Learn to Say "No"

Next time you get asked to do something that just doesn't sound right for you or may bring up uncomfortable feelings, try simply responding, "No thanks." No explanation is necessary unless you want to share why your answer is no. Know that being honest about how you feel shows love for yourself and can inspire others to do the same. In today's world full of overwhelm and burnout, prioritizing yourself could be one of the kindest acts possible.

Trust Your Instincts

Before making decisions or plans with someone else, check in with what your gut tells you first. Maybe there aren't any red flags yet. But sometimes things change, and it's better to err on the side of caution than ignore that inner voice that quietly whispers warnings. Goals or expectations may shift suddenly, too. You can always revisit later, once the dust settles. But if initial reactions say to avoid or proceed with care due to negative vibes, pay attention.

Prioritize Self-Care

Think about setting aside some fun time dedicated solely to your enjoyment. It's okay to stick up for yourself, to take breaks without guilt, and to make choices based on personal growth or happiness goals—not just obligation! These actions actually lead to a greater ability to handle life's challenges in stride and find contentment along the way. Let yourself off the hook from constant giving and expecting nothing in return, and see transformation start within yourself first.

Practice Consistency

Let's say you want people to take their shoes off outside instead of coming right through with dirty feet. If they already see you carrying out this rule consistently (like not allowing people in until the shoes come off), it sets up a pattern or expectation, so next time they think twice before just walking straight in without stopping at the door; it helps you remember, too! So yes, sticking with rules and boundaries means showing self-discipline, but it also shows others what you mean since actions speak louder than words! And that way, over time, everyone learns how to treat you better!

Gradual Implementation

Start small and grow big. Start implementing healthy boundaries little by little. It's totally normal! As you experience the benefits of boundaries on your inner peace and happiness, you'll feel braver to make bolder choices in saying "yes" or "no." Just go with your gut and do what feels best for you along the way.

Be Open to Negotiation

In dealing with boundaries, sometimes there's room to negotiate and reach an agreement that works out best for everyone involved, just like finding a solution through active listening and talking stuff over together! Remember, flexibility doesn't mean giving in but rather finding another path forward together. Open discussion keeps lines of communication strong for current issues, future ones, and overall trust between one another.

Be Self-Compassionate

Be nice to yourself when facing obstacles or criticism when establishing new boundaries. Setting up rules to protect yourself is essential self-care, similar to eating fruits, washing hands often, brushing teeth daily, and so forth. Carry self-compassion alongside you like a security blanket, so don't give anyone permission to shame or judge your sincere effort toward guarding your emotional safety just as much as your regular hygiene.

Embrace Uncomfortable Conversations

Some chats where sharing boundaries might cause some unease, however, are vital steps you're taking for developing resilience, so embrace the slight squirminess as evidence of progress on your road to uber-self-confidence.

Letting Go of Perfectionism

In this world, sometimes people expect nothing less than perfection from each other, but truthfully, nobody has ever achieved such a thing or lived happily trying. You may start comparing yourself to others based on their photoshopped appearance or edited life story, putting pressure on yourself. This mentality might make you focus mostly on criticism of yourself instead of compliments, lowering your confidence and happiness. These unrealistic expectations bring out negative emotions, making everything look gloomy. Try not to aim high all the time, but shoot low now and then.

Recognize the Roots

As part of growing up, many factors push us to think perfection or flawlessness should be the goal; however, the reality remains far off from these ideals. Explore why you have higher expectations of yourself, maybe by thinking about how your environment and background shaped your beliefs. Maybe we should also remind ourselves of stories where imperfect events turned out okay. Small steps every day going against these old teachings could break the rules written in childhood and allow growth without fear of failure.

Reframe Mistakes as Growth

When someone does something wrong, they usually feel guilty or frustrated. But what if mistakes were welcomed as chances to improve next time? Try seeing errors as helpful guides, teaching us another way that didn't work, and then find ways to adjust or learn new skills around similar subjects. Enjoy exploring while moving forward little by little.

Set Realistic Goals

Setting hard targets for yourself leaves no room for flexibility or forgiveness for being human. What if tiny pieces built big dreams one brick at a time, so reaching their destination felt easier due to numerous successful small milestones celebrated along the road? Actions broken down help gain confidence, too. Make targets reachable yet exciting, and track your way with cheerful checkpoints.

Celebrate Imperfection

Everyone has strengths and weaknesses, just as snowflakes differ slightly. Pursuing absolute flawlessness misses great bits already present, so remember that charming peculiarities exist within, too. The effort put into accepting these traits creates space for recognizing inner gifts unique to each individual. Each person deserves love despite flaws hidden behind a mask of self-expectation. Uncovering quirky traits allows others to see the true colors underneath the shell.

Challenge All-or-Nothing Thinking

Oftentimes, folks approach situations like a task must come out perfectly well, or it'll amount to zero; this "black and white" thought process makes it harder to cope during slight slip-ups since it sounds like there are only two possible outcomes. However, actual life experiences show various degrees between extremes, which means we get the chance to correct our course during a mix of successes and partial failures called living! It helps to replace harsh "perfect or none" thoughts with flexible "gradually improving" types of perspectives.

Embrace Flexibility

Rigid expectations block any hope for handling sudden changes outside plans; embracing flexibility promotes peace, allowing unexpected moments to turn up, leading to fresh adventures. The power lies inside our reactions, determining whether smooth adjustments occur or stress dominates. So, keep options open while having a clear direction to maintain strong yet malleable spirits.

Practice Mindfulness

In order to be truly aware of yourself and your actions, take part in activities that encourage full attention to current occurrences. This nurturing of mindfulness enables conscious recognition without criticism of mental contents or emotions, which leads to undoing obsession over making things faultless. By focusing on currently existing conditions, we free our minds from constantly seeking ideal results, thus enabling serenity when pondering about the specific situation at hand.

Affirm Your Worth

Keep telling yourself every day that you have value regardless of successes or shortcomings; doing affirmations of personal significance works wonders for battling doubt from trying to meet excessive standards, which causes low opinions of ourselves. Making a habit of speaking positive truths aloud (either to yourself or in writing) will eventually lead the subconscious mind to believe factual good points.

Embracing Self-Compassion

Learning how to treat ourselves right is like weaving many different colored strings together to make a beautiful picture. But there are some colors (bad memories) we wish weren't there, so rather than cutting them away, we use the gold thread (self-compassion) to remember flaws that do exist even within beautiful creations. Accepting and dealing with the bad parts brings peace. Having a better relationship with yourself helps you deal with hardships in life.

Cultivate Self-Awareness

When troubles come around, notice how you chat internally because the way we think directly affects our feelings, too, as we discussed earlier. Do you comfort yourself like a trusted friend or scold yourself? Tune into your self-talk to catch patterns because fixing starts here. Awareness of behavior changes attitudes. Loving yourself is not just saying sweet words; it reflects actions like listening to yourself.

Replace Self-Criticism with Self-Kindness

Treat yourself exactly the way you want friends to be treated when facing difficulties: supportive, patient, and kind. How would you react if a close friend went through failure, compared to how you react when you fail personally? Remember, when friends are hurt, they get cared for. Similarly, love yourself enough to take steps to help in times of struggle.

Offer Yourself Forgiveness

Nobody should go through life burdened by regrets. Learning involves accepting that mistakes were made. We learn new skills every day, so our past errors look bizarre since we have changed so much over the years. Nevertheless, harboring regrets prevents us from moving on to new opportunities. Letting go means growing further. We can't go back and change what happened yesterday, but clearing our minds today will make tomorrow better!

Befriend Your Inner Critic

Instead of fighting with your inner critic all the time, why not make friends with it? Did you know that sometimes our inner critics are just trying to keep us safe? But we don't have to be afraid or fight them off; by being kind and understanding toward ourselves, we can turn those harsh voices into soft whispers of self-care and love. Giving some TLC to that critical part inside us will help change its tune for good.

Key Takeaways

- Ditching societal expectations frees you to follow your own unique adventures by preserving individual rights to select your own destiny. This enables you to go after your goals while being true to your moral principles.

- Setting boundaries strengthens the self-preservation actions required when social traumas cause psychological numbness.

- Instead of seeking approval, try to be sincere in your expressions. By being honest with yourself and others, authenticity supports the emergence of attuned connections.

- Eliminating perfectionistic inclinations removes a source of ongoing self-criticism that might result in unhealthy levels of anguish or disquiet brought on by unmet expectations of oneself.

- A powerful strategy to support positive feelings about yourself is to show compassion for yourself. Building inner resources capable of handling future upheavals requires being mindfully kind to yourself.

In order to become emotionally intelligent, we have learned how to stop caring excessively about what other people think. In the chapter that follows, let's explore how EQ can improve our professional abilities.

Chapter 5:
How Emotional Intelligence Can Improve Your Work Skills

CEOs are hired for their intellect and business expertise and fired for a lack of emotional intelligence.

–Daniel Goleman

Warren G. Bennis believed that emotional intelligence plays a critical role in determining one's success at work. He claimed it contributes significantly—between 85 percent and 90 percent—to achieving professional excellence (Wann, 2023). While possessing a certain level of IQ is necessary, it alone may not guarantee exceptional performance. In contrast, having high levels of emotional intelligence could increase an individual's chances of becoming successful.

When it comes to succeeding in today's working world, being technically skilled in just one area isn't enough anymore. Understanding the human aspect of things is what really sets apart individuals because when you do, incredible things happen. In this chapter, we'll look at how having strong emotional abilities can improve your relationships with people, make you happier at work, and help you achieve more in general.

Effective Communication and Conflict Resolution Skills

Strong connections and solving problems at work often come down to two big talents: speaking clearly and handling disagreements wisely. These aren't just important for any job; they're vital for building great professional relationships, too. And what do both have in common? They need good emotional skills from you first!

Effective Communication

Communication should go beyond just talking and exchanging information! Listening helps, too. People always react differently due to their diverse experiences growing up or whatever they experienced that day. If you wish to better connect with them and get along, pay attention to their expressions and body language during conversation; read between the lines; and ask why or how they got there. Show some emotions in return; empathize so that together, you find a solution that leaves everyone content.

- Emotional awareness: Knowing your feelings, controlling them, and recognizing other people's emotions are all parts of being emotionally intelligent. This understanding is the basis for productive communication. In essence, developing emotional aptitude equips you to handle your emotions proactively and respond thoughtfully to co-workers. Through increased communication, EQ promotes deeper interpersonal bonds.

- Active listening: Listening actively plays a critical role in efficient conversation. Doing so means focusing entirely on the speaker while making an attempt to understand their feelings, body language, and concealed meanings. By applying emotional intelligence, people engage in deeper appreciation and comprehension of the individual they are interacting with. Embracing active listening encourages meaningful exchanges rooted in compassion, comprehension, and engaged dialogue.

- Empathy and perspective-taking: Developing your emotional intelligence helps grow your empathic abilities—the ability to fully grasp and experience other people's sentiments. Sympathy elevates your capability for heartfelt correspondence that is sincere and humane. When talking with someone facing trouble or going through difficult times, empathetic responses help them feel acknowledged and understood, which might lessen distress or sadness.

- Clear expression: Through improved emotional intelligence, people acquire the capacity to articulate their viewpoints, needs, and limitations with assurance while being conscious of how their words affect other people. Positive connections with others are strengthened, and reciprocal respect is supported by effective self-expression. Assertiveness combined with regard for others' emotional welfare allows individuals to advocate for themselves adeptly, fostering honest discussions while nourishing interpersonal harmony.

Conflict Resolution

Navigating disputes demands emotional intelligence that leads to constructive resolutions through heightened levels of empathy and receptivity to alternative viewpoints, coupled with a resolute dedication to discovering shared interests. Those possessing strong emotional intelligence consistently arrive at favorable outcomes due to their exceptional capability to perceive conflicting sides and effectively collaborate toward solutions agreeable to all parties involved.

- Empathic approach: Understanding people's sentiments will enable you to treat them appropriately. Diverse viewpoints are heard and treated with respect when empathy is displayed. The empathetic method fosters productive workplaces that promote development and unique experiences.

- Active listening in conflict: By genuinely listening to each person's viewpoint and feelings in a conflict, you open the door for open discussion and the pursuit of solutions that respect everyone's needs.

- Constructive communication: Even in tense talks, emotional intelligence enables you to communicate your thoughts clearly without discounting or minimizing the sentiments of others. This results in dialogues that are useful and mutually beneficial.

- Seeking win-win solutions: Having emotional intelligence means thinking beyond yourself and considering everyone else's perspectives, too. In conflicts or negotiations, aiming for win-win solutions ensures that nobody gets hurt or is left behind.

Enhancing Leadership Abilities

Leading teams successfully in modern times relies on understanding people's feelings and needs, promoting inclusion, and encouraging creativity through harmonious working together. Emotional skills like listening deeply, empathy, and appreciating different backgrounds make all the difference nowadays. With them, leaders foster strong bonds and adaptable climates where ideas flow freely for everyone to grow professionally or personally.

Connecting on a Deeper Level

Think about how powerful it would be if you could really connect with your colleagues on a personal level. If you had high levels of emotional awareness, you'd grasp what drives and troubles each person in ways no one else might sense or notice. You could then use that insight to help individuals shine by capitalizing on talents they never knew existed or addressing limitations before they escalate.

Empathetic Leadership

Try picturing yourself guiding others while putting your heart into truly comprehending their experiences firsthand, seeing things from various angles so adjustments will benefit all aspects of staffers' lives simultaneously, mindsets included. Adeptness in relating to folks on such a deep level unites people as they witness management genuinely care about overall happiness beyond mere work performance metrics.

Inspiring through Example

Picture the impact of leading by example versus solely speaking to encourage change. Emotional intellect helps ensure alignment between expressions and behaviors, which influences employees significantly more profoundly than mere verbal guidance ever would alone. Through living as someone worth replicating through sincerity, openness when struggling or feeling overwhelmed, and keeping calm under pressure, the whole group rises collectively toward excellence through reciprocal influence.

Adapting to Diversity

Emotional intelligence helps you value diversity and appreciate unique perspectives. By embracing inclusion, you can create a safe haven for all team members. Emotional intelligence enables leaders to build strong bonds between different cultural groups so they trust one another enough to come up with creative solutions or strategies together.

Nurturing Growth

Emotional intelligence enables you to support the growth of your team. You are able to offer assistance that considers the sentiments and individuality of each person. Your direction creates chances for people to grow both personally and professionally. This style of leadership encourages team members to work more closely together while achieving personal fulfillment.

Handling Challenges with Grace

Having emotional intelligence means you are prepared to face difficult times. It lets you remain calm when things get tough and keep going without losing control or confidence. Keeping your cool under pressure will encourage those around you to do the same and tackle setbacks collectively.

Fostering Teamwork and Collaboration

When it comes to forming strong and productive work teams, emotional intelligence is key! It involves being able to sense, comprehend, control, and make good use of our own emotions, along with everyone else's. With emotional intelligence, we can handle tricky interactions better by showing more care and understanding for each other, leading us all toward greater harmony. But don't forget, emotional intelligence doesn't apply only to individuals; its power is what keeps professional groups bonded and thriving through shared trust, respect, and clearer communication overall.

Building Trust Through Empathy

When people on a team show lots of empathy, it helps them trust each other more since everyone feels cared about enough to listen carefully and take people's thoughts seriously. That trust helps build stronger connections among workers, so they happily support and push each other ahead at work, turning your boring job into a fun chance for friends to lift each other up!

Navigating Conflict

Working in a team sometimes means running into disagreements or issues. Though these disputes may occur naturally, how they are resolved affects team spirit. Having emotional intelligence, as we discussed earlier, gives people the know-how to settle arguments peacefully. This approach turns challenges into chances to grow closer and stronger.

Leveraging Diversity as a Strength

People with diverse backgrounds, experiences, and perspectives bring unique qualities to a team. From varying life stories to unique ways of doing things, this mix helps make a group more dynamic. The secret ingredient is your emotional intelligence. This helps you see others' differences as positives. It lets you celebrate various skills while ensuring everyone feels valued and heard.

Inspiring a Positive Team Culture

Team feelings flow like wildfire. Just as you can catch a cold from someone nearby, you can catch emotional vibes from fellow workers; even a leader's mood strongly influences the climate. How? Well, smart leaders tune into their inner feelings and show they care about yours. Such awareness, plus managing personal mood, make great chemistry for happy, inventive efforts. That's why emotionally wise bosses create an upbeat, go-get-em workplace that gets results.

Nurturing Growth and Resilience

Tough times come just as autumn follows summer! Teammates facing storms need all the support they can get to stay on course. Thankfully, emotional prowess grows with experience and practice. Overcoming obstacles or disappointments becomes easier when people know how to feel and act. Sure bets when everyone shares this ability to be flexible, adjust to unexpected twists, and learn from mistakes. So, whether the path ahead looks smooth or rough, groups upheld by emotionally savvy souls stay steady and ready to steer forward.

Managing Stress and Emotions in the Workplace

Stress at work can seem familiar to lots of people. Since job expectations keep rising, our nerves tend to go up too, with productivity and happiness taking hits, as well as physical health problems sometimes cropping up. Those who possess emotional intelligence, though, are equipped to take on tough times much better since they learn to regulate their upset feelings and respond to pressure in useful ways.

Recognizing and Addressing Stress

Work stress takes many forms and affects us daily at work—tight deadlines, plenty on our plates, or conflicting priorities—but emotional intelligence helps us realize these pressures in ourselves and others around us. When EQ kicks in, people connect over this tough stuff and support each other more easily. By pooling ideas for dealing with these hassles, we become stronger together than when struggling alone. Through all this, emotional intelligence makes challenges feel less daunting because we face them as a united crew.

Embracing Self-Regulation

When it comes to handling our often intense feelings like worry or annoyance, emotional intelligence comes in mighty handy. Instead of letting frustration swallow us whole, EQ lets us take charge and channel how we react to situations positively, making smarter decisions. Remaining cool under high intensity also protects our mental clarity, so that even when things are really heating up, we stay collected inside. In short, emotional intelligence keeps us self-regulated when facing job stress because we can manage our inner reactions better.

Empathy as a Bridge

Workplaces bring together lots of different kinds of people who come loaded with ups and downs. Emotional intelligence inspires us to see the world as others do. Thinking about and caring about friends' moods and troubles leads to a climate where hardships get talked out, easing problems that trouble coworkers deeply. Empathy supports team spirit best when people know they aren't going it alone through rough patches.

Cultivating Resilience

Tough times hit everyone at work sometimes. Problems might slow you down or trip you up. But having emotional intelligence means turning those hurdles into helpful chances to build courage. You grow wiser from mess-ups by examining what went wrong and becoming braver next time around. Your spirits lift despite troubles because you keep a confident eye on your goals. That's why EQ is important: it helps you rise again after life gets tough.

Key Takeaways

- Emotional intelligence can help facilitate better communication between people.

- EQ also makes it easier to work out disagreements when we listen carefully and acknowledge other perspectives; this boosts problem-solving.

- Emotional intelligence enhances your leadership skills.

- It strengthens respect across various backgrounds, helping everyone feel included and creating harmony.

- EQ keeps us calm during difficult times, resulting in personal happiness.

In the following chapter, let's discuss how EQ can help us in building family relations and friendships.

Chapter 6:
How to Build Family Relationships and Friendships

When dealing with people, remember you are not dealing with creatures of logic but with creatures of emotion.

–DALE CARNEGIE

In our personal lives with loved ones, feelings tend to be intense. This is where we show our true selves. If not handled well, it can lead to chaos and frustration. But if we use emotional intelligence, we can turn those close connections into warmth and kindness. In this chapter, we discuss the pivotal role EQ plays in cultivating family bonds and friendships. We plunge into the importance of this skill in assisting streamlined interactions, resolving disputes, and creating a sense of unity and contentment that radiates throughout our lives.

Emotional Intelligence in Family Relationships

Family bonds act as pillars in human interactions, forming our identities and guiding our lives. Every feeling on the emotional spectrum—from happiness to frustration, from love to conflict—is felt in the warmth of our families. The use of emotional smartness emerges as a ray of hope inside these relationships, directing us toward interactions that are healthier and more peaceful.

In Marriage

Marriage is a profound union where emotional intelligence carries great significance. Navigating life together as a married couple involves being sensitive to one another's emotional necessities. EQ entails active listening, empathy, and comprehension, as discussed in the earlier chapters. It involves sincere communication and giving value to your spouse's emotions, just like yours. By cultivating emotional intelligence inside your marriage, you establish a serene environment where affection, respect, and confidence can thrive, promoting a loving relationship that becomes sturdier over time.

For Parents

Being a parent and raising kids is a distinctive bond strengthened by fond memories and occasional miscommunications. Emotional quotient serves as a bridge across age gaps, allowing parents to grasp their children's thoughts and sentiments. Practicing EQ as a parent includes paying attention, showing empathy, and recognizing your youngster's emotions. Adapting your communication approach to fit their emotional prerequisites helps develop a supportive ambiance where heartfelt conversations are welcome. By being emotionally intelligent, mothers and fathers build a solid foundation of mutual understanding, friendship, and care with their kids that transcends traditional family dynamics.

Bridging the Generational Gap With Grownup Kids

The transition from childhood to adulthood often creates a divide between generations, potentially resulting in communication barriers. However, applying emotional intelligence can help overcome this gap by emphasizing empathy, appreciation, and understanding. Acknowledging that life encounters vary among ages does not negate anyone's emotions or opinions. Emotional intelligence allows adult children and parents to engage in conversations with patience, compassion, and admiration. By adopting emotional intelligence, families can convert possible disputes into chances for shared development and fortify intergenerational bonds.

Cultivating EQ within familial connections demands self-awareness, empathy, and deliberate efforts. Begin by becoming aware of and accepting your own emotions. Comprehend how your emotional reactions influence your interactions. Practice active listening, offering complete focus to your loved ones' words without criticism. Empathize by putting yourself in their shoes and honoring their standpoints. React graciously and patiently, shunning reactions driven by unfavorable emotions.

Embracing emotional intelligence in family relationships brings about numerous benefits. It cultivates understanding, warmth, and honest dialogue. Conflicts become possibilities for growth and learning.

An environment characterized by emotional awareness, strong attachments, and enhanced links emerges. Family members collaboratively face life's obstacles while supporting one another through affection, support, and love.

Emotional Intelligence in Friendships

Friendships represent the soft fabrics that enhance the color and texture of our existence. These unbreakable alliances offer comfort, backing, and happy memories. In the sphere of amity, emotional intelligence functions as a navigator, directing us toward stronger affiliations, comprehension, and meaningful interactions.

Navigating New Connections

Making new friendships can evoke mixed feelings of excitement and nervousness. At this stage, emotional intelligence takes great significance. EQ promotes attentive listening and empathy—essential components of fruitful conversations. When meeting with new people, it is imperative to approach them with an open mindset, asking thoughtful queries that reveal authentic curiosity in their ideas and experiences. By showing empathy and understanding, you form an ambiance where the individual feels appreciated, laying the foundation of a potential friendship.

Conversations With Existing Friends

Existing friendships flourish on shared memories, similar passions, and a profound bond. Emotional intelligence fortifies these links through efficient communication. While interacting with friends, emotional intelligence makes you concentrate attentively, focusing on their verbal and nonverbal indicators. Additionally, it entails being sensitive to their emotions, providing aid during challenging times, and celebrating their triumphs with genuine enthusiasm. By applying emotional smartness, you show your friends that you truly care, nurturing a relationship built on mutual understanding and respect.

Perspective-Taking

Perspective-taking enables you to perceive scenarios from your friends' perspectives, resulting in improved understanding and reduced disputes. Through exercising empathy and perspective-taking, you build the foundation for strengthened bonds and enduring friendships.

Managing Conflicts and Misunderstandings

Even the strongest friendships encounter bumps along the way. Nonetheless, emotional awareness furnishes you with the tools needed to navigate misunderstandings elegantly. Rather than responding instinctually, emotional intelligence motivates you to take a moment, contemplate your emotions, and tackle the circumstance with empathy and an unbiased outlook. This process defuses stress, promotes straightforward chats, and averts differences from intensifying. By managing clashes with emotional skills, you reinforce the basis of confidence and interaction in your friendships.

Setting Boundaries With Family and Friends

In family relationships and friendships, boundaries carry the role of fragile but indispensable strands that outline our personal space, well-being, and autonomy. Establishing limitations is an act of self-care and self-esteem, a means to respect our requirements while nurturing wholesome connections. Nevertheless, the process of boundary-setting could be intimidating, particularly when it pertains to families and friends. Here is where EQ comes into play as a beacon of direction, empowering us to traverse this complex landscape with compassion, awareness, and grace.

The Balance of Boundaries

Boundaries represent the parameters that distinguish what is acceptable and comfortable for us in relationships. They constitute the bedrock of healthy connections, permitting us to safeguard our individuality while engaging in meaningful connections. Emotional smartness imbues this idea with an added level of complexity by providing us with the capability to determine and convey boundaries while taking into account the feelings and viewpoints of others.

Self-awareness as the Starting Point

Effective boundary establishment originates from self-awareness—a fundamental element of EQ. We must acknowledge our very own necessities, values, and limitations. EQ directs us to examine our emotions and grasp what causes discomfort or unease. This consciousness of ourselves lays the groundwork for our boundaries; boundaries that secure our psychological well-being and uphold our genuineness.

Empathy and Effective Communication

Empathetic emotional skills enable us to walk in the shoes of others. When determining limitations with family and friends, empathy assists us in appreciating their points of view and feelings. It enables us to communicate our boundaries with compassion, decreasing the possibility of misinterpretation or dispute. By articulating our requirements while recognizing theirs, we develop a bridge of understanding that promotes regard and straightforward conversation.

Navigating Family Dynamics

Navigating boundaries with loved ones can be specifically complicated because of the complicated dynamics involved. EQ motivates us to tackle these discussions with delicacy. It makes us communicate our boundaries in a non-confrontational manner, highlighting that our objectives stem from self-care instead of critique. EQ helps us realize that although establishing limitations might be novel or uncomfortable for certain family members, it's an action of development and self-regard that advantages all in the long run.

Balancing Friendship and Boundaries

Friendship, similar to family relations, requires mindful consideration when determining limitations. Emotional skills prompt us that true buddies respect and support our well-being. It encourages transparent conversations regarding boundaries, where we can share our needs without worrying about judgment or dismissal. EQ facilitates us to steer these conversations with empathy, guaranteeing that our friendship stays solid and sincere despite the fact that boundaries are developed.

The Art of Flexibility

The emotional quotient instructs us that boundaries are not inflexible barriers but adaptable frameworks that could change along with changing circumstances. As we grow and our connections evolve, our boundaries might alter, too. EQ provides us the power to deal with these adjustments with openness and comprehension. It aids us in communicating our evolving needs with honesty and empathy, nurturing a perception of mutual growth and relationship.

Key Takeaways

- In the realm of family associations and friendships, EQ is the pulse that maintains honest connections. It's the capability to apprehend and react to emotions—our personal and those of our cherished ones—that enrich our bonds and cultivate a society of understanding and admiration.

- Empathy is the elixir that bridges gaps, cures mental wounds, and nurtures trust inside family and friendship groups. By walking in the shoes of our family members and friends, we create an atmosphere where emotions are recognized, valued, and discussed, laying the foundation for more powerful, more caring associations.

- Honesty and open communication is a keystone of any wholesome relationship. EQ motivates us to convey our emotions, ideas, and boundaries in a way that's empathetic and non-confrontational.

- Conflict is bound to happen in any relationship, yet EQ helps us to handle it with elegance.

- Emotional quotients illuminate the significance of developing healthy boundaries within family connections and friendships. It educates us that creating boundaries is an act of self-care, a means to safeguard our wellness without damaging the bonds we cherish.

Now that we discussed emotional intelligence in family relations and friendships, let's learn how to talk to anyone and understand people's emotions through emotional intelligence.

Chapter 7:
How to Talk to Anyone and Understand People's Emotions

He who knows others is wise; he who knows himself is enlightened.

–Lao Tzu

Whether it's a brief discussion with a stranger or a deep talk with a loved one, correspondence is the string that collectively binds the texture of human connections. However, actually comprehending somebody's emotions calls for a deeper level of involvement, one that goes beyond shallow chat. Here is where emotional knowledge comes in as a leading power, assisting us to navigate the intricacies of human emotions and develop a connection that reverberates at a profound level.

Every discussion is a chance to bridge gaps, exchange experiences, and build bonds that improve our lives. Nevertheless, the craft of talking to anyone and genuinely knowing their emotions moves beyond simple words—it's a combination of empathy, active listening, and emotional knowledge. In this chapter, we plunge into the deep world of interacting with others and unraveling their emotions through the lens of emotional quotient.

Recognizing that various folks need diverse approaches is a cornerstone of effective communication. Similar to how individuals possess distinctive choices and communication styles, their emotional requirements likewise differ. Some might prefer to reveal freely, while others could discover convenience in listening. Emotional knowledge makes us tuned to these distinctions, permitting us to adapt our communication style to match the individual before us. By identifying these variances, we create a room where conversations flow naturally, promoting a feeling of ease and common understanding.

Tailoring Communication to Individual Preferences

In human relationships, the charm rests not just in the words exchanged but also in the harmony of understanding. Every individual brings their unique communication style and personality traits to a discussion. The art of effective communication goes beyond speaking; it's about crafting a dialogue that resonates with the recipient. In this exploration, we delve into the profound realm of tailoring communication to individual preferences, a practice guided by empathy and enriched by emotional intelligence.

Recognizing Diverse Communication Styles

In communication, acknowledging and adjusting to an individual's preferences and propensities is a vital element of developing meaningful connections. Some individuals are verbal communicators, sharing themselves mostly through words, while others communicate their feelings via nonverbal signs such as gestures, facial expressions, and physical body language. Comprehending these distinctions is the initial action toward crafting communication that echoes.

Talkative vs. Reflective Individuals

Communication preferences differ between talkative and reflective individuals. Some people find comfort and relationships through a vibrant exchange of thoughts, while others require a moment of reflection before they can share themselves. Emotional knowledge motivates us to value these distinctions and change our approach appropriately. While talkative individuals flourish in participating in discussions, reflective individuals may enjoy times of peacefulness to collect their thoughts before sharing.

Detail-Oriented vs. Big-Picture Thinkers

The way we process information shapes our communication style as well. Detail-oriented individuals focus on specifics and nuances, while big-picture thinkers tend to see the broader context. Emotional intelligence encourages us to bridge this gap by finding common ground. Acknowledging details while also discussing the larger narrative ensures that both types of thinkers feel heard and valued.

Impact of Personality Traits

Personality qualities also have an impact on how we relate to and interact with others. Knowing these characteristics can aid us in having sensitive and empathic conversations.

Introverts vs. Extroverts

Introverts may choose solitary or small group interactions, appreciating stronger connections over a bigger social circle. Extroverts, on the other hand, flourish in social setups. Emotional knowledge motivates us to produce comfy areas for introverts to open up, offering them the moment they need to share their ideas. For extroverts, it involves developing an atmosphere where their excitement is accepted.

Sensing vs. Intuitive Individuals

Sensing individuals rely on tangible information, while intuitive ones lean toward patterns and possibilities. Emotional knowledge helps us to bridge this gap by utilizing language that corresponds to both kinds. Integrating concrete instances for sensors and exploring potential scenarios for intuition guarantees that everyone really feels consisted of and recognized.

Thinking vs. Feeling Personalities

Thinking characters prioritize logic and analysis, while feeling personalities value emotions and relationships. Emotional knowledge radiates here, advising us to think about both viewpoints. Structuring discussions with logical reasoning while acknowledging emotional effects develops a well-balanced approach that connects with both thinking and feeling individuals.

Strategies for Adapting Communication Styles

Adapting our communication styles involves a combination of awareness and responsiveness.

- Flexibility in conversation initiation: Emotional intelligence encourages us to initiate conversations in ways that align with the recipient's preferences. Some might appreciate straightforward questions, while others might select a more casual approach.

- Asking open-ended questions: Encouraging engagement with open-ended questions opens the doorway for meaningful conversations. It allows individuals to share their thoughts and feelings without feeling constrained.

- Allowing space for silence and reflection: In a fast-paced world, silence can be a powerful tool. Emotional intelligence prompts us to allow for pauses, giving individuals the space to collect their thoughts and respond authentically.

Understanding Emotions Through Active Listening

In human communications, the exchange of words often barely scratches the surface of what truly lies beneath. Emotions shimmer just beneath the surface of conversations, waiting to be uncovered and understood. In this emotional exploration, active listening emerges as the compass that guides us to the heart of another's feelings. As an integral aspect of emotional intelligence, active listening is not just about hearing words—it's about understanding the emotions that run within them.

The Components of Active Listening

Active listening is a multi-faceted skill that involves several components, each contributing to the depth of understanding.

- Attending verbal cues: Active listening starts with focus. It involves concentrating on the speaker's words, tone, and nuances. Verbal clues, such as breaks, emphasis, or modifications in tone, offer beneficial understandings of the underlying feelings being conveyed.

- Paraphrasing and reflecting: Paraphrasing and reflecting on the content of what has been shared demonstrate that you are fully engaged. It involves rephrasing what you've heard to ensure you've understood properly. This not only validates the speaker but also encourages them to dig further into their feelings.

- Empathetic responses: Empathy is the soul of active listening. Responding with empathy involves recognizing and acknowledging the emotions being conveyed. It's about expressing understanding and compassion, creating a safe space for the speaker to open up further.

Techniques for Improving Active Listening Skills

Enhancing active listening skills requires intention, practice, and a genuine desire to connect on a deeper level.

- Minimize distractions and maintain eye contact: In a world filled with distractions, active listening demands our complete presence. Minimizing distractions, such as putting away devices and maintaining eye contact, signals to the speaker that they have your undivided attention.

- Avoid interrupting and premature judgments: The desire to interrupt or offer solutions can obstruct efficient listening. EQ leads us to resist interruptions, allowing the speaker to completely express themselves. Furthermore, preventing preliminary judgments ensures that we approach the discussion with an unbiased mindset.

- Demonstrate genuine interest through body language: Our body language talks volumes regarding our involvement. Moving ahead, nodding, and making positive gestures show sincere interest and motivate the speaker to share even more openly.

Key Takeaways

- By stepping into others' emotional shoes, you create a room where feelings are recognized and connections are nurtured.

- By focusing on verbal cues, reflecting, and reacting compassionately, you create an atmosphere where emotions are valued and comprehended.

- Customizing your approach based on whether somebody is chatty or reflective, detail-oriented or big-picture concentrated, demonstrates emotional knowledge. This adaptability promotes comfort and connection in chats.

- By determining emotional triggers and practicing methods to stay calm and composed, you contribute to constructive interactions. Handling your emotions guarantees that interactions continue to be productive and concentrated.

- With authentic connections, conversations come to be genuine exchanges where emotions are identified and accepted.

As you learn how to talk to people and understand their emotions, it's also important to understand your own emotions and thoughts, which we are going to discuss in the following chapter.

Chapter 8:
Understanding Your Own Emotions and Thoughts

Care for your psyche... know thyself, for once we know ourselves,
we may learn how to care for ourselves.

      —SOCRATES

Emotions, the raw currents that flow through us, reflect our inner conditions—from happiness to sadness, from pleasure to uneasiness. Thoughts shape our views, beliefs, and actions for the globe around us. Discovering this dynamic interplay unveils the deep connections that affect exactly how we experience and navigate life. In the ocean of emotions, it's natural for waves of negativity to wash over us at times. The path to understanding begins with a compassionate pause—a moment when we don't hastily react to these emotions. This chapter emphasizes that when feeling overwhelmed or upset, it's often best to avoid taking immediate action. Rather, acknowledge the feeling and allow it to be, accepting it as a part of your human experience. This break acts as a shelter, offering the room we require to later reflect and gain deeper insights.

The Power of Reflection

Living life can feel busy and fast-paced, so stopping to think about things sometimes feels like a waste of time. But if we want to better understand our feelings and thoughts, slowing down and thinking deeply can help a lot. In fact, paying attention to your inner world helps make you a kinder and more aware person overall!

Mindful Reflection

Mindful reflection can involve spending some quiet time focusing on how you feel and what's on your mind. It involves being open-minded and nonjudgmental toward whatever shows up during those moments of introspection. Essentially, it provides space for you to get acquainted with yourself better and cultivate emotional awareness for healthier relationships outside of yourself.

Take Time Before Acting

The push for speedy decisions might suggest that delaying action seems odd. Yet, making time for emotions is crucial for growing emotional awareness. Resisting urgency creates an opportunity to ponder and process feelings. Reflection permits understanding them better, which helps avoid rash replies influenced by fleeting moods.

Navigating Negative Emotions

When it comes to emotions, negative ones are just as natural and inevitable as the rise and fall of waves on the seashore. It's like an ocean—sometimes calm but mostly turbulent waters that stir up different emotions inside us—joy vs. sorrow, contentment vs. worry. Avoiding these emotions is not easy; what really helps is being aware and patiently working through them with self-kindness and wisdom! This will help you sail through life and handle your emotional roller coaster ride much better, balancing your head and heart!

Human emotions can be quite tricky sometimes, but no matter what we feel—good or bad—they form a lovely patchwork quilt. Even though certain emotions may seem unwanted, they still have value, like those dark clouds before a rain shower brings coolness. Sometimes, we get upset for no apparent reason; irritation or feeling low easily become part of our daily routine! All these emotions do give us character depth by showing how sensitive and intelligent we are. Having them shows strength and honesty toward everyone else, too! The more we understand these emotions, the more ready we are for the ups and downs we encounter throughout life. We owe this to ourselves, after all, since we only live once, right?

Negative emotions can trick us, push us hard when something bothers us, and sometimes hurt us deep within if left alone. Oftentimes, this inner urgency demands quick reactions, such as fighting back or running away. But then here's another option: understanding those hidden emotions and observing how they truly affect us; pause yourself so you know why you feel that way; maybe look deeper into those thoughts and realize that acting rushed might result in bigger problems later than temporary relief. Take some time instead—don't brush off what hurts or ignore what feels overwhelming. Instead, try to listen to your body's signals because, ultimately, it knows best at times! Your gut always wins anyway.

The difference between impulsive actions and reflective solutions stands at the center of managing negative emotions. Impulsiveness typically results in actions driven by the intensity of the moment, actions that might not line up with our values or lasting well-being. Reflective solutions, on the other hand, arise from the pause we grant ourselves. By giving ourselves time to comprehend our emotions, we change our reactions right into responses. These responses are based upon emotional expertise, formed by our understanding of our emotions and their triggers.

Emotional intelligence acts like a beacon when navigating negative emotions. Like using a map and compass together in the wilderness, emotional literacy allows you to pause, reflect, and move forward more thoughtfully instead of blindly reacting based on old habits. The insight gained by digging deeper can lead to healthier responses to setbacks or triggering situations. Exploring your inner world aids personal growth and a clearer sense of identity, too! Just think how easy it would be to hike knowing exact directions and terrain features. Having clarity always makes things easier! That's what emotional intelligence brings to the table!

The Reflective Process

Amid the daily chaos lies a sanctuary where one goes beyond the surface-level thoughts and feelings to delve deep, analyze, and understand themselves better. This place is called reflective procedure, and its process involves expressing yourself through writing or journaling, analyzing your own ideas and feelings honestly with empathy, and finally connecting the dots through intuitive thinking. As a result, not only do individuals develop emotional awareness and cognitive insights, but they also enhance their self-worth and well-being overall!

Reflecting on Emotions and Thoughts

The self-reflection process simply means taking a closer look at yourself and getting familiarized with various methods to figure out your true personality traits, along with recognizing any triggers that drive behavior patterns! As the days pass by, this self-discovery mission results in better emotional regulation and gracefully managing those inner chattering thoughts that used to cause distress earlier!

- Pause and acknowledge: Begin by acknowledging your emotions and thoughts without judgment. Recognize that they are part of your experience, neither good nor bad—simply a reflection of your human complexity.

- Journaling as a tool for capturing feelings: Writing acts as a bridge between the internal and the external. Journaling enables you to catch your emotions and ideas in a concrete way, creating a canvas for reflection. Through words, you give shape to the intangible, making it simpler to discover and comprehend.

- Analyzing triggers and underlying beliefs: Dive further into your emotional panorama by examining triggers—the occasions or scenarios that set off specific emotions. Investigate the beliefs or assumptions that underlie these reactions. By determining these underlying beliefs, you uncover the origins of your emotional reactions.

- Recognizing patterns of reaction: Patterns often emerge as you navigate your emotions and thoughts. Reflect on whether you tend to react in similar ways to different triggers. Recognizing these patterns is a pivotal step toward conscious change, enabling you to respond rather than react.

- Cultivating self-compassion: Throughout the reflective process, take care of yourself with compassion. Emotions and thoughts, whether positive or negative, are part of your experience. Accept them with empathy, creating an environment of understanding and approval.

Key Takeaways

- By consciously exploring your inner self, you acquire insights that allow you to navigate life's complexities with knowledge and sincerity.

- When confronted with extreme emotions, the wisdom of pausing before reacting ends up being priceless.

- Through journaling, evaluation, and introspection, you illuminate the complicated nuances of your inner world, untangling patterns and triggers that mold your responses.

- Analyzing your emotions and ideas reveals even more compared to superficial reactions. By evaluating triggers and probing right into underlying beliefs, you obtain an understanding of the origins of your emotional responses, opening the doorway to mindful adjustment.

- Emotions, whether optimistic or negative, are a natural component of your human experience. Welcome them with empathy and also acceptance.

It's time to navigate conflicts with emotional intelligence, which we're going to discuss in the following chapter.

Chapter 9:
Navigating Conflict with Emotional Intelligence

The quality of our lives depends not on whether or not we have conflicts,
but on how we respond to them.

–THOMAS CRUM

Conflict is a natural outcome of human connections. It originates from our distinctiveness, differing viewpoints, and varying aspirations. However, beneath the area of conflict exists a narrative—a story interwoven with emotions, beliefs, and inspirations. To genuinely handle disputes, it's important to recognize the factors driving everyone's stance. Emotional intelligence furnishes us with the tools to uncover the emotions and ideas that fuel disputes, permitting us to look beyond the surface and connect with empathy.

Resolving conflicts isn't really about eliminating disagreements; it has to do with discovering paths that result in mutual growth and tranquility. Emotional intelligence leads us in the direction of strategies that promote beneficial discussions and long-lasting options. This chapter dives into the art of dispute resolution through the lens of emotional knowledge, leading us in the direction of a course where disputes are converted into bridges that encourage empathy, collaboration, and enduring solutions.

Understanding Your Opponent's Reason for Conflict

Disagreements often arise from deeply rooted emotions, beliefs, and inspirations that shape our distinctions. Comprehending your opponent's factors for dispute is a vital element of emotional knowledge that empowers you to connect the space between varying viewpoints, encourage empathy, and look for solutions that vibrate with sincerity and mutual advancement.

Peering Beyond the Surface

Conflict commonly shows up as a clash of opinions or desires, yet the genuine essence remains concealed in emotions and underlying inspirations. Emotional knowledge encourages you to go much deeper, to peel back the layers and reveal the reasons behind your opponent's stance. This procedure isn't about winning or losing; it's regarding acknowledging the human complexity inside every one of us.

The Power of Empathy

Empathy is the spirit of recognizing your opponent's factor for conflict. It's the capacity to step into their shoes, to view the world through their lens, and to acknowledge the feelings that fuel their position. By embracing empathy, you go beyond the restrictions of evaluation and assumption, creating a space where relationships and interaction can flourish.

Listening With Open Ears and Open Hearts

Genuine understanding arises when you actively listen. It's greater than simply hearing words; it's regarding being completely present, allowing them to reveal themselves without disruption or judgment. Through active listening, you welcome their feelings and ideas to the surface, offering an atmosphere for sincere understanding.

Curiosity as Compass

Adopting curiosity during conflicts allows you to explore the underlying principles and emotions guiding your opponent's views. In doing so, you demonstrate respect for their perspectives and pave the way for collaborative problem-solving rather than negative interactions.

Finding Common Ground

Understanding your opponent's reasons for dispute does not suggest neglecting your very own worth or beliefs. It's about discovering common ground—the bridge that connects differing points of view. Emotional intelligence motivates you to seek areas of agreement, shared objectives, or shared passions. This common ground comes to be the structure upon which you construct options that honor both parties' needs.

Conflict Resolution Strategies

Conflicts are actually excellent chances to increase both interpersonal skills and emotional competence if handled smartly rather than impulsively or ignoring entirely out-of-discomfort zone fears! In this section, learn effective ways to tackle issues head-on without hurting anyone's sentiments but rather fostering open dialogue between parties involved. Imagine the positive outcome possibilities waiting behind resolving the deadlock peacefully, exciting, right? Let's get cracking, then!

Assertive Communication

Mastering assertive communication is crucial for resolving conflicts peacefully. Using "I" statements enables you to convey your perspectives while respecting the viewpoints of others, promoting an exchange of ideas without blaming fault or belittling the other person. This will create a welcoming atmosphere for transparent discussions.

Maintain Emotional Balance

Navigating heated disputes requires self-regulation skills. Recognizing and managing your own emotions is crucial. Mindful practices like deep breathing, pausing, or staying aware help manage emotions and promote considered replies instead of reflexive reactions.

Win-Win Solutions

Conflict resolution isn't about one person triumphing over the other. Instead, emotional intelligence directs our focus toward mutually satisfying outcomes by identifying common interests, shared objectives, or points of concurrence. These foundations support cooperative problem-solving.

Creativity in Problem-Solving

When tackling conflicts, emotional intelligence inspires innovative approaches to problem-solving. A flexible attitude uncovers options that value both parties' views, leading to novel resolutions that might not have been immediately apparent.

The Power of Apology and Forgiveness

Showcasing emotional intelligence through apologizing and forgiveness has the power to restore damaged connections. Honest apologies acknowledge accountability for your actions, whereas forgiveness releases both individuals from the weight of the conflict and facilitates healing and growth.

Assertive Communication Techniques

Assertive communication isn't about dominance or aggression; it's about voicing your thoughts, feelings, and needs with confidence while still honoring the viewpoints of others. It's a skill rooted in emotional intelligence—one that navigates the delicate balance between passivity and aggression, opening doors to effective communication.

Using "I" Statements

At its core, assertive communication hinges on utilizing "I" statements. Starting sentences with words like "I feel," "I think," or "I need" frames your thoughts as personal experiences, fosters a non-confrontational space of consideration, and avoids accusatory attitudes.

Expressing Emotions With Clarity

By embracing assertive communication, you learn to articulate your emotions clearly. Expressing how you feel when upset, nervous, or joyful helps you communicate more effectively rather than suppressing them and invites your conversational partners to understand your emotional state.

Setting Boundaries with Confidence

Mastery of emotional intelligence involves establishing boundaries with grace and assertiveness. Articulating your limitations safeguards your well-being and dignity. At the same time, assertive communication encourages you to be receptive to the boundaries of others and cultivates reciprocal understanding.

Fostering Open Dialogue

Assertive communication entails initiating open discussions that encourage active listening and mutual sharing. Both sides must feel safe to divulge their thoughts, emotions, and requirements without apprehension or consequences. Open dialogue thus paves the way for comprehension and connection.

Key Takeaways

- Emotional intelligence works as a bridge between conflicting parties by inspiring empathy.

- Recognizing the emotions, beliefs, and motivations behind different viewpoints produces a base for effective conversations and solutions.

- By acknowledging your very own emotions and those of others, you acquire an understanding right into the triggers and underlying causes of the disagreement.

- Emotional knowledge changes your emphasis from succeeding in conflicts to discovering solutions that profit both parties. This state of mind motivates teamwork and also encourages you to look for options that appreciate the requirements of all parties.

- Emotional intelligence empowers assertive communication—revealing ideas and feelings with self-confidence and respect.

Being emotionally intelligent also entails having patience and managing stress, which we'll cover in the following chapter.

Chapter 10:
How to be Patient and Stressless

Patience is the road to wisdom.

–Kao Kalia Yang

Modern living's hectic pace commonly causes us to compete against time, regularly attempting to examine tasks and achieve milestones. Amid all this chaos, the craft of patience and stresslessness usually goes unnoticed. Nevertheless, within the domain of emotional understanding, patience ends up being a light of peacefulness that guides you through life's obstacles with grace and tranquility. In this chapter, we take a journey to developing patience and calmness—a journey that consists of mindfulness, stress management, self-reflection, and time management.

Mindfulness and Meditation Practices

Finding calm amid turmoil appears like an uphill task. But hang on; learning mindfulness and meditation opens doors to serenity and self-understanding! Such techniques bring together gentle energy aimed at alleviating stress instead of adding more pressure or complexity. Try practicing them soon and watch the magic unfold gradually as though someone is applying oil to rusty hinges, bringing back joyous smiles. Remember, consistency is key here because these methods don't work overnight but ultimately help strengthen your mental fortitude and endurance when facing life's trials down the road!

Deep Breathing

Our breath keeps us grounded in the present. Devoting only three minutes to partake in deep inhalations and exhalations could promptly pacify your nervous system, lessen worry, and concentrate your ideas. By focusing on the pattern of your breath, you can calm the constant stream of ideas that keep your brain racing and recenter yourself in the here and now.

Sensing

Engaging your senses—sight, hearing, smell, taste, and touch—is key to unlocking the richness of the present moment. Being mindful encourages you to fully take in your surroundings and experiences. Through mindful observation, you can see the ordinary, promoting a feeling of thankfulness for the world surrounding you.

Listening

True listening is uncommon in a world where everyone is always talking. The goal of mindful listening is to hear the words that are stated while also comprehending the feelings and intentions behind them. We build deeper connections, foster empathy, and bolster relationships by being totally present during talks.

Observing

We frequently walk through life not really seeing. Mindful observation allows you to pause and cherish the atmosphere. There is wonder in everyday things, like the way the leaves rustle in the breeze or how the lights flicker. Such observations ground us, allowing us to value the elegance that unfolds moment by moment.

Introspection

Taking moments to observe your inner voice connects you to your intuition or gut feeling, providing direction whenever needed in complex situations! The more you tune into those quiet whispers, the simpler decision-making gets. Self-observation further equips you to handle tricky circumstances with poise and wisdom, all the while stepping outside societal judgments or limiting beliefs that cloud your vision too much.

Walking

Walking mindfully alters a daily task into a meditative exercise. With each step, you harmonize your breath, physical body, and mind. Walking mindfully allows you to discard interruptions and take pleasure in the rhythm of life, one step at a time.

Eating

In our hurry, we frequently neglect the simple act of eating. Mindful eating helps you to enjoy each bite, participating in all your senses. By enjoying textures, flavors, and aromas, you create a more powerful connection with your nourishment, stimulating gratitude for the sustenance you receive.

Meditation

Sitting quietly and following your breath for merely five minutes could result in deep changes. Meditation is the foundation stone of mindfulness, providing a space to grow inner serenity amid life's consistent movement. Through this method, you discover how to observe your ideas without judgment and create a haven of peace inside.

Stress Management Techniques

Life's demands can typically lead you down a route of stress and anxiety; however, you possess the capacity to find comfort and reclaim your balance. Stress management techniques provide a range of useful tools that enable you to navigate life's obstacles with resilience and grace. With practices like yoga, progressive muscle relaxation, workouts, biofeedback, aroma therapy, and concentrating on getting enough rest, you can develop a harmonious association with stress and promote your health.

Yoga

Yoga is an ancient practice that connects the soul and the body, offering a sanctuary of calm among turmoil. Yoga helps you to be present in your physical being and embrace the moment through a sequence of postures, breathing techniques, and meditation. This practice doesn't solely enhance adaptability and strength but additionally helps a closer bond with yourself, calming the mind and dissolving pressure.

Progressive Muscle Relaxation

In the tumult of life, we regularly carry anxiety inside our bodies, showing up as physical discomfort and psychological pressure. Progressive muscle relaxation is a strategy that includes tensing and, afterward, progressively releasing various muscle groups. This procedure not only promotes physical relaxation but also creates an alertness of the body-psyche relationship, empowering us to unfasten the clasp of worry.

Exercise

Physical activity can be really helpful for managing stress! Exercise releases feel-good chemicals called endorphins that improve your mood. Doing activities you enjoy, like walking, working out at the gym, or even dancing around your living room, will help turn negative feelings into positive ones. These types of movements also boost confidence and make you feel good about yourself. So, get moving to help manage stress naturally.

Biofeedback

Biofeedback is an approach that enables us to acquire command over our physiological replies to stress. With the aid of modern electronic devices, we get real-time details regarding our heart rate, muscle tension, and other physical functions. By finding out how to consciously influence these attributes, we reclaim control over our stress reaction, resulting in a much more well-balanced and durable condition of mind.

Aromatherapy

Aromatherapy utilizes the power of fragrance to affect mood and reduce stress. Specific essential oils, such as lavender and chamomile, possess soothing qualities that can induce relaxation. Breathing in these smells or applying them in massages can set off a sensory experience that delicately steers you far from stress and toward tranquility.

Sleeping Enough

Amid our occupied lifestyles, sleep is frequently given up, causing a waterfall of stress-connected troubles. Prioritizing enough rest is crucial for your physical and mental health. A properly-rested entire body and psyche are superior and geared up to manage stress, nurturing emotional equilibrium and cognitive clarity.

Cultivating Patience Through Self-Reflection and Reframing

Our lives have ups and downs like rollercoasters. Sometimes things go wrong or it takes longer to get what you want, which can make us feel grumpy and tired. But thinking about why this happened and looking at different ways to solve your problem helps you stay calm and believe more in yourself. It makes you strong, even when everything seems hard. See problems as chances to do better next time.

Reframe Setbacks as Learning Experiences

Sometimes setbacks can drag you down. They might make you question everything you do and feel like giving up entirely, but hang tight! Setbacks aren't roadblocks or game-overs; they're chances to revamp your route forward. No matter how bumpy things appear, always remember that you still possess skills gained from previous adventures or experiments. If one plan doesn't hit its target, it doesn't mean you should stop trying because another idea might rock.

Be Kind to Yourself During Difficulties

Troubles are everywhere, and no one seems immune. But here's something positive you might want to consider: Everyone makes mistakes! We all feel unsure at times, too because nobody knows all the answers. That's okay—we humans need reminders every now and then to pat ourselves on the back! Why? Because recognizing the good intentions hidden inside mistakes prepares you for something that will happen sooner or later in life. Your inner dialogue will turn kinder and more supportive as you move ahead without fear.

Practice Mindfulness for Calmness

Mindfulness allows you to focus right where you are. It keeps your thoughts grounded, so worries won't cloud your vision and make you miss the beauty around you. The advantages are clear head space while gaining peace of mind since distractions disappear when you are intentionally fully involved in what surrounds you versus letting anxious ruminations ruin your day. Start paying closer attention—little moments add value if acknowledged!

Create a Culture of Patience, Tenacity, and Learning

Get together with people in a culture passionate about perseverance, like learning, growing through challenges, and encouraging curiosity, since surrounding yourself with patient people tends to rub off!

Besides, there's nothing better than a heartfelt discussion over shared quests and fresh perspectives to help you understand your potential. Their presence boosts courage simply because camaraderie builds strength, so don't shy away from welcoming a circle rich with insightful vibes!

Practice Deep Breathing Exercises

Simple steps to harvest tranquility include daily doses of quiet moments focused on being present instead of running mental replays or jumping into what-ifs. Consequently, breath control lessens frantic feelings, nourishing mental serenity alongside physical energy. As the weeks drift by, this easy habit stamps a brand new sense of poise onto old routines.

Accept Your Current Circumstances

Patience needs the pillar of acceptance! What does that mean? It means taking things as they come, without grumbling, even when some events seem unfair or disappointing. Embrace acceptance of whatever comes up next. Adopting this flexible attitude leaves room for smart problem-solving free of added worry and negative impact on family and friends.

Develop Tolerance for Discomfort

Patience requires tolerance for discomfort. Embrace situations that challenge your comfort zone, and you'll gradually develop resilience against restlessness. Embracing discomfort with an open heart opens doors to unexpected growth.

Slow Down in Moments of Rush

Slow down in life's hurry! Even though zipping through tasks often seems more effective, pause right there: taking your time pays better dividends! Why? This deliberate practice fosters patience, which makes sure we wisely react to twists instead of acting recklessly due to fear, anxiety, or pressure. Besides noticing benefits like improved clarity and peace by not dashing, we usually spot niceties passed by in hectic momentum.

Immerse Yourself in an Absorbing Project

Find projects that hook you into focused involvement! Since getting fully involved in such interests moves distractions far away and directs attention to the process itself, it naturally leads to patience.

How exactly does it do that? Engrossing ourselves in something absorbs both body and mind, thus keeping impatience away since no other worries have space!

Time Management Strategies

In this busy world, precious moments can escape quickly, leaving us stressed and scattered. Exploring ways to manage time helps us regain peace in our crazy schedules. A little investment in understanding tips boosts efficiency, making use of minutes more meaningful and giving a clearer perspective on tasks that help you achieve those goals that are important to you (a happy home, career success, and so on). Every day's a fresh start to put into action ideas to maximize your time!

Recognizing the Value of Time

Emotional intelligence prompts us to recognize that time is a precious resource—a currency that we invest in various aspects of our lives. The way we manage our time directly impacts our well-being, productivity, and the quality of our relationships.

Set Clear Priorities

Time management starts with knowing what really counts! Decisions based on EQ point us straight toward important things since these decisions determine immediate versus less pressing needs to be taken care of first. Attending high-priority issues equals having extra mental peace and time to relax or tackle another task.

The Power of Planning

Plan away! Putting thoughts into list form keeps distracting interruptions to a minimum and also reminds the brain what comes next. Having a map makes unclear days much easier with greater focus and purpose. So, when things pop up unexpectedly, you adjust your plans without wasting excessive time thinking about multiple options. You already made choices earlier; now, just stick to the original schedule unless circumstances seriously change the major items listed previously.

Break Tasks into Manageable Steps

Big tasks seem tough until they break down bit by bit. This habit decreases intimidation and boosts determination by showing progress built upon completed portions. Patting yourself on the back after checking off several parts feels positive and motivates your personal drive to keep at it! Applying the idea to your actions could prove very fruitful.

Embrace the Pomodoro Technique

One cool technique for being efficient uses work segments followed by brief pauses—the Pomodoro technique. It keeps momentum going yet prevents exhaustion, resulting in higher-quality work overall! You might enjoy experimenting and putting its principles into practice.

Eliminate Time-Wasting Habits

Our inner voice guides us toward good life decisions, including where exactly we place our energies. Finding which habits steal time without adding value may even leave us unhappy. Unveiling such actions clears space, ready for something better, replacing the former void with richer experiences.

Balance Work and Rest

Time management isn't solely about productivity; it's also about finding balance. Emotional intelligence emphasizes the importance of incorporating rest and leisure into our schedules. Balancing work with moments of rejuvenation enhances our overall well-being and creativity.

Embrace Flexibility

While time management strategies provide structure, emotional intelligence reminds us to embrace flexibility. Life is unpredictable, and being rigid can lead to frustration. By being adaptable, we navigate challenges with resilience and ease.

Key Takeaways

- Patience is being able to wait nicely without getting upset. It helps you handle tough situations better and feel closer to yourself and others.

- Being more aware of what's happening right now can make you less stressed and help you relax, even when things are busy.

- To deal with stress better, try taking deep breaths, exercising, planning your day, and saying no to extra tasks sometimes.

- Thinking about why you get impatient can also help you be more patient.

- Understanding that some things take time and accepting that will make you happier.

To take care of our mental health, we need to learn to say "No" to the things that could harm our mental health. We will learn how to say "no" to things that can drain up our souls in the following chapter.

Chapter 11:
How to Say "No"

You have to create little pockets of joy in your life to take care of yourself.

—Jonathan Van Ness

Our lives are composed of numerous factors, much like the threads that make up a carpet. Sometimes, they blend so thoroughly that we feel trapped and unsure of where to start. However, among all of this chaos, we must take care of ourselves. Saying "no" when you need to is crucial because if you don't, you'll put your needs last while attempting to take care of everyone else. Since you secretly despise doing all those things, saying "yes" too frequently also makes you unpleasant to be around. This chapter talks about how to put ourselves first nicely and be able to tell others "no."

Mastering Assertiveness

As discussed in the earlier chapters, at the heart of all meaningful relationships lies the art of being assertive, a talent that paves the way toward concordance and genuine discussion. Asserting your needs and desires forms the bedrock of emotional aptitude, enabling you to interact with others in a manner that honors your own dignity while embracing empathy.

Asserting yourself links two vital skills: Setting clear limits and the capability to converse easily. Being assertive doesn't mean aggressively pushing views, nor should you avoid expressing yourself truthfully. When executed effectively, this trait smoothly blends boundaries with kind conversations. Balancing these traits adds to the overall happiness quotient! Incorporating awareness of emotional aspects into social interactions creates harmony with confidence levels.

Balance Self-Respect and Empathy

Mastering self-assertion involves appreciating your own significance and relating sensitively with others. It doesn't mean forgetting or dismissing others' perspectives but standing up for your own rights gracefully. Striking equilibrium between these conflicting desires assists growth personally and interpersonally through healthy connections that nurture overall emotional well-being.

Express Desires and Boundaries

Learning to be confident in stating wants and boundaries promotes positive conversations. Using "I" sentences with a level-toned expression during chats keeps discussions going without misunderstandings brewing because all feel heard and acknowledged!

Navigating Difficult Conversations

Boundaries must be discussed in order to explain limitations, which could provoke tension, but learning EQ makes it easier. Showing compassion to understand another's point of view, actively listening, and striving for agreement brings resolution.

Utilize Nonverbal Communication

Body signals assist the message behind spoken words through nonverbal cues. Looking someone directly in the eyes and keeping open body language demonstrates poise, strengthening convictions expressed through assertiveness skills. Applying this concept will boost your effectiveness in communicating what you truly believe while coming across naturally.

The diversity of communication skills relies on the capacity to adapt to a variety of situations, both personal and professional. The skill of speaking your mind while also considering other people's points of view leads to effective communication. Emotional intelligence ensures that having clarity and treating people with respect through assertiveness benefit any exchange.

Effective Communication When Declining Requests

Occasionally, dealing with people may be challenging. There may be times when you must decline a request, but you don't want to offend the person or sour your friendship with them. This is when emotional intelligence is useful. Effective communication, even when you have to refuse someone, is a crucial component of emotional intelligence. This entails being understanding of the other person's emotions while remaining aware of your own needs and boundaries.

The Delicate Balancing Act

Declining requests is not about shutting doors; it's about balancing your priorities and capacities while nurturing connections. Emotional intelligence recognizes that effective communication in these moments is pivotal to avoiding misunderstandings and fostering respect.

Choose Words With Care

Choosing responses thoughtfully when unable to do something prevents hurt feelings. Actions may speak louder than words; however, words are powerful enough to alter the course of relationship dynamics. Sensitive selection of speech and tactful actions equals a strong bond strengthened through clear and kind actions.

Honesty and Transparency

A transparent explanation helps clarify the motives behind declining a request. When your reasoning matches another person's perspective, a healthy and satisfying discussion follows, leading to better understanding. Honest opinions and genuine intent lead to stronger relationships.

Express Appreciation

When someone makes a request, saying, "Thank you for thinking of me," can go a long way. It shows that you appreciate their effort and consideration, which can help ease any disappointment they might feel if you ultimately can't do what they ask. Emotional intelligence plays a role in these kinds of interactions by helping you communicate clearly and empathetically.

Empathetic Listening

When talking with someone, really hearing what they have to say is just as important as sharing your thoughts. Opening your mouth alone won't do it; you also need to open your ears. Being aware of and interested in another person's viewpoint demonstrates your respect for them and their emotions. This approach is essential to building strong, lasting connections.

Suggest Alternatives

When turning someone down, suggest an alternative solution or task that matches your abilities and resources while still fulfilling their overall goal. This demonstrates flexibility, collaboration spirit, and problem-solving skills. Plus, it keeps doors open in case future possibilities arise, with potential benefits for everybody involved. Using emotional intelligence throughout the whole process enables constructive dialogue, keeping people comfortable even despite initial disappointment due to rejected inquiries.

Maintain a Respectful Tone

The tone used when exchanging ideas plays a crucial role. Respectful tones allow both speakers to emerge feeling appreciated and validated. While keeping conversations amicable helps each grow socially and emotionally, it also leads to fruitful relationships.

Avoid Over-Explaining

Transparency is significant, yet nobody wants long explanations! It's fine to decline without overexplaining your reasons. Saying less keeps chat concise and doesn't affect companionship. Keeping the right balance helps preserve the conversation's focus.

Overcoming Guilt and People-Pleasing Tendencies

Guilt and pleasing others are two issues many people face in relationships. These challenges can come from societal expectations or past negative experiences. But in reality, they only lead to frustration, exhaustion, anxiety, and depression. They hold you back. But emotional intelligence offers ways out. By breaking free from those patterns, you liberate yourself and build stronger bonds based on true closeness and care without hidden agendas or fear of rejection. Embracing honesty and vulnerability will attract those who truly love and accept you. That said, finding the right balance requires courage to confront destructive habits, practice self-compassion, and create assertiveness tactics tailored to your unique needs. Investing time in exploring and growing emotional intelligence pays off big time!

Understand the Roots of Guilt

Sometimes, we feel guilty because we worry about letting others down or falling short of their standards. That pressure can come from outside sources like society, family members, or peers. It can also stem from messages we picked up early in life or fears rooted deep within ourselves. These kinds of emotions can get in the way of living a fulfilling life and carving out paths true to our individual hearts. You can better negotiate these psychological complexities by developing emotional intelligence, which results in a life that is more free, tranquil, and satisfying.

Recognize the Impact of People-Pleasing

People-pleasing tendencies can cause you to put others' needs ahead of your own, which can leave you feeling emotionally exhausted and cut off from your true self. Emotional intelligence emphasizes the importance of understanding this effect and the toll it has on your overall well-being.

Unearth Authentic Desires

Overcoming guilt, and people-pleasing starts with unearthing your authentic desires. Instead of chasing everyone else's nod of approval, find which paths light your spark. Inner strength develops quickly when brave decisions fueled by genuine yearnings are acted upon.

Separate Self-Worth from Others' Approval

Emotional intelligence empowers you to separate your self-worth from others' approval. By recognizing that your value isn't determined by meeting external expectations, you liberate yourself from the grip of guilt.

Embrace the Power of "No"

Mastering the ability to confidently say "no" despite potential guilt is a valuable tool. This skill arises from emotional intelligence, which involves learning how to set firm boundaries around your personal space, develop confidence in stating your opinions and desires plainly, and empathize deeply with others.

Honor Your Well-Being

Learning to overcome feelings of guilt and people-pleasing tendencies requires recognizing that taking care of yourself is actually an expression of self-worth rather than egotism. Embracing self-care as an aspect of self-esteem helps you understand that looking after yourself isn't just acceptable but necessary for your overall health and contentment. Emotional intelligence teaches you that your well-being is a priority.

Shift Perspectives on Disappointment

Disappointing others is a part of life, but being wise lets you look at it in another way: instead of thinking of it as a mistake or failure, take it as a chance to open communication and grow from the experience.

Alternatives to Saying "No" and Nurturing Self-Care

Saying "no" is a crucial piece of human interaction; however, it must be done tactfully, particularly in close associations. At the point when you use expressions other than "no," it causes others to feel seen and regarded, accordingly reinforcing relational bonds. This capacity to converse in complex manners is what we would refer to as passionate insight. Emotional knowledge is an intriguing theme loaded with significant standards for each sort of connection. Whenever used appropriately, you create more grounded ties, experience less struggle, and impart more successfully.

Understanding the Nuances of Alternatives

"No" straight up may sometimes work best, yet other alternatives expand possibilities, granting flexibility, especially when combined with empathy. Making considered choices helps you adapt responses that match each situation and the individuals involved. Thoughtful decisions adjust according to diverse circumstances, avoiding one-size-fits-all and honoring various preferences. Personalized answers treat everyone uniquely, offering customized care since variety truly does spice up human interactions!

Offering Compromises

Finding common ground creates cooperation since emotional smarts allow you to suggest compromises, creating room for differing views while still honoring your boundaries. Offering suggestions that meet both sides alleviates tensions without stepping too far in either direction.

Negotiating Timelines

Time can be a crucial factor in some situations. By negotiating deadlines that benefit both parties, emotional intelligence encourages you to show your commitment to the request while taking into account your other obligations.

Prioritizing and Reframing

Emotional intelligence can help you handle difficult situations by framing them in a positive way. When you say, "I want to do it, but I have other important things to focus on right now," you are being honest about what matters most without offending anyone. This kind of communication shows that you respect everyone involved and their feelings too.

Embracing Self-Care Practices

Taking care of yourself is like planting seeds for happiness that you'll harvest over time. It's not about feeling guilty or selfish if you think your emotions need refilling because the truth is, no one can pour from an empty cup. So, keep taking moments to pause, reflect, and feel your emotions—whether it's loneliness, anger, or excitement—and know that showing empathy for yourself will lead to strengthening connections with people.

Creating Sacred Spaces

Creating cozy spots where you can unwind and feel calm helps you relax better inside your own homes. When you take the time to arrange quiet corners and decorate them soothingly, you end up with little hideaways that become havens away from stressful thoughts or distractions.

Setting Digital Boundaries

Digital devices often intrude upon the self-caring actions you practice each day. To prevent this, you need to learn ways to separate yourself from the digital interference since technology can crowd out the valuable moments of restoration you all require. A smart approach involves setting digital boundaries between online interactions and moments spent getting restored and focusing only on your true self.

Embracing Leisure and Joy

Enjoying free time and happiness recharges the emotional batteries. By learning emotional intelligence, you do things that make you content since happiness comes in various forms, like reading books or planting seeds, as well as cherishing bonding moments with dear companions. Simply anything that brings cheerful smiles to faces!

Key Takeaways

- Making yourself a priority by saying "no" is not being selfish. It enables you to put your health first and keep your emotions in check.

- How you say "no" is just as crucial as the actual act. Relationships can be preserved by using straightforward, sympathetic, and respectful communication.

- Boundaries must be established and upheld in order for relationships to be healthy. A strategy for enforcing those limits is to say "no" when it's necessary.

- Being honest with yourself and your limitations gives you the freedom to make decisions in line with your priorities and values.

- Overcoming the guilt that comes with saying "no" is a path to self-empowerment and a greater appreciation of your worth.

Chapter 12:
Raising Kids With Emotional Intelligence

The best inheritance a parent can give their children is a few minutes of their time each day.

—ORLANDO A. BATTISTA

Being a parent is a complex journey full of joy, difficulties, and a great responsibility to support your children's emotional development. You set off on a journey into the expansive world of parenting children with emotional intelligence in this chapter. Here, we examine educating kids about emotional literacy while encouraging empathy and compassion, giving them tools for handling conflict, and encouraging emotional control and self-awareness. We explore the fundamentals of fostering a loving and emotionally mature home setting where your kids can thrive.

Teaching Emotional Literacy to Children

Emotions are an inherent part of the human experience. Teaching children emotional literacy is like handing them a map of their emotional landscape. It equips them with the tools to navigate the highs and lows of their feelings, fostering resilience and mental well-being.

The Vocabulary of Emotions

One of the first steps in teaching emotional literacy is introducing children to the vocabulary of emotions. By helping them name what they feel—whether it's happiness, anger, sadness, or fear—you validate their emotions and empower them to communicate their feelings effectively.

Emotions as Messengers

Teaching children emotional intelligence involves assisting them in realizing that emotions aren't necessarily negative. Instead, they really contain incredibly valuable messages that educate us about our needs, wants, and potential limitations. Children will be better equipped to make wise decisions and come up with solutions when they encounter problems if you teach them how to pay attention to these messages coming from their emotions.

Modeling Emotional Literacy

As a parent or caregiver for kids, you play a big role in showing them how to deal with emotions. You have two jobs here: First, just being open about your own feelings and expressing them in healthy ways; second, talking to the kids about how you feel so they learn that having feelings isn't something to be afraid of. If you act this way, it shows young people that it's alright to experience all kinds of different feelings inside.

Empathy and Emotional Literacy

Empathy is the capacity to comprehend and relate to the sentiments of another person. The good news is that if you put effort into teaching your children how to understand and manage their own emotions through emotional intelligence, they will naturally improve in their ability to perceive how other children around them are feeling as well. That makes it simpler to establish friendships and determine how to conduct appropriately in social circumstances.

Emotion-Focused Activities

Kids love games and activities. Luckily, there are lots of emotion-focused activity ideas that can help kids get better at dealing with and understanding their emotions without even seeming like school-work—like drawing pictures of how various feelings look facially, reading stories together about characters going through all types of moods, or playing card games where the objective revolves around recognizing certain emotions. These sorts of exercises provide entertainment while still making sure that little minds absorb key lessons regarding managing their internal states.

Validation and Empowerment

Teaching emotional literacy is not about telling children how they should feel. It's about validating their emotions, letting them know that their feelings are valid and acceptable. This validation empowers them to trust their emotions and themselves.

Emotional literacy is a lifelong skill that serves children well into adulthood. Not only does it help them create positive connections with their family members and friends, but it also allows them to steer clear of complications, remain firm under pressure, and grow up strong both physically and mentally!

Promoting Empathy and Compassion in Kids

Children benefit enormously if encouraged early on to develop an empathetic and compassionate approach since empathy plays a crucial role in helping humans interact socially and establish meaningful connections. Acquiring this attribute at a tender age promotes nurturing favorable relations among peer groups while paving the path for their evolution as emotionally astute entities possessing excellent interpersonal communication abilities.

Modeling Empathy

As a parent, you serve a significant influence in shaping future generations; therefore, it is imperative to demonstrate qualities such as empathy during today's life events. Young brains tend to adapt observed habits quite rapidly, thus presenting an ideal chance for implementing values through practice instead of mere theory dissemination. Henceforth, incorporating sympathetic behaviors into regular activities exhibits an effective style, constructively influencing juveniles to acquire the same traits, resulting in fruitful interactions alongside community fellows.

Teaching Perspective-Taking

In order for children to develop empathy, which is the capacity to see events from other perspectives, it is helpful to engage them in activities that will help them develop this capacity. Curious questions like "How do you think they feel?" and similar ones are examples of this. You can help young minds comprehend other points of view and grow into kind, caring individuals in the future by implementing these little modifications.

Storytelling and Literature

Stories have a significant influence on aiming to foster empathy, especially in children who may have had exposure to situations outside of their comfort zones through literature or oral tales. Such findings considerably broaden perspectives and increase understanding of the complexities included in our communal lives. Books and fictional narratives show themselves to be powerful tools for developing a broader perspective on the many facets of the human experience.

Encouraging Acts of Kindness

As parents and guardians, encourage your children to perform acts of kindness, whether it's helping a friend, sharing a toy, or even caring for a pet. Executing such pleasant tasks grants tiny souls insights regarding the consequences brought forth by individual selections made by them upon fellow earth dwellers.

Active Listening

Teaching kids active listening skills is a fundamental part of promoting empathy. Encourage them to truly hear what others are saying, ask questions, and show that they care about the feelings being shared.

Cultivating Self-Compassion

Empathy begins at home. Teach children to be kind to themselves and to recognize and validate their own emotions. Self-compassion is the foundation upon which empathy for others is built.

Building Emotional Intelligence

If you want kids to grow up knowing their own feelings and being kind to other people's feelings, too, then as parents and guardians, you must help them. You can start a chat about how everyone is feeling and remind them that it's always fine to share what's happening inside their hearts with you. This way, you're teaching them about emotional intelligence, along with empathy.

Conflict Resolution Skills for Children

Fights happen to everybody, even children. But guess what? It's totally okay because arguments can be handled nicely. As a parent, you can help kids master some techniques to resolve disagreements in a friendly manner. That's called conflict resolution skills, and it's an awesome tool that can bring a lot of peace and love into friendships and create a more harmonious world.

The Importance of Conflict Resolution Skills

Having conflict resolution skills does not include being silent and disregarding issues. Instead, you must teach kids to develop excellent communication skills, to put themselves in other people's situations, and to find solutions that benefit everyone. Building solid, long-lasting connections is made possible when you teach them how to do this properly.

Identifying Emotions

Conflicts usually stem from desires going unnoticed. Helping children realize and point out their emotions makes things less likely to escalate. Then, encouraging them to think deeply about the way others feel will help settle issues promptly. Understanding the emotional aspect of conflicts is the first step toward resolution.

Encouraging Open Communication

Teach children the value of open communication. Encourage them to talk about their true emotions honestly and respectfully; sharing honest feelings won't only enhance connections but also make life fuller since hearts aren't overflowing with hidden grief.

Teaching Problem-Solving Skills

Conflict resolution often involves problem-solving. Guide children through the process of defining the problem, brainstorming solutions, and evaluating the pros and cons of each. This teaches them to approach conflicts with a constructive mindset.

Emphasizing Win-Win Solutions

Conflicts happen when people disagree, but that doesn't mean someone has to be the loser. Show kids how to find answers that make everyone happy—win-win solutions. This helps them work together better and understand others' feelings better.

Modeling Conflict Resolution

Kids copy what they see. So, if you want them to handle fights nicely, do it yourself. Let them know it's alright to have arguments sometimes, but we can fix them peacefully without fighting. Also, tell them that saying sorry is good if we mess up.

Role-Playing

Role-playing can be super fun for learning! Make scenarios with problems and let the kids act out how to solve them. They will get better at hearing each other, thinking of smart ideas, and figuring out ways everyone can be happy.

Reinforcing Positive Behavior

When you see your kid doing a great job handling conflicts nicely, acknowledge and reward their efforts, and give them something special as a treat. Positive reinforcement helps them internalize these skills. Doing this makes them feel good inside, so they keep being awesome at fixing problems!

Handling Bullying and Peer Pressure

Teach children to recognize and respond to bullying and peer pressure appropriately. This includes assertiveness skills to stand up for themselves and others while still promoting empathy and understanding.

Fostering Emotional Regulation and Self-Awareness in Kids

To be able to regulate and control our emotions is to be able to engage in emotional regulation. To put it simply, it entails learning how to react positively and constructively in the face of highly emotional situations. This capacity has several benefits, including improved social relationships, emotional wellness, and even physical well-being. For instance, kids with good emotional control frequently create stronger relationships, perform mentally better than their classmates, and engage in fewer conflicts.

The Importance of Self-Awareness

Children gain much benefit from becoming aware of their inner world—their emotions, thoughts, and habits. Observing oneself offers a vital building block for growing emotionally savvy since it provides insight into what makes each unique individual tick. Once a child appreciates their internal landscape, they will have an easier time identifying requirements (like solitude or companionship) and discerning how their conduct affects loved ones and acquaintances alike.

Creating Safe Spaces for Expression

Children must feel safe to share how they feel. You should create environments where they won't worry about showing off their upset feelings. You should explain to them that no matter what they feel inside, all feelings are valid.

Mindfulness and Emotional Regulation

Mindfulness practices can be highly effective in teaching emotional regulation. Taking some time each day for mindfulness exercises such as deep breathing, meditation, or pausing to think about things can really help kids learn how to control their feelings.

Teaching Coping Strategies

Kids need healthy coping strategies to handle the strong emotions they feel. Show them ideas like taking a break, exploring outside, or doing something fun with their hands or brain (like drawing, writing, or building). These strategies provide outlets for emotional expression.

Emphasizing the Mind-Body Connection

Help children understand that what they're thinking and feeling affects not just their thoughts but also how their bodies feel. Explain how our emotions can manifest physically, such as if they have scary or worried thoughts sometimes, it might make their tummy squeeze up, even though nothing bad is happening right now. This awareness can help them regulate their emotions.

Encouraging Self-Reflection

Children can use self-reflection as a potent tool to examine their ideas, feelings, and behavioral patterns. They can build a solid basis for developing emotional literacy by being encouraged to examine their own feelings. Asking inquiries that are specifically focused on emotional triggers is one strategy. Questions addressing the "why" behind a particular feeling might ignite deeper reflection. An illustration question could be: What happened today that led to these sensations? In-depth investigation makes it easier to appreciate the causes of certain emotional reactions, eventually fostering a child's capacity to control and understand sentimental encounters.

Creating a Supportive and Emotionally Intelligent Family Environment

A family should aspire to become a safe haven where kids thrive. This relationship of attachment might become a productive ground for growing emotional intelligence with shared commitment and effort. Within your family, nourishing feelings bloom into powerful ties built on empathy. It takes work to establish a flourishing home environment, but if everyone in your family shares this goal, your family's emotional well-being will also blossom.

The Power of a Supportive Family Environment

Supportive families provide an environment where individuals can express themselves genuinely. They recognize and discuss emotions comfortably while offering ample affection. This environment allows children to develop the skills necessary to cope well under challenging circumstances while also being thoughtful and discerning regarding their inner experiences.

Embracing Emotions

In an emotionally smart household, all types of feelings are welcome. Train everyone that it's okay to feel sadness, irritation, or fear are typical results of occurrences in everyday life. These feelings come naturally.

Creating Family Rituals

The repetition of family rituals and celebrations within households instills a perception of security and a sense of connection among family members. Developing cherished memories unites folks through festive events and regular pastimes. Turning occasions into long-lasting practices fortifies kinship ties.

Emotionally Intelligent Discipline

Disciplining your child plays a crucial role during child-rearing; however, this practice should not mean inflicting suffering upon them. Rather, utilize discipline as an opportunity to teach children about cause-and-effect scenarios and their impacts on those near them. When handled wisely, this method leaves behind enduring life lessons.

Individuality and Acceptance

Every family that has high levels of emotional intelligence values distinctiveness by celebrating the individuality and talents inherent in every individual. Encourage family members to pursue their passions and interests.

Quality Time

Spending quality time without disturbances establishes lasting affinity. Unplugging gadgets and focusing complete attention on one another enables fulfilling interrelationships. Engaging in enjoyable mutual undertakings further solidifies relationships.

Key Takeaways

- Family plays a crucial role in nurturing emotional intelligence in children. Parents and caregivers are the first teachers, modeling emotional regulation, empathy, and conflict resolution.

- Helping kids recognize and articulate their feelings builds self-awareness, communication abilities, and coping mechanisms. Teaching children emotional literacy, including recognizing and naming their emotions, ensures they don't bottle up problems but rather ask for guidance when necessary.

- Nurturing empathy in children prepares them to connect on deeper levels. Developing a sense of compassion for others leads to positive social bonds and harmonious communities. Children trained in empathy grow into adults capable of valuing diverse perspectives, resolving issues constructively, and strengthening human connections.

- Conflict is a natural part of life. Teaching children conflict resolution skills empowers them to communicate effectively, listen actively, and find mutually beneficial solutions.

- Emotionally intelligent families provide secure environments for youth to share experiences without fear or shame. With open communication, warmth, and acceptance, families cultivate resilient individuals versed in constructive interaction. This fertile soil yields loving relationships rooted in tolerance and a deep comprehension of fellow humans.

Developing emotional intelligence is crucial, and we'll talk about it in the following part of the book. An exercise that works for one person might not work for another because we all are unique. That's why there is a range of exercises in which you can choose what suits you best and practice it.

PART 3:
EXERCISES FOR ENHANCING SELF-AWARENESS

Exercises 1:
Enhancing Self-Awareness

Breath Awareness

Objective

Utilizing the breath as the primary focus, this practice develops present-moment awareness.

Instructions

- Choose a peaceful location that allows for sitting or lying down comfortably.

- Close off external distractions by closing your eyes. Follow this up with some deep, calming breaths aimed at restoring inner balance.

- Focus your awareness on the rhythmic patterning of your breathing; simply acknowledge each inhale and exhale without trying to change it.

- As you breathe, observe the sensation of the breath entering and leaving your nostrils or the rise and fall of your chest or abdomen.

- If your mind starts to wander, gently bring your focus back to the breath without judgment.

Duration

Begin with 5-10 minutes and gradually extend the practice.

Body Scan

Objective

This practice promotes awareness of your body's many physical feelings.

Instructions

- Lie on your back with ease.

- Breathe deeply a few times to calm your nerves.

- Shift your attention to the lower parts of your body, starting from your toes.

- Take note of any sensations like heat or numbness.

- Gradually shift your focus up through each part of your body, focusing on any distinct sensations that surface.

- By doing this, you can discover areas where there might be some discomfort, but try not to let it bother you. Simply acknowledge these feelings. End at the peak of your head.

Duration

Depending on your preferences and free time, this workout might last anywhere between 10 and 30 minutes.

Mindful Eating

Objective

Promoting mindful awareness of the senses during a common activity like eating.

Instructions

- Select a tiny snack like a grape, a slice of apple, or a piece of chocolate.

- Search for a serene corner apart from diversions to sit undisturbed.

- Before eating, examine the food closely, employing every sense. Notice the color, texture, and fragrance.

- Nibble slightly. Chew leisurely, savoring the flavor and the sensation of chewing.

- Do not hurry, enjoy each mouthful totally.

Duration

Depending on how quickly you want to eat, you may do this activity in 5 to 10 minutes.

Gratitude Journal

Objective

Cultivating gratitude and focusing on positive aspects of your life.

Instructions

- Every single day, carve out some personal space, no matter how short, say four to five minutes max, to contemplate the blessings bestowed upon your life.

- During this self-introspection, pen down three elements you feel grateful for in a paperback diary. It could be anything minor, ranging from a steamy hot cup of coffee to heartwarming words from a friend to mesmerizing sundown scenery.

- Spare ample thought behind the reasons for this gratification and also jot down the emotional rollercoaster experienced because of it.

Sensory Awareness

Objective

Become more conscious of your immediate surroundings.

Instructions

- Find stability by either standing or sitting comfortably.

- Inhale deeply and exhale completely several times.

- Gently open your gaze while fixing your interest on only one of your five senses at a time: sight, hearing, texture (touch), smell, or taste.

- Investigate the details of what you are seeing, followed by tuning into the sounds around you. Next, feel the textures against your skin, pick out individual fragrances in the air, and lastly, detect different flavors present within your mouth. Make sure to pause before shifting to another sense.

- Linger over each perception without passing judgment regarding its significance.

Duration

This exercise may take 5 to 10 minutes.

Walking Meditation

Objective

Combining mindfulness with physical movement.

Instructions

- Choose a peaceful area indoors or outdoors solely for strolling around.

- Start treading gradually compared to habitual swiftness.

- Pay attention to the feeling during each step. Experience touchdown feet meet the ground, muscle motion, and bodily equilibrium.

- In case your mind starts to wander, kindly retrieve concentration onto the walking procedure.

Duration

Start out with a 10 to 15-minute stroll and progressively extend it as you become used to it.

Loving-Kindness Meditation

Objective

Cultivating feelings of love and compassion toward yourself and others.

Instructions

- Look for somewhere comfortable to sit.

- Close your eyes and breathe deeply several times until you calm down inside.

- Quietly think nice things about yourself, like wishing for happiness, health, and safety, then start doing it for folks around you, like kin, buddies, strangers, and lastly, everyone alive. For example, "May I be happy, may I be healthy, may I be safe."

- Let all pleasant feelings come automatically.

Duration

Depending on your preferences, this meditation might last anywhere between 10 and 20 minutes.

Journaling Prompts for Self-Reflection

Gratitude

- What are the three things for which I'm thankful today?

- Recently, who or what has been uplifting in my life?

- How can I show someone my appreciation for improving my day?

Self-Discovery

- What traits or abilities do I find admirable in other people, and how might I develop them in myself?

- Which pursuits or adventures help me feel fully alive and lose sight of time?

- What goals or desires would I pursue if I were unrestricted?

Emotional Awareness

- How am I now feeling, and what may be causing these feelings?

- What self-care practices have I lately practiced, and how did those experiences make me feel?

- Do I need to let go of anything or forgive myself in order to move on?

Challenges and Growth

- What recent difficulty did I encounter, and what did I learn from it?

- What factors helped me grow as a person over the past year, and how?

- What small things can I do right now to further a bigger objective or aspiration?

Relationships

- Who are the people who support and improve the happiness in my life?

- Is there a relation that requires my attention or a discussion that must take place?

- How can I express my love and gratitude to those who mean the most to me?

Mindfulness

- What time during the day did I feel wholly absorbed in the experience?

- What can I do to include more mindfulness in my regular activities?

- What can I do on a hectic day to find calm and peace?

Identifying Personal Triggers and Emotional Patterns

Objective

To increase awareness of your emotional triggers and patterns so that you may react to circumstances more consciously and in control.

Instructions

- Find a place where you may write in peace and quiet while carrying a journal.

- Start by considering recent events that made you feel emotionally heated. Make quick notes on these things, including who was involved, when and where they happened, and your feelings.

- Look more closely at each incident you've described to determine the precise triggers that set off your emotions.

- Now consider how these triggers make you feel. Think back on your emotions and responses in each circumstance.

- Consider your past to see if any events may have influenced these emotional patterns and triggers.

- Look for patterns or commonalities in your emotional reactions and triggers.

- Throughout this procedure, be kind to yourself. Avoid judging and criticizing yourself.

- As you develop an understanding of your emotional patterns and triggers, consider future appropriate responses.

- Write down your findings, including the triggers, emotional patterns, and any methods you intend to use in the future.

Personal Values Inventory

Objective

Determining and making clear your basic beliefs, which act as a foundation for major life decisions.

Instructions

- Begin in a peaceful and comfortable place by remembering major moments or occurrences in your life when you felt completely gratified, proud, or sincerely satisfied.

- Ask yourself what values were at work during those key moments.

- Start making a list of the values that stand out to you after reflecting on them.

- Review the list you've made for a moment. Now order them according to your importance to you.

- Spend some time writing out what each value on your list means to you individually.

- Think about the choices and conditions in your life right now. Consider how well they fit the ideals you've identified.

- Set plans for how you wish to live and make decisions going ahead based on your clear principles.

Exercises 2:
Building Social Awareness

Active Listening

Objective

To increase focus and understanding while listening.

Instructions

- Select a 10 to 15-minute-long audio clip, podcast episode, or TED talk.

- Play the audio and try to concentrate on listening without any outside noise.

- Note important details, fascinating information, or comments from the speaker while you listen.

- After the audio is finished, pause to consider what you learned or found most useful.

Reflective Listening

Objective

Practicing reflecting back on what you've heard to ensure you understand and validate the speaker's message.

Instructions

- Get together with another individual so you both take turns speaking and listening.

- The first person talks about something important to them that they want to share. Pick whatever topic you fancy!

- Use a stopwatch and speak without pause or interruption by another party for a fixed stretch, let's say, five minutes.

- While your friend is talking, just don't disturb them and hear them out properly. Mind their verbal cues, their voice's pitch and volume, and how their body moves.

- Once the speaker finishes their spiel, use phrases such as, "So essentially, you said…" or "What I inferred was…."

- The speaker confirms or denies that the listener correctly caught the meaning intended.

- Swap roles and perform a similar process once more.

Paraphrasing Exercise

Objective

Practicing paraphrasing to ensure comprehension and demonstrate empathy.

Instructions

- Prepare a few short stories or concepts that are around three to five lines long.

- Pick a partner with whom to work. One person gets to talk, while the other person gets to listen.

- When the listener is ready to hear, the orator reads one of the prepared speeches.

- The listener mirrors what was said, trying to accurately capture the most important ideas.

- The speaker examines the reflected data and verifies its accuracy. Speaking clarifies situations where there is uncertainty.

- Change roles, then repeat the assignment.

Nonverbal Cues Observation

Objective

Improving your capacity for instantaneous nonverbal cue detection and interpretation.

Instructions

- Pick a public area with lots of interaction potential, such as a mall, coffee shop, or park.

- Find a quiet location where you can watch without drawing attention to yourself.

- Observe individuals or groups without making them feel uncomfortable by staring at them. Observe their body language, facial expressions, gestures, and overall demeanor.

- Mentally record your observations. Note things like posture, eye contact, hand movements, facial expressions, and any other nonverbal cues you notice.

- Try to decipher what their emotions, goals, or behaviors could be communicating through these nonverbal signs.

- After some time has passed, stop and reflect on what you saw.

The Perspective-Taking

Objective

Improving your ability for empathic observation of circumstances.

Instructions

- Select a certain scenario or circumstance. It may be a regular occurrence in life or something more particular, like a situation at work or a family reunion.

- Put yourself in the position of another person involved in the incident. Take into account their sentiments, ideas, and viewpoints.

- From this person's perspective, compose a little story. Describe the possible thoughts and emotions they may be experiencing at that time.

- If it is comfortable, talk about the experience and share your story with a friend or family member.

Exercises 3:
Strengthening Relationship Management

The Roommate Disagreement (A Role-Playing Scenario)

Context

You live with a roommate in an apartment. There have recently been problems with responsibility and cleanliness.

Roles

- Person X: You want to solve the problem without escalating the conflict. You want to find a solution because you value the friendship.

- Person Y: You've been under a lot of work-related stress, but you weren't aware that your messiness was contributing to it.

Find a solution that will allow for peaceful coexistence.

Team Project Dilemma

Context

At the office, you are collaborating on a project. The project's direction has been a source of dispute.

Roles

- Person X: You have an idea of what you want the project to be, and you think it's crucial to follow the original strategy.

- Person Y: You see things differently and believe a fresh strategy would be more successful.

Find a solution that honors everyone's viewpoints and results in a project that is effective.

Giving Effective Feedback

Objective

To become more adept at providing balanced, constructive criticism.

Instructions

- Choose a situation where feedback could be required. It could have anything to do with your job, a side project, or a relationship.

- Begin by listing at least two positives associated with the situation.

- Next, choose one area where something can be changed or improved. Offer precise advice that can be put into practice.

- Reiterate the positives and provide words of support or encouragement to close.

- Role-play through the situation with a friend while trading off on the feedback.

Random Acts of Kindness

Objective

Spreading love and compassion to strangers and friends.

Instructions

- Set a goal for how many acts of kindness you want to conduct in a certain period of time.

- Write out all the kind things you can do. Simple examples include opening doors for others, complimenting a coworker, or putting a motivational note in a public area.

- Pick one good deed from your list to perform every day.

- Consider your feelings and any observations you may have had on the recipient's response after each deed.

Exercises 4:

Building Emotional Intelligence in Family Relationships

Feelings Check-In

Objective

To engage in open and honest conversation regarding feelings.

Instructions

- Locate a peaceful, comfortable area where you won't be disturbed.

- The speaker speaks first, followed by the listener.

- The speaker expresses their thoughts on a particular subject or their overall emotional condition. Utilize "I" statements, such as "I feel…" or "I felt…"

- The listener uses active listening techniques. Avoid interrupting and concentrate on figuring out how the speaker is feeling.

- The listener validates their understanding by reflecting on what they heard after the speaker has finished speaking. Respect their sentiments to validate them.

- Change positions and do the exercise once more.

Feelings Charades With Kids

Objective

Encouraging kids in a playful and participatory approach to identify and express their feelings.

Instructions

- You'll need cards or pieces of paper with the words "happy," "sad," "excited," "angry," and "surprised" written on each one.

- Tell the kid that you're going to play a unique game of charades.

- Act out an emotion to start. Let the kid try to guess the emotion you're feeling.

- Alternate roles. Allow the child to express an emotion while you guess.

- After each round, discuss your feelings. Ask the youngster whether they've ever experienced that emotion and what may have caused it.

- Spend a minute expressing your own thoughts and feelings. This promotes free communication and normalizes emotions.

Storytime with Emotions

Objective

Using storytelling as a way to explore and discuss different emotions with kids.

Instructions

- Choose books or tales that are about emotions and feelings.

- Read the story aloud to the youngster while you are sitting down. As you read, pause to talk about the characters' feelings.

- Invite the kid to express their ideas. Ask questions such as, "How do you think the character feels right now?" "Have you ever experienced it before?"

- Connect the emotions in the story to real-life experiences. Describe your personal experiences if they are pertinent.

- Ask the kid to express their feelings by drawing, writing, or speaking after the reading.

Collaborative Problem-Solving

Objective

Working together with your family to find mutually acceptable solutions to conflicts.

Instructions

- Clearly state the issue or disagreement that needs to be resolved.

- Encourage everyone in the family to brainstorm potential fixes. Without passing judgment, jot them down.

- Talk about the advantages and disadvantages of each option on the list. Select the course of action that best suits everyone.

- Implement the selected solution and agree to review it later to determine if any revisions are required.

- Check in with one another later to see how the chosen solution is performing.

Taking a Time-Out

Objective

Giving everyone involved in the conflict time and space to cool down and reflect.

Instructions

- In a family situation, whenever emotions get intense and rational conversation seems improbable, suggest a little break.

- Decide as a group on a specific time period for rest (say, 30 minutes or one hour).

- Encourage other family members to spend the break engaging in relaxing, enjoyable pastimes.

- After the break, get back together and discuss the issue again, but this time with calmer minds.

- Post-break, try to understand your own psychological state and try to see things from someone else's perspective.

Gratitude Circle Ritual

Objective

Cultivating gratitude ritual and appreciation tradition within the family.

Instructions

- Set up a specified time every day or week to participate in the Gratitude Circle with your family.

- Locate a place where everyone can sit in a circle in comfort. This might take place at a table or on cushions on the ground.

- Everyone takes a turn sharing something for which they are thankful. It may be a particular memory from that day or just a general expression of gratitude.

- The rest of the family listens intently and expresses thanks as each member speaks.

- You may enhance the ceremony with a symbolic element, such as lighting a candle to symbolize the warmth of appreciation.

- End the ritual by expressing gratitude for each other's presence and the moments of thankfulness when everyone has finished speaking.

Memory Jar Ritual

Objective

Making a ritual for creating a tangible collection of cherished family memories.

Instructions

- Provide a huge glass jar, some pieces of paper, and a pen.

- Encourage each member of the family to write a memory or an act of gratitude on a piece of paper.

- After folding, put the paper in the jar. Contributions can be anonymous or signed, as desired.

- Gather as a family every so often to read the compiled memories, possibly on a significant occasion or at the end of the month.

- After reading each recollection, pause to think about it and express any feelings it evokes.

Exercises 5:
Emotional Intelligence in Challenging Situations

Mindful Breathing

Objective

Calming the mind and bringing awareness to the present moment, helping to manage overwhelming emotions.

Instructions

- Pick a peaceful area where you won't be bothered.

- Choose a comfortable position to sit or lie down. Close your eyes if it's more comfortable.

- Take note of your breathing. As you breathe in and out, notice how it feels in your body.

- Breathe deeply and slowly. Take a big breath in with your nose, hold it for a second, and then gently let it out through your mouth.

- Count each inhalation and exhalation as you breathe. Maintain a constant beat, if possible.

- Recognize any challenging feelings you may be going through while keeping your attention on your breath. Don't judge them; just watch.

- Breathe in good vibes and let go of bad ones. Imagine letting go of the challenging emotion with each exhalation.

Duration

Practice for at least 5-10 minutes, or until you feel a sense of calm.

The Emotional Journal

Objective

Providing an outlet for expressing and processing difficult emotions.

Instructions

- Set aside a diary just for this practice.

- Spend some time writing about the emotions that are overwhelming you. Without any censoring or filtering, let the words flow.

- To describe the emotion you're feeling, use evocative words. How does it feel inside of you? What triggered it?

- Investigate potential causes of the emotion. Was it a conversation, an event, or a memory?

- Write about constructive coping mechanisms for this feeling. It could happen through meditation, physical activity, talking to a loved one, or another method.

- Finish the entry by mentioning something uplifting or for which you are thankful.

Visualization and Grounding

Objective

Shifting your focus away from overwhelming emotions and reconnecting with the present moment.

Instructions

- Choose a comfortable position to sit or stand.

- Close your eyes if it makes you more comfortable. If not, a soft look might be used to keep the eyes open.

- To calm yourself down, take a few slow, deep breaths.

- Think about a location where you feel fully secure and comfortable. It may be a warm room, a beach, a forest, or any other area that makes you feel at ease.

- Imagine yourself in this environment. What do you hear, smell, see, and feel? Use each of your senses.

- Permit yourself to lose yourself entirely in this visualization. Spend as much time as necessary in this secure place.

- When you're ready, gently return your focus to the present.

The Reflective Response

Objective

Practicing active listening and responding to criticism in a constructive and non-defensive manner.

Instructions

- Choose a partner you can trust and feel at ease with.

- Make a decision on who will be the giver and who will be the receiver of feedback.

- With the recipient, the giver imparts some helpful criticism. Make sure it's clear, precise, and behavior-focused rather than personality-focused.

- The receiver keeps quiet while doing active listening. Instead of composing a response right away, concentrate on comprehending the feedback.

- The recipient confirms understanding by reflecting back on what they heard after receiving the input. If necessary, they can also make a clarification request.

- Regardless of the feedback's content, the recipient acknowledges the sender.

- Replicate the procedure by switching roles.

The Empathy Response

Objective

Responding to criticism with empathy and understanding.

Instructions

- Before replying to criticism, take a minute to calm yourself by practicing mindful breathing.

- Thank the individual for their input.

- Imagine yourself in their position. Consider their perspective and the reasons they might hold it.

- If the criticism is not totally obvious, request further information or specific instances.

- After thanking them for their input, express your own viewpoint. Be courteous and collected when responding.

- To continue, look for points of agreement or compromise.

- Even if it was difficult to hear, thank the person for their contribution.

Progressive Muscle Relaxation

Objective

Releasing physical tension and promoting a sense of calmness.

Instructions

- In a quiet area, sit or lie down in a comfortable position.

- To calm yourself down, take a few long, deep breaths.

- Beginning with your toes. As much as you can, tighten the toe muscles, hold the squeeze for a brief period of time, and then relax. Till you reach your head, gently work your way up your body, tensing and releasing each muscle group (calf, thigh, abdomen, and so forth).

- Pay special attention to how each muscle group feels when it is tense or relaxed.

- Take a big breath in and let it out gently as you relax each muscle group.

- Repeat the technique if you're still feeling tense.

Box Breathing

Objective

Regulating and controlling your breath helps to calm the mind.

Instructions

- Sit with your back straight in a calm area.

- Inhale deeply through your nose slowly for four seconds. Consider drawing a box's top side.

- For an additional four seconds, hold your breath. Consider drawing a trace of the box's right side.

- Exhale via your mouth gradually for a duration of four seconds. Consider drawing a trace of the box's bottom side.

- Once more, hold your breath for four seconds. Consider tracing the box's left edge.

- Repeat this pattern until you feel more at ease or after several rounds.

The Five Whys Technique for Problem-Solving

Objective

Diving deep into the root cause of a problem and identifying potential solutions.

Instructions

- Pick a specific issue or difficulty you're dealing with. It could be about your job, your personal life, or anything else you want to better.

- To begin, ask yourself why the issue occurs.

- When you have an answer, follow it up by asking "why" once again. Follow this procedure five times. For instance, "I'm frequently stressed at work" is the issue.

- Why? Since I have a lot of work to do.

- Why? I don't prioritize my duties well.

- Why? Because I have a hard time telling the difference between urgent and significant activities.

- You'll likely have a greater grasp of the fundamental issue after asking "why" five times. This is the root problem you should address.

- Think of possible solutions or coping mechanisms based on the root of the problem.

- Select one or more solutions to use. Evaluate the performance of your selected strategy after some time.

The Mind Mapping Exercise

Objective

Visually organizing thoughts and ideas around a specific problem.

Instructions

- In the middle of a sheet of paper, jot down the exact issue or difficulty.

- Like a tree's branches, draw lines that branch out from the primary issue. Each branch needs to stand for a distinct facet or dimension of the issue.

- Write down potential solutions, tactics, or other aspects of that component of the problem on each branch.

- Connect similar concepts or potential solutions by drawing lines. This makes dependencies and linkages easier to see.

- Examine your mind map and note the most promising answers or tactics. Put them in order of importance depending on their viability and impact.

- Start implementing the solutions on the list, starting with the ones that appear most practical and effective.

Exercises 6:
Emotional Intelligence in the Workplace

The Situational Analysis

Objective

Evaluating your emotional intelligence in various work-related scenarios.

Instructions

- Make a list of frequent situations that arise at work, such as handling a challenging coworker, providing and receiving criticism, managing a tight deadline, and others.

- Consider your emotional response in each situation. Use a scale of one to five, with one representing "Not Effective" and five representing "Very Effective."

- Consider your replies for a moment after evaluating each scenario. Take into account what went well and any potential areas for development.

- Analyze the trends in your answers. Are there particular situations where you perform well or poorly?

- Set specific objectives for enhancing your emotional intelligence in work-related circumstances based on your reflections.

The Feedback Loop

Objective

Gathering feedback from trusted colleagues or supervisors to gain insights into your emotional intelligence.

Instructions

- Select a small group of coworkers or managers you can rely on to provide you with genuine and helpful feedback.

- Ask for specific input on your emotional intelligence in work-related circumstances from each person you speak with one-on-one. If required, give examples or instances.

- When getting feedback, pay close attention without defending yourself. If further information is required, ask.

- Spend some time considering the feedback you received. Think about the recurring patterns and the areas that might be better.

- Make a strategy for how you can work to improve your emotional intelligence at work based on the comments.

The Emotional Intelligence Journal

Objective

Tracking and reflecting on your emotional intelligence in real-time work situations.

Instructions

- Set aside a diary just for this practice.

- After significant work interactions or events, make notes on the details of the situation, your emotional response, and your actions.

- Think about how your feelings affected your actions and choices in each circumstance.

- Make a note of any trends or circumstances that keep coming up where you'd like to strengthen your emotional intelligence.

- Set precise, doable objectives for enhancing your emotional intelligence in similar circumstances in the future based on your reflections.

Resolving a Conflict (Role Playing)

Objective

Practicing resolving a conflict between two colleagues in a constructive and empathetic manner.

Instructions

- Employee X: You believe that your colleague, Employee Y, doesn't respect your thoughts. You wish to deal with this situation and figure out how to cooperate more successfully.

- Employee Y: Although you don't mean to ignore Employee X's suggestions, you work in a distinct style. You're interested in figuring out how to collaborate more efficiently.

- Employee X, start the discussion by voicing your thoughts and worries. Employee Y pays close attention and offers sympathetic responses. Find a compromise or a solution that enables better collaboration by working together.

Addressing Performance Issues

Objective

Practicing addressing performance issues with a direct report in a constructive and supportive manner.

Instructions

- Manager: You've seen that a team member's performance has fallen short of what was anticipated. To offer feedback and encourage progress, you want to have an open discussion.

- Team Member: Your performance has been impacted by a personal issue you've been dealing with. You're open to talking about it and coming up with solutions.

- Manager: Start the dialogue by expressing your concern with the work.

- Team Member: Please describe the personal problem and pledge to become well.

- Create a support and improvement strategy together.

The Human Knot (Team Activity)

Objective

Promoting communication, problem-solving, and teamwork.

Instructions

- Have everyone stand shoulder to shoulder in a circle.

- Each participant should stretch across the circle and take hold of someone else's hand, but not the one that is immediately next to them.

- The goal is to free everyone from the human knot without releasing go of their hands.

- Encourage discussion and cooperative problem-solving among participants as they attempt to disentangle themselves.

- Discuss what tactics succeeded and what might have been improved after the exercise. Stress the value of cooperation and communication.

Two Truths and a Lie (Team Activity)

Objective

Building trust and getting to know team members on a more personal level.

Instructions

- Every team member takes a turn disclosing two truths and one untruth about themselves.

- The rest of the team tries to determine which statement is false once someone has shared their information.

- Repeat this process until everyone has had an opportunity to speak.

- Discuss what shocked folks or what they discovered about their coworkers after the activity.

Escape Room Challenge (Virtual or Physical)

Objective

Encouraging problem-solving, collaboration, and teamwork.

Instructions

- Split the team up into smaller groups, either physically at an escape room location or digitally via an online escape room platform.

- Within a certain amount of time, each group collaborates to resolve a number of puzzles and challenges.

- Stress the need for effective collaboration and clear communication in order to complete the assignment.

- Gather the team after the challenge to review the tactics that were successful and how they may use these abilities at work.

Time Management and Prioritization

Objective

Reducing stress by effectively managing tasks and responsibilities at work.

Instructions

- Make a list of the things you need to do at the beginning of each day. Put them in order of importance and urgency.

- Large tasks may be too much to handle. Divide them into more manageable, smaller steps.

- Set aside timed intervals to do each activity. This aids in maintaining attention and minimizes multitasking.

- Work on one project for 25 minutes, then take a 5-minute break. Continue this cycle.

- Recognize your daily limitations and set reasonable goals. Avoid overcommitting yourself to work.

- Review your accomplishments at the end of each day and make any necessary adjustments to your strategy.

Exercises 7:
Emotional Intelligence and Conflict Resolution at Work

The Neutral Mediator

Objective

Practicing mediating a conflict between two parties.

Instructions

- Roles: Person X (with conflict), Person Y (with conflict), and mediator

- Person X and Person Y each explain their side of the story to the impartial mediator.

- Ensuring equal opportunity for input from everyone involved, the mediator steers the dialogue.

- To assist with comprehension and harmony, the mediator actively listens and rephrases what has been said.

- With guidance from the mediator, the conflicting parties explore shared viewpoints or overlapping interests.

- Potential answers to the problem are generated through collaborative idea generation led by the mediator.

- Assisting all individuals in achieving joint consensus as well as developing next steps is handled by the mediator.

The Reflective Mediation

Object

Practicing reflective listening and empathy in conflict resolution.

Instructions

- Persons X and Y portray a hypothetical argument they are having right now. The impartial mediator carefully considers each side's arguments while remaining neutral.

- The thoughtful conciliator summarizes the main aspects of such comments after hearing all sides of the argument.

- The reconciler expresses empathy by echoing the thoughts and concerns expressed by each participant.

- The impartial mediator creates a greater understanding of the subject at hand by adopting a bird's-eye perspective, assisting opposing parties in understanding one another's perspectives.

- Rivals set off on an exploration to find workable solutions, led by the observant peacemaker.

- As the sympathetic catalyst, the cool-headed mediator helps adversaries who have become allies create a consensus and then provides them with a road map for prosperous times to come.

Salary Negotiation Role Play

Objective

Practicing negotiating a salary offer.

Instructions

- Individual X was offered a position but wants to negotiate for better pay before accepting.

- Individual Y, the hiring manager, is fine with discussing finances to get the best deal possible.

- Individual X starts talking nicely about how much they want this job, then talks confidently about why they deserve more pay than what was originally offered.

- Individual Y hears them out and takes everything they say into account; they might give a new figure or suggest other perks instead.

- Both people try really hard, so in the end, everyone feels okay about where things landed financially (individual X gets enough money and benefits that make sense given the company budget).

- Keep chatting back and forth till you decide together that something works perfectly regarding payment details and anything else tied into the employment contract.

Business Partnership

Objective

Practicing negotiating the terms of a business partnership.

Instructions

- Person A and Person B want to start a company together, but they can't agree on some things (like who owns how much of it or who does what).

- Both talk about what they want from this partnership—their hopes and dreams as well as their worries.

- Both listen closely to one another and ask lots of questions so they understand better. This makes sure no misunderstandings happen later down the line!

- Your goal is to figure out something fair for everyone involved. That way, everyone feels good about the decisions made around money, workload, and so on. It should be a win-win situation!

- If needed, have more discussions until all the details are nicely ironed out between you two without anyone being unhappy.

Vendor Contract Negotiation

Objective

Practicing negotiating terms and conditions with a vendor.

Instructions

- The task of negotiating a contract with a supplier of products or services falls to person A.

- As the vendor's advocate, person B is amenable to compromise.

- The dialogue is started by person A by explaining the requirements, targets, and preferred terms of the business.

- Person B listens to the company's requests while presenting the vendor's proposal.

- Both sides collaborate to come to terms on pricing, delivery intervals, and service levels that are acceptable to both.

- Negotiations will continue until a good contract is reached.

Empathy Cards

Objective

Practicing expressing empathy through written communication.

Instructions

- Give each participant a set of blank cards, some markers, or colored pencils.

- Give the group a list of potential conflict situations or problems. These could be made up or true.

- Invite participants to write a message of understanding and support on a card in the form of an address to the individual experiencing the conflict after selecting one conflict scenario.

- Participants can present their empathy cards to the group and provide a brief justification for their word choice. Explain how writing about empathy may be a useful strategy for resolving disputes.

- Highlight the value of empathy in written and verbal dispute communication.

Exercises 8:
Parenting with Emotional Intelligence

Emotion Color Wheel

Objective

Helping children identify and express their emotions using colors.

Instructions

- Give kids an empty color wheel worksheet or a drawing of a segmented circle.

- Create a list of common emotions (such as joy, sorrow, anger, excitement, and so on) and give each one a color (such as yellow for joy, blue for sorrow, and red for anger).

- Ask the kid to color the wheel's parts in accordance with their feelings. For instance, kids could color in the "happy" part with yellow if they're feeling pleased.

- After they've finished coloring, talk to them about the colors they used and the feelings they symbolize. Encourage them to explain the reasons for their feelings.

- To assist kids in developing their vocabulary and emotional awareness, repeat this practice frequently.

Emotion Charades

Objective

Encouraging children to express emotions through body language and facial expressions.

Instructions

- On separate cards, note the various feelings.

- Allow the kid to select one emotion card at random without revealing it to you.

- Ask the kid to express the selected feeling silently. They can communicate using gestures, body language, and facial expressions.

- Try to determine which emotion they are displaying. Encourage your kids to express themselves and be creative.

- Talk to each other about the selected emotion after each round. Find out whether they have experienced this recently and why.

Emotion Journal

Objective

Helping children track and reflect on their emotions over time.

Instructions

- Provide a special notebook or diary for your kid to record their daily emotions.

- Encourage the child to document their emotional state every day using whatever form of expression works best for them (words, drawings, or stickers).

- Help the child develop an emotional vocabulary by encouraging them to label their feelings specifically (such as happy, sad, and angry) and providing guidance if they struggle with this.

- Regularly review the child's recorded emotional experiences with them, looking for trends or shifts over time.

- Use these documented emotional experiences as a springboard for discussing and validating the child's feelings and offering support when necessary.

Emotion Regulation Toolbox

Objective

Creating a toolbox of coping strategies for different emotions

Instructions

- Give out a box, container, or shoebox that has been adorned.

- Assist the kid in making cards with various coping mechanisms inscribed on them. Include exercises like painting, taking a stroll, chatting with a trusted friend, deep breathing, and so on.

- Allow the kid to personalize their toolbox. Encourage individuality and inventiveness.

- Discuss various feelings and the potential triggers for them. Align coping mechanisms with certain emotions (such as deep breathing for anger).

- When the youngster is experiencing powerful emotions, encourage them to use the toolbox. They can select a coping mechanism that seems comfortable for them.

Feelings Thermometer

Objective

Helping children recognize and label their emotions on a scale.

Instructions

- On a sheet of paper, sketch a thermometer. Name the bottom "Calm" and the top "Intense."

- Ask your kid to place various feelings on the thermometer as you discuss them. For instance, happiness may be lower on the scale, while rage may be higher.

- Talk about how their bodies are feeling at various points on the thermometer. For instance, they could feel at ease when they are calm, but they might feel stiff or heated when they are intense.

- Encourage your child to express and identify their feelings using the thermometer. They can display their position on the scale.

- Discuss several techniques they might employ to help themselves become calmer while experiencing strong emotions.

Sibling Disagreement (Role Playing)

Objective

Practicing resolving a disagreement between siblings.

Instructions

- Younger and older siblings argue about using a shared area or object (like a game or a bedroom).

- The siblings convey their opinions and feelings by acting out their disputes.

- The mediator ensures that both sides are heard by listening to them both and facilitating the dialogue.

- Encourage the siblings to come up with a solution that takes into account each other's preferences and requirements.

- After the role-play, talk about the results and potential alternative approaches.

Parent-Teen Communication

Objective

Practicing effective communication between a parent and a teenager.

Instructions

- A parent and teen do not see eye-to-eye on something related to home life. This is okay and can be used as a learning opportunity!

- Both act out the disagreement but practice active listening skills and assertive communication techniques during the role-playing.

- Both of you should feel comfortable sharing your inner thoughts while trying hard to understand where the other may come from, working collaboratively toward a compromise acceptable to both of you in the dispute-resolution process.

- Discuss what happened well and what may have been handled differently after the role-play.

Extended Family Gathering

Objective

Practicing conflict resolution in a larger family setting.

Instructions

- During a gathering, there is a dispute or misunderstanding among the family members (such as about the schedule and the allocation of tasks).

- In order to foster polite dialogue and a resolution, the family members role-play the conflict.

- Encourage them to collaborate in order to find a solution that takes into account the requirements and opinions of every family member.

- Discuss practical methods for resolving disputes in large families after reflecting on the role-play.

Emotion Bingo

Objective

Enhancing emotional vocabulary and recognition in kids.

Instructions

- Prepare bingo cards with a variety of emotions (such as happy, sad, thrilled, concerned, and so on) inscribed in the squares.

- You can use phrases like, "You received a surprise gift," "You lost a favorite toy," and so forth to describe various circumstances. On their bingo card, the kids note the feelings they anticipate experiencing.

- Discuss the emotions that were selected after each scenario and how various circumstances might affect how people feel.

- The first kid to receive a line (horizontal, vertical, or diagonal) screams "Bingo!" and describes how the feelings on their card apply to them.

Emotion Stories

Objective

Encouraging kids to create stories that involve various emotions.

Instructions

- Set up a series of scenarios for the kids, such as "You come upon a lost dog," "You get caught in the rain, and you don't have an umbrella," and so on.

- Instruct them to write short stories with characters who are affected by emotions in response to the prompts.

- Have each kid tell their tale. Discuss the characters' feelings and the reasons behind them after each story.

- Ask the kids to think about how they would react if they were in the same position.

Exercises 9:
Applying Emotional Intelligence in the Digital Age

Mindful Tech Check-In

Objective

Promoting awareness of your tech usage patterns.

Instructions

- Begin your day by committing to being conscious of your technology usage.

- Create reminders or alarms on your device to remind you to check in with yourself every hour.

- When the alarm goes off, pause to consider how you utilize technology. Ask yourself:

- What am I feeling at this moment?

- Is my use of technology purposeful or just a matter of habit?

- Do my aims and beliefs and how I utilize technology match up?

- Make any required modifications to how you utilize technology in light of your reflections. This can mean taking a break, establishing limits, or doing something thoughtful.

- Consider how you used technology during the day before going to bed. Take note of any trends or revelations that emerge.

Tech-Free Zone

Objective

Creating designated tech-free spaces in your environment.

Instructions

- Choose one or more locations in your house or place of work where technology will not be permitted. Examples include a reading area, the dining room, or the bedroom.

- Inform your family, coworkers, or any visitors of the no-technology zone.

- Use this area to practice mindfulness by doing anything like reading a book, journaling, or just being present.

- Observe how it feels to be in a place without technology. Any feelings of tranquility or relaxation should be noted.

- Consider your feelings after you've spent some time in the no-technology area. Think about making this a regular habit.

Tech-Free Mealtime

Objective

Cultivating presence and connection during meals.

Instructions

- Set an intention to be totally present during the meal without being distracted by technology.

- Make taking a deep breath or expressing thanks for the meal a part of your pre-meal ritual.

- To avoid disturbing the meal, turn off or put away all electronic gadgets.

- Eat carefully and slowly, focusing on the tastes, textures, and feelings of each bite.

- Take part in meaningful discussions if you're with others. Share your ideas and emotions while actively listening.

- Consider how the experience differed from other meals that use technology after the meal. Keep an eye out for any connections or satisfaction.

Digital Detox Day

Objective

Taking a break from digital devices and engaging in offline activities.

Instructions

- Decide on a day (maybe a weekend day) for your digital detox.

- You should let your loved ones and coworkers know that you will be offline today.

- Make a list of the things you enjoy doing in the physical world, such as reading a printed book, taking a stroll, painting, cooking, being outdoors, or anything else.

- Place your cell phone, tablet, and laptop somewhere out of sight and reach.

- Immerse yourself in the chosen activities all day long. Keep your focus firmly on the here and now.

- Consider how you felt throughout the digital detox at the end of the day. Keep an eye out for any rises in awareness, inventiveness, or clarity.

Empathy in Written Communication

Objective

Practicing expressing and recognizing empathy through written messages.

Instructions

- Select a person to be your online contact from your friends, family, or coworkers.

- Consider their possible feelings in light of what they've shared before replying to a message.

- Recognize their emotions and offer an empathic response. For instance, "I can see how difficult that must have been for you."

- Think back on how successfully you managed to express empathy once you've finished your message. Think about whether there are any areas that may use improvement.

- If appropriate, inquire about your discussion partner's opinion of your empathy.

Gratitude and Appreciation

Objective

Expressing gratitude and appreciation in online interactions.

Instructions

- Commit to showing thankfulness or praise toward someone daily via digital platforms.

- Contact an assortment of people, like loved ones, coworkers, or internet buddies.

- Be clear on what exactly you're grateful for and its importance when saying thanks.

- Observe the reactions to your expressions of thankfulness and their role in enhancing virtual connections.

- Record these incidents and feelings in a journal dedicated to thankfulness for reflective purposes.

Reflect and Define Your Digital Boundaries

Objective

Establishing and clarifying personal digital boundaries.

Instructions

- List all regular internet tasks (like social media, work emails, and games).

- Score the comfort degree from 1 (unhappy) to 5 (contented) per task.

- Mark those that are underrated (less pleasing). They might require boundary-fixing.

- Decide on distinct limits. Like restricting Instagram use to particular hours every day.

- Share these rules with your close ones if they impact them.

- Regularly review and revise rules to keep them aligned with requirements.

Mindful Tech Usage Practice

Objective

Cultivating mindfulness while using digital devices.

Instructions

- Decide before using electronics why you want to use them, whether for fun, office work, or chatting.

- Use an alarm to remind you to see how well you are sticking to the plan regarding internet usage.

- To prevent tired eyes from too much screen time, blink often and gaze far away at stuff twenty feet off for over twenty seconds every 20 minutes. This is called the "20/20/20 rule."

- Ask yourself while internet surfing, especially when on places like Twitter or Instagram.

- Does this benefit me?

- Does this match up with things I want to know or do?

- Is there value added?

- Once night falls, reflect on the entire day. How successful were your attempts at managing boundaries around screen time? Where else can you tweak settings so tomorrow goes even better?

Exercises 10:
Building Emotional Intelligent Mindset

Empathetic Reflection

Objective

Strengthening your empathy by reflecting on others' perspectives.

Instructions

- Choose a specific encounter that took place with an individual today, such as a talk with a coworker or a message from a friend.

- Think about the interaction from the other person's perspective. Think about their needs, feelings, and likely motivations.

- Create a response in your notebook while acting like that person, expressing your feelings and points of view.

- After writing from the other person's perspective, look for beginning similarities that line up. Watch for deviations.

- If appropriate, discuss interaction specifics with the individual in question to get a different perspective.

Gratitude With Positive Affirmations

Objective

Cultivating a positive and appreciative mindset.

Instructions

- Write down three things you are grateful for every day, big or small!

- Say positive affirmations to yourself that help motivate you, and think about those a lot during the day.

- At night, remember all the good things you did and celebrate them.

- Try to be nice to yourself, even if you feel like you mess up sometimes. You deserve some support.

- Write everything good down in a book to read later to cheer yourself up.

Morning Mindful Reflection

Objective

Starting the day with intention and self-awareness.

Instructions

- Locate a calm place to spend five minutes undisturbed.

- Close your eyes and breathe slowly but deeply. Center your focus on the intake and output of air.

- Ponder your plans for the day. What are your intentions today? How should you behave toward everyone?

- Evaluate your inner feelings. Recognize emotions without negativity.

- Picture a triumphant day full of self-belief, empathy, and optimism.

- Pick a positive affirmation and mentally recite it several times.

- Document plans, sentiments, and messages in diary form. This logs your initial musings.

Evening Gratitude and Reflection

Objective

Cultivating gratitude and reflecting on the day's experiences.

Instructions

- Before sleeping, put pen to paper and recall three great happenings from the day. It doesn't have to be major; it can simply be small delights or grand occasions.

- Revisiting the day by reflecting about how things unfolded. Dwell upon events that turned out well and also those that didn't go as planned. Reflect on the emotions triggered that day.

- Delve into the hardships faced and notice your own resilience in dealing with tough circumstances.

- Applaud yourself for smaller feats accomplished and bigger targets achieved; each counts!

- As you prepare for the new dawn, contemplate the objectives you intend to pursue.

- Treat yourself softly, just as you pamper your bestie. A bit more consideration wouldn't harm anyone, right? Especially after a taxing day.

The Three-Question Daily Check-In

Objective

Quickly checking in with yourself and building self-awareness.

Instructions

- Ask yourself these questions throughout the day:

- What emotions am I experiencing currently?

- Which topics occupy my brain right now?

- What do I need for myself instantly?

- Spend short durations sincerely answering the above questions.

- According to replies reflected inside your head, make changes in attitude, actions, or personal rejuvenation methods opted for by you.

- Optionally, write down your replies either on a pocket-sized notepad or digitally saved on a mobile phone device through an app designed especially for writing notes.

The Resilience Journal

Objective

Developing a habit of reflecting on and building emotional resilience.

Instructions

- Choose a notepad that is just for increasing mental resilience.

- Always write down three things for which you are grateful each day and one accomplishment.

- Consider your past issues. Take note of your own strengths and the coping skills you've used to overcome challenges that once appeared insurmountable.

- When faced with difficulty, don't run away. Take notes about the entire scenario in your diary. Explain in detail how you are handling that period and how it makes you feel.

- Determine how to reframe each challenge in a way that is more uplifting or growth-oriented.

- Make precise goals for yourself in terms of resilience. These objectives can be to manage stress, deal with changes, or get over phobias.

- Review older notes frequently to keep up with the emotional resiliency process. Also, rejoice at the mini victories attained.

Resilience Mindset Visualization

Objective

Strengthening your belief in your ability to bounce back from challenges.

Instructions

- Find somewhere comfortable and peaceful to sit undistracted.

- Breathe slowly and deeply multiple times until relaxed.

- Visualize dealing confidently with hardships while feeling strong. Picture things going well despite difficulties.

- Concentrate on succeeding by imagining all the details, such as sounds and feelings, involved during this process.

- Think happy thoughts after winning against problems! Believe strongly inside yourself that you are capable of handling tough situations.

- Say encouraging stuff like "I can do it!" again and again, so remember that true power exists within yourself, always ready whenever needed.

The Growth Journal

Objective

Developing a growth mindset through daily reflection and self-encouragement.

Instructions

- Get a special notebook just for dedicating yourself to cultivating a growth mindset.

- Every day, write down three good things that happened and something new you learned—even if it's tiny!

- If something hard happens, write about it in your notebook. Say what you thought and felt at first.

- Look out for mean things you might think or say to yourself. Try to change those thoughts into helpful ones instead.

- Write about mistakes or times when things didn't go well. Think about what they taught you and what you can do better next time.

- Make some goals for learning and getting better at stuff. It could be anything related to skills, knowledge, or personal development.

- Read through your old writings sometimes to see how far you have come with your progress in developing a growth mindset! Be proud of all the work you are doing.

Growth Mindset Affirmations

Objective

Reprogramming your thought patterns with growth-oriented affirmations.

Instructions

- Make a collection of growth mindset positive affirmations that remind you to keep trying and getting better. Like:

- Challenges help me learn.

- It's okay to mess up; I'll get better next time.

- I can do new things by practicing and working hard.

- Pick one or more of these affirmations each day and say them to yourself. You can do it in the morning or whenever you feel like you need a little encouragement.

- While saying the affirmations, imagine yourself acting out what that sentence says. If the affirmations are about learning from challenges, picture yourself trying really hard at something, even though it's difficult.

- Write down examples of when you acted like the affirmations. Maybe there was a problem you had to solve, but instead of giving up because it seemed too hard, you remembered that challenges help you learn, so you kept trying until you figured it out.

- Keep using your affirmations every day. Change them if you want, or add new ones as you develop your growth mindset.

The Growth Challenge

Objective

Intentionally seeking out challenges and embracing the process of learning and growing.

Instructions

- Choose an activity or task that will make you learn something new or improve your skills. It should be a bit scary but also exciting.

- Make a step-by-step plan to complete the task. Consider who or what can help you during the process.

- Always remember that while working on this task, success isn't everything; the most important part is having fun while learning and growing.

- Take breaks now and then to look back at your journey till now, notice your progress, and celebrate how much better you have gotten.

- No matter the final result, be happy that you took this adventure to learn and grow. You did a great job!

The Gratitude Garden

Objective

Visually representing and nurturing gratitude in your life.

Instructions

- Find a little booklet and some colorful pens or crayons for drawing.

- Inside the booklet, draw a garden filled with blank flowerpots.

- Every day, pick something or someone you are thankful for. Maybe it's a friend, a family vacation, or even just having ice cream after dinner!

- Put what you are grateful for inside one of the flowerpots in your garden. Use symbols, pictures, or short words to show what it looks like.

- Keep making your garden prettier by putting more gratitude flowers in all the empty flowerpots.

- After doing this for lots of days, your garden will be full of pretty colors and drawings showing everything that makes you happy. Looking at your beautifully drawn garden helps you remember how lucky you are to have so many wonderful things in your life!

The Emotion Tree

Objective

Visually representing and exploring emotions.

Instructions

- Grab a pad of plain paper and colored pens or crayons.

- Draw a tree complete with trunk, branches, twigs, and leaves on a page. Label each branch or leaf with names of feelings like "happy," "angry," "scared," and so on.

- Throughout the day, pay attention to your feelings. Pick the label from your tree that matches how you feel.

- Use a pen or crayon of a matching color to ring the branch or mark the leaf.

- With time, all the labels on your tree will disappear under circles and marks. The rings and marks will form unique patterns. These patterns show how you've been feeling over time.

- Try looking at your tree diary every night before bedtime.

PART 4:
THE LAST
BUT NOT THE LEAST

Chapter 13:
Movies for Practicing Emotional Intelligence

Cinema is a mirror by which we often see ourselves.

–ALEJANDRO G. INARRITU

Movies are essentially storytelling mediums for human experiences. With elements like joy, sorrow, love, and personal growth entangled throughout each movie's storyline, viewers meet complex characters who must make difficult choices while navigating interpersonal dynamics. This ultimately leads to self-discovery and empathetic understanding among one another, with the end result being mirrored reflections that resonate strongly with audiences due to the relatability found within those same shared life events depicted on screen.

Movies let you practice feeling different emotions safely because they're not happening to you but to someone on the screen. It teaches you how other people might act when something good or bad happens to them. You get to think about whether you would do the same thing if you were in their place.

Choosing which movie to watch matters here since everyone has different types of feelings inside. Some movies will make you laugh a lot, and some will tear you apart. Movies teach you how to read others and know better ways to treat your fellow humans. There are sure to be many chances waiting once popcorn starts popping.

Some movies are really great because they talk about feelings and situations that anyone can relate to. For example, there may be characters dealing with tough things like navigating complex relationships or fighting with friends; some might show bravery even when times get hard—all while figuring out more about themselves along this journey called life. These types of films act almost like practice sessions where you can work toward becoming a more emotionally aware individual!

Life has many different kinds of feelings mixed together, both good and bad. Watching certain movies helps you explore those various emotions in an interesting way—like looking into a big image made entirely out of small pieces, each telling its part within it all! You end up learning so much, not only about other people but also yourself, through such experiences captured within film frames. They reflect back on your personal experiences, making everything seem closer to home than ever before!

When you finish seeing a movie, it's nice sometimes to stop and think about what happened in the story and how it made you feel inside yourself. Try thinking about why people do things in movies and see if anything similar has happened to you before. Doing this will make watching movies more fun because, afterward, you will know yourself a little better, too.

Sometimes, when you watch movies, they make you cry, laugh, or maybe even be scared, which is okay because this means the movie was able to touch something inside of you—your emotions! Art does this kind of thing, whether paintings, music, books, or whatever. It opens up our hearts and minds so that we can feel other people's feelings too, like putting yourself in someone else's shoes without leaving yours behind, you know what I mean. Anyone watching lots of movies will learn about life and stuff.

There are several films that can aid in developing emotional intelligence. Particularly effective learning tools are movies that feature characters who experience challenging circumstances but ultimately come to understand themselves or others better by the conclusion. By seeing such plots develop on the screen, you will not only learn more about your own emotional states but will also develop mental acumen-related skills.

Chapter 14:
How to Continue the Process of Self-Improvement

Life isn't about finding yourself. Life is about creating yourself.

–George Bernard Shaw

We all want to improve ourselves and be stronger inside. This can happen by growing and trying to do things better each day. In fact, sometimes just keeping track or understanding what you did before helps. The main point of all these efforts isn't reaching some kind of impossible perfection but rather actually seeing improvement over time! When emotional intelligence starts really working well, life gets happier!

This chapter explores in depth how to carry on the process of progress. It's a path that prioritizes improvement over perfection, charts your development, and recognizes the telltale indicators of a burgeoning emotional intelligence. With each stride forward, we reaffirm our dedication to improving upon who we already are while accepting the flaws that make us human.

Perfection is an Enemy of the Good: Expect Success, Not Perfection

When we try to get better, it might feel like it's hard because we haven't reached "perfect." But don't worry too much—you only need to go one small bit at a time! Even something very small still counts toward doing good work overall. That's definitely worth celebrating.

Thinking that everything has to be absolutely perfect can hold you back if you want to move ahead with your goals. If instead, you focus solely on whether it works out successfully, then there may actually be many opportunities waiting around every corner where failure could provide valuable lessons learned that contribute greatly toward achieving personal development objectives, ultimately enabling you to reach heightened levels of performance capability beyond limits previously thought possible. This clearly shows why aiming high should always stay a top priority when striving toward self-betterment, regardless of whatever roadblock appears along the way!

People often get caught up thinking only perfect results count, but failures teach a lot. Take Thomas Edison, for instance, who kept trying until he succeeded in finding the right stuff for light bulbs. Every mistake brings you closer to solving the problem. The same happens in any field or aspect of life—experiments show wrong paths, making the proper direction clearer. Don't fear admitting you fell short on your first attempt; everyone does occasionally. Perseverance pays off eventually. Remember, true growth happens by accepting not knowing everything already, constantly acquiring knowledge, skills, and abilities, and overcoming obstacles head-on.

It's crucial to acknowledge and value the work and advancement that have been made rather than concentrating entirely on perfection. No matter how small, every action represents development and advancement. By adopting this viewpoint, you can develop more self-compassion and obtain a better understanding of your individual growth journey. The path to success is rarely easy, but by celebrating tiny successes and remaining resilient, you may realize your goals and experience the gratifying feeling that comes with achievement.

How to Know That You Are Progressing? Track Progress

Taking baby steps every day shows how far you have come in making yourself a better person than yesterday. Realize that getting worse actually doesn't happen here. Keeping notes helps you remember exactly what you did, so next time similar situations arise, use the old trick! Knowing better today compared to the old days proves true dedication and commitment to positive growth.

Keeping track of how you're doing helps a lot. For one thing, it shows you all the good things you have already done. When you feel like giving up, it reminds you how strong and hardworking you really are. Plus, looking at what you did before helps you figure out what works best so you can do even better next time.

Also, seeing how well you're doing makes you happy and excited to do more. Rejoicing over little wins keeps you going stronger. You also start feeling proud and sure that you're moving ahead in life.

Don't forget—getting better isn't always easy and straightforward. Sometimes, you might stay still or slip back some before moving forward again, and that's alright, too. Keeping track of where you went wrong helps you see those ups and downs and know that they happen to everyone trying to get better at something.

Pick a way that works for you to keep track—write things down, use a list, or choose an app. Use tracking as a helper along the road to being better at things, and remember, each tiny step ahead shows just how committed and brave you truly are.

When You Can Say Your Emotional Intelligence is Improved

Knowing how much better you are at understanding and controlling your feelings is something only you can judge. It doesn't depend on what other folks think or say but on how different you feel deep inside yourself and see changes happening while talking with friends and family.

One of the first signs of improved emotional intelligence is heightened self-awareness. You can tell better why and when certain emotions happen and how they work. This knowledge lets you deal with your feelings nicely and smartly instead of just acting without thinking.

Also, you start having an easier time putting yourself in other people's shoes and figuring out how they must be feeling. This lets you connect better with friends, family, coworkers—everybody! These relationships turn out warmer and stronger because of that.

You can also tell you're getting better at EQ by managing arguments and problems. Instead of fighting or yelling, you act nice and peaceful, wanting to solve issues and not cause more trouble. That shows you are controlling your emotions better and learning how to talk about stuff properly.

As you keep working on understanding and controlling your emotions better, you end up being really great at talking to other people. You share your thoughts plainly, stand up for what you need, and also listen closely to what others have to say. This makes friendships and relationships way stronger and truer.

You'll know your emotional intelligence is at an expected level when you see a positive shift in your overall well-being and relationships. Your life is happier, and your friendships and love affairs are healthier and stronger. Keep growing and evolving; don't ever stop! Each baby step counts toward making you the best version of yourself—stronger, smarter, kinder, braver, and happier.

Key Takeaways

- Attempting to be flawless is impossible, so keep that in mind. Instead, concentrate on tweaking and enhancing whatever you are doing in minor ways.

- Don't stress about performing everything perfectly at once. Simply establish modest goals and rejoice when you achieve them. Continue making little by little progress.

- Your progress toward achieving your goals should be documented in writing or with photographs. You may keep your enthusiasm for your tasks up by looking at them.

- Spend some time identifying your strengths and areas that require improvement. This enables you to identify the sections that require the greatest focus.

- There are instances when things won't go precisely as you planned. But don't use them as an excuse to give up. They teach us important things we can use to make our next try even better!

Conclusion

The journey is never ending. There's always gonna be growth, improvement, adversity; you just gotta take it all in and do what's right, continue to grow, continue to live in the moment.

–Antonio Brown

Now that we have reached the finish line of this adventure, let's take a moment to ponder the giant leap you made in terms of comprehending and mastering your emotions. You've explored the key aspects of EQ through theory and practice; you've ventured into unfamiliar territories of soul searching and self-reflection; you've blossomed and matured as an individual and as a social creature. Look back and marvel at your wonderful feats and victorious march toward self-realization and emotional liberation.

Above all else, never lose sight of the fact that every little bit of progress matters way more than aiming to reach impossible standards of perfection. Despite society telling you otherwise, disregard being flawless! The real fun lies in learning from mistakes, celebrating mini-wins, and constantly morphing into an upgraded version of yourself.

All those exercises weren't merely tasks but special keys to help you delve deeper inside yourself, sympathize with others, and bond better in any sort of relationship. They showed you ways of avoiding squabbles, chatting effectively, and developing finesse when dealing with feelings—both others and yours.

Understand once and forever that self-betterment isn't a straight road or a quick trip. It's all about never ceasing to expand your horizons, gain fresh wisdom, and bend with the twists and turns of existence. Even seemingly bad luck can teach you priceless lessons. Learning how to say "no" to people nicely, raising kids with lots of warmth and comprehension, remaining cool and collected amid modern tech chaos—you've trained yourself diligently to excel at these areas.

As you advance farther along your chosen pathway, recall fondly everything you learned and practiced beforehand. Allow those exercises and role-playing to act as lanterns, leading you safely forward. Remember, above all, that working on yourself is actually super powerful and inspiring!

It's time to take what you've learned and start using it. Think back on which parts spoke to you the most. Then, start putting them into practice. Pay attention to yourself and listen carefully to others. When disagreements pop up, look at things from their perspective. Don't worry too much about being perfect; just focus on moving forward. You can use these skills at work or at home, wherever you feel they would be helpful. Watch as you see results because of how well you manage your emotions.

As you close this book, know that learning more about managing your feelings and connecting well isn't done after reading here. Each new day has a chance to improve. Be proud of any little bit of progress, and bounce back quickly when something doesn't go as you hoped. Remember, you have strength, so don't give up trying to do great things. Have compassion for yourself even while working hard. May the road ahead bring good changes both around you and deep down inside you.

BOOK 3

The Art Of Critical Thinking, Logic, & Problem-Solving

15 Everyday Exercises To Enhance Your Cognitive Potential, Conquer Logical Fallacies, & Polish Decision-Making Skills For Success In Work & Life

Introduction

"People can be extremely intelligent, have taken a critical thinking course, and know logic inside and out. Yet they may just become clever debaters, not critical thinkers because they are unwilling to look at their own biases."

- CAROL WADE.

A few years ago, I was at a conference that centered around including more women in STEM spaces. My daughter was keen on becoming a groundbreaking scientist, and this was the best way to support her. I felt like the world's best dad as I walked her through the stands, ensuring I got as many pamphlets as possible. And when she was not rolling her eyes at my enthusiasm, I could tell she was grateful for my involvement. I was the perfect dad, right? I felt so proud of myself as I was challenging gender norms and paving the way for my daughter to be what she wanted. Boy, was my smugness short-lived!

The conference included a panel discussion that centered on bias. Rather than focus on gender bias, the moderator expanded the focus to all kinds of bias and happily gave some examples. Then, without missing a beat, she turned to the crowd and asked, "Who can confidently say that they do not have bias?" The room fell silent, with most people shying away from looking at the moderator. The tension was evident, and I felt my shoulders slump. How could I raise my hand when I knew the obvious?

Bias - we all have it, no matter how much we want to think we don't. So, it was not a surprise that nobody raised their hand. In those minutes, we were all equal in this one wrong that often blurs our thinking.

How bad is the situation?

Let's start with gender bias as an example. A World Bank (2023) study focusing on political, educational, economic, and physical integrity factors found that at least 90% of people had one bias in gender social norms. Most people had 3 to 4 indicators, and this did not even touch on gender diversity but instead focused on cis-gender men and women.

If you think that's bad, let's move to something most of us have been guilty of at some point - ageism. Usually, people think of ageism as discriminating against the old, but it also happens to young people. I've seen brilliant young minds turned down because they were "too young." And older adults are not enjoying much luck either. An American Psychological Association (2022) report showed that at least 93% of older adults (aged 50 to 80) had faced ageism, especially in the digital world. If this is hard to picture, think about it this way: How often have you seen an older adult with a digital device and wondered if they needed help using it? - Or seen them handling a task and felt compelled to help even if they had a handle on things?

The context gets even more interesting once we look at bias against ourselves, which we often call self-sabotage. Many people fail to make decisions, explore excellent opportunities, or even ask for help because they do not think they deserve such good things.

So, when you consider these and more biases, can you genuinely say you are unbiased?

Are we just hardwired for bias?

Unconscious bias is not accidental. We start developing attitudes towards people different from us at an early age. It begins with our school and home experiences and continues growing as we become more ingrained in society. You see the stereotypes in movies, social media, books, etc., and without knowing it, you develop implicit bias. Then, one day, you pass someone over for a promotion based on their gender, age, or some other factor that has nothing to do with the job description or their skills. Or you hire someone because you have an affinity bias - their culture aligns with yours, and they feel like a safe decision. It goes both ways.

The problem with bias is that it seeps into our lives in all aspects. It affects how you approach your family, engage in relationships, maintain friendships, handle conflicts, what you do when you have problems at work, and even how you interact with your neighbors.

Worse still, it spills over to your **decision-making**. Think about it. How often do you look at the facts? If you are like most people, you base your decisions on what you feel. So, you favor people you like and dismiss the ones you don't, even without reviewing the data. Take an example of a fight between friends. Do you often side with the person who has been wronged, or do you favor the person you like better? Bias is everywhere, which explains why decision-making becomes difficult in all other aspects of our lives.

Is Critical Thinking the Solution?

"He just can't do it!" came the curt reply. We had been in a meeting for about thirty minutes, during which we discussed whether a developer should put up a high-rise hotel in our neighborhood. Everyone was okay with the idea except for one gentleman with no sound argument. He stood his ground, claiming that the hotel would result in lower property values despite the data showing that the hotel would result in as much as a 100% value increment. Of course, the development continued as planned, and we later discovered that the gentleman's issue with the developer was personal. They had once pitched to the same investor, and the developer had won - there was nothing wrong with the hotel plan; it was plain bias.

And while it might be easy to judge the gentleman, we have all been guilty of such biased arguments. So, what are our options? You can sit back, go with the flow, and blame everyone else for the bad things in your life. You have probably seen those people who always delegate blame - their alarm did not go off, someone was too slow in traffic, their boss hates them, and the list goes on. Or you can accept that you are human and subject to bias. By doing this, you can find a way to approach situations with a clear mind and be more critical in your approaches. In this way, before you retaliate, you will have time to review the logic of your decision. *Are you not inviting Allan to the barbecue because you don't like him, or are you envious of his new home? Are you truly angry at your boss for the warning letter, or did you deserve it after your behavior at the last office party?*

In the gentleman's case, was he against the hotel or the developer? Because everyone who analyzed the hotel's benefits saw that the cons did not outweigh the pros. If he had used the same logic, he could have saved himself and everyone a lot of time.

I don't praise critical thinking over biased decisions because I have lived a perfect life. In fact, it's more of the opposite. For many years, I worked a stressful job with routine tasks - anyone in the banking field will tell you that some weeks feel like a maze. I was stuck and angry and blamed everyone and everything for the dark cloud that hung over me. Simple decisions were often hard to make and usually resulted in negative outcomes. My relationship with my wife and kids was strained, and I was on my way to a very dark place. I lived in limbo for many years before I finally sought help from a therapist who was into philosophy. Without knowing it, she guided me into the world of stoicism, and I never looked back.

I learned that I was not a pawn in my own life - I had a say in what I did and said. People did not have the power I had given them, and I could take it back by making sound decisions. When faced with a problem, I could look at it from different perspectives instead of playing the victim and counting it as another negative thing in my life. It was a long and fulfilling road that finally enabled me to better my relationships with my loved ones, pursue a career I enjoy, and live the life I never knew I wanted. I'm not saying that I no longer have bias - I am just more aware of it and have learned how to ensure it does not take over my life. And I now want to share these skills with you.

What's in the book?

Critical thinking is not a formula you can apply to your decisions. Instead, it requires you to be introspective in each situation. You must address your bias, be aware of your emotions, communicate properly, be honest with yourself, avoid conformism or selfishness, and focus on the facts. On top of all this, you must be receptive to different ways of thinking. Of course, achieving this balance is not easy. This book covers the importance of all these skills and how to employ them while paying particular attention to bias. By the end of reading the book, you will:

- Understand how bias works and discover the many ways you may have allowed it to shape your decisions,

- Uncover what critical thinking entails and address any misconceptions you may have about it,

- Delve into the importance of critical thinking in the society,

- Find ways to ask the important questions and challenge your biases,

- Discover the power of logic and understand how to craft good arguments,

- Become a good problem solver by learning how to conduct good analyses and present your findings logically,

- Figure out how to sift information in this digital age and navigate conversations in the digital realm,

- Learn how to communicate with other people and resolve conflicts and

- Embrace a life of learning.

The change does not happen overnight. You won't suddenly stop arguing with people in traffic (yep, this was me) or start getting along with your colleagues. Instead, it takes time. You start learning more about your shortcomings, how to put yourself in other people's shoes, where to spend your energy, and how to harness positivity by taking the lead in your decisions. Critical thinking is not just about winning arguments but also about figuring out what decisions best align with your purpose and goals.

The chapters in this book will help you build a solid foundation in your rationale that will benefit you in all areas of your life. You will also have exercises at the end of each chapter - you can keep returning to these to reinforce your foundation long after finishing the book.

Are you ready to become a sound critical thinker? Let's start flipping the pages!

PART 1:
THEORY OF CRITICAL THINKING

Chapter 1:
What Critical Thinking Really Is And What It Is Not

"The unexamined life is not worth living."

- SOCRATES.

Looking at the average job ad in this digital era, you'll see terms like "critical thinker." So valued is this skill that an AACU (2013) report showed that critical thinking skills ranked higher than undergraduate majors for job candidates! However, while many companies have stood by these and more critical thinking stats, one thing is clear: the definition of critical thinking is as vague as problem-solver, team-oriented, and other broad terms used at work or in social settings. Only a few people know what it means, yet many applicants cheekily add it to their CVs to get a boost - who wouldn't? But rather than go with the flow that's now made its way to HR offices everywhere, let's uncover what employers really mean when they argue the benefits of critical thinking and how you can fit the bill.

Section 1: What is Critical Thinking?

Assume you lie about your critical thinking skills and find your way to the interview stage for your dream job. Then, one of the interviewers asks you to define critical thinking. What would you say? Well, the long explanation goes into the critical thinking concepts I will later break down. Or you could keep it simple and go with "rational." A critical thinker is rational, and that about sums it up!

Simplifying Critical Thinking Components

What does **rationality** mean? What separates a rational person from an irrational one? It all comes down to how people approach situations or people. Critical thinkers use the following thought-out processes:

→ They observe the situation or person,

→ They analyze the data available to them,

→ They process the data to make sense of it,

→ They come to a conclusion based on the data, their knowledge, and their (or other people's experiences),

→ They communicate their findings to the other people involved, and

→ They work with other people to solve the problem.

As a critical thinker, your work is to understand the logic in a situation, eliminate assumptions, work past your biases, and review the implications behind all arguments and decisions. Now, let's see this in action using an everyday example. You walk in and find your friends, Tommy and Brian, arguing about who owes the other person money. Based on your experiences, you know that Brian tends to borrow money from his friends and fail to repay it. But does that make him the guilty party? Not at all. The critical thinking approach requires you to listen to both parties and get facts from both of your friends. Even better, you can tabulate the data so everyone can understand the outcome. Doing this paves the way for a fact-based conversation where you can all work towards the solution.

Of course, you can't just butt into an argument and start deriving equations and offering solutions. In later sections, I will show you how to judge situations before offering your two cents.

Common misconceptions about critical thinking

"Critical thinkers are heartless - they don't consider people's emotions." That was an argument posed by a grad student in a seminar I attended. Some people were for the notion, others were unsure, and others disagreed with him. It's natural for critical thinking to face misconceptions as it is a unique way of solving problems. Here are some other misconceptions you may encounter:

a. ***It's a glass-half-empty way of thinking:*** Since critical thinking requires people to cover all sides of the coin without dismissing ideas, some think critical thinkers are often out to uncover flaws. However, you can't truly be rational without covering all the bases, as your analysis won't be objective.

b. ***It comes naturally to some people***: Have you heard of the notion that leaders are born and not made? Some people follow the same school of thought in critical thinking. Luckily, enough research shows that people can learn to be critical thinkers. Take the Henley (2020) report on Finnish schools as an example. They start the students in critical thinking from as young as six years - by the time they are in their teens, they are so good at fact-checking that you cannot fool them with Wikipedia articles!

c. ***It only cares about facts:*** Being rational does not take away your humanity - you can't just make decisions based on numbers or scientific findings. Instead, you must be empathetic enough to understand other people's positions and curious to find sustainable solutions to problems. Think Solomonic wisdom.

d. ***It is neutral:*** Remember my focus on bias in the introduction? Often, people think that critical thinkers do not allow their feelings or beliefs to get in the way of their decisions. But that could not be further from the truth. Luckily, when people are aware of their bias and do not ignore it or let it control them, they can still make the right decisions.

e. ***It's impractical for everyday living***: Some people think critical thinking only makes sense for professionals and academics. But don't we need critical thinkers everywhere? - School, at work, the neighborhood grocery store, the line in Disneyland, on social media. Rationality would solve many world problems.

PS: While the above are misconceptions, they can also be true for someone who has not embraced the entirety of critical thinking. For example, you are not a critical thinker if you often lean towards the negative aspects of situations instead of viewing all the options. I'll explain how you can embrace skepticism while remaining open-minded in the third section of this chapter.

Section 2: The Elements of Thought

When someone acts irrationally, others often ask, "***What were you thinking?***" They seek to understand the reasoning behind the perceived poor judgment shown by the other person. If you are a critical thinker, answering this question should be easy, as you can base your decision on the Paul-Elder critical thinking framework, as evidenced by the University of Louisville (2010). It considers the following elements and how they come into play:

1. **Purpose**: Your thinking should start with what you want to achieve. For example, your purpose could be to take a one-month holiday with your family. With that, you can derive related

and objective questions, e.g., *where will you vacation? How much money do you need? When you have a purpose, everything else takes shape.*

2. **Point of view**: How we see things and other people often hinges on our understanding of the world and our experiences and hopes. Our point of view is simply a combination of our primary values and biases and often does not change. It thus makes sense that when thinking about situations that include other people, we must step away from our points of view and consider different perspectives. *For example, if you want to invite your sister on vacation, what would make her want to be part of it? It comes down to understanding what appeals to other people.*

3. **Information**: The best way to arrive at a decision is to get accurate information from raw data, statistics, statements, experiences (yours and others), or observations. It should be free of bias, come from credible sources, and show all sides of the coin such that it challenges your assumptions and forces you to rethink your stance. Let's go back to our holiday purpose. *You can get accurate data from airlines, hotels, tour operators, and people who have traveled to places you'd like to visit. At the same time, consider how much your family can afford to use on a trip.*

4. **Concepts**: Suppose you were to pitch a business idea; you'd use ROI formulas to argue your case. It's not by chance - theories, laws, principles, models, and definitions help everyone understand things more clearly and are integral to highlighting the objectivity in ideas. As such, you should consider concepts that can guide and support your reasoning. Back to the holiday - *a savings plan is ideal. For example, you can propose that everyone save $200 a month for ten months for a trip to Mexico.*

5. **Assumptions**: We all believe some things to be true, even without evidence. *E.g., you may assume your boss will give you a month off work. Or you can automatically use your miles to save on travel costs.* Now is the time to challenge these beliefs by checking if you can verify them. Those you can verify become information. E.g., if your boss grants you time off work, this is verifiable data. You must decide if it's justifiable to maintain assumptions you cannot verify by assessing their impact on the overall decision in the next section.

6. **Inferences and interpretations**: Our points of view are so different that two people can look at the same data and develop contrasting solutions. For example, you could propose your holiday idea to your brother, who suggests you travel the next month and save $2,000 in one month despite your plan to save the same amount in 10 months. Thus, using the available data to determine the most reasonable solution is important as you will likely need to support your

position. To do this, you must consider different approaches to the problem and assess their suitability. *For example, why choose Mexico over Bali? Why save $2,000 instead of $1,500?*

7. **Implications and consequences:** Before making your decision, consider its implications. How will people feel or act when they hear it? *For example, will people accept your holiday idea? And what happens if they accept it?* The implications and consequences you arrive at should be logical and should follow the elements of thought we have discussed. Your experiences can also help you with this, e.g., *if your family is always eager to go on trips, you might deduce that this time will be similar.*

See? Critical thinking is relatively easy. If someone were to ask you what you were thinking, you'd guide them through all the steps without batting an eyelid! In the next chapters, I will walk you through all the elements to help you understand decision-making better.

Section 3: Cultivating a Critical Mindset

"To know is to know that you know nothing. That is the meaning of true knowledge."

- CONFUCIUS

Is a critical thinker the loudest person in the room who thinks they have answers to the universe? Not at all. Being a critical thinker means you understand that your knowledge has limitations, hence the need to develop the following skills:

1. **Embracing curiosity**

We've had our cat, Mus (my daughter named him), for many years. And each time I open the fridge, he's there, peering inside, trying to figure out the meals we've prepared and assessing the structural integrity of this cooling machine. Deep down, I am envious that he can maintain such curiosity every day. I am not suggesting that you become as curious as a cat - we all know how that ends. But here are some ways you can unearth more knowledge:

→ *Ask yourself and others questions*: When you seek answers, you start thinking much more deeply and go down paths you never would have considered. For example, instead of assuming you know how your favorite wine is made, read about it.

→ *Become an active listener:* Hearing what people say and actually listening to them are different things. Often, people listen to stories, thinking they must have a response. How about taking in the information without thinking of what to say? For example, if your friend is talking about a new ad they are launching, be the audience, and you will discover interesting tidbits.

→ *Stimulate your brain:* In the digital age, it's easy to get lost scrolling social media as you watch people bake, dance, eat, - even sleep! Take a break from your phone and explore the world - go on a walk, attend a show, buy fresh veggies from the local farm - these experiences leave you curious and help you learn more.

Most importantly, accept that you don't know everything. You know some things, but a lot exceeds your imagination, so be open to discovering more.

2. Becoming a skeptic

Your journey to curiosity will take you down a rabbit hole. If you are not careful, you may accept ideas that are not necessarily true. So, how do you stay on your toes - skepticism! Here's how you do this:

→ *Check your sources*: Good information sources often have qualified research. But those that do not hold any water usually tend to tug at your emotions by introducing bias. So, is your source informing or swaying you? What do they stand to gain if you buy into the messaging? What do you stand to lose?

→ *Use the "is it too good to be true" approach*: Take weight loss ads as an example - some even claim to help people lose 10 pounds in two days! When faced with such information, do a deep dive and uncover the facts instead of going with the claims.

→ *Note your bias:* Sometimes, cynicism takes over when the person or situation attracts our bias. For example, if your nemesis at work gets accused of slacking on the job, you're likely to accept the allegations. The best way to remain objective is to look at the information that conflicts with your views, e.g., talking to someone who thinks your nemesis is innocent.

In a later chapter, I will get more into how you can assess information sources and check your bias.

3. Developing open-mindedness

Remember when people would say things like, "It's either my way or the highway?" Well, that does not work in critical thinking. Open-mindedness is essential in embracing curiosity and skepticism as it forces you to acknowledge that you don't know everything. But how does it work? You need to become more aware of your biases, learn to see things from other points of view, ask more questions, connect with people with different perspectives, be open to different media, and refrain from negative thinking. Achieving this balance takes a while, and in later chapters, I will show you how to do this by exploring all of these concepts.

4. **Practicing intellectual humility**

Being wrong is often a hard pill to swallow - we go through life being punished for being wrong. This thinking thus takes shape from our school grades, our punishments from our parents, being shunned in social settings when we make wrong decisions - the list goes on. It is thus easy to understand why many people have difficulty asking questions or admitting they are wrong. But as we covered in elements of thought, a critical thinker must be willing to explore different solutions while noting that their viewpoints limit their process. Your ideas will sometimes be wrong, and your biases may get in the way. If someone points this out, be ready to welcome their viewpoints. And if you learn from such experiences, thank them for educating you. Sometimes, the teachings will come from younger people, less educated people, and people with fewer resources than you do. By avoiding bias, you can learn a lot and become a much better thinker from such interactions!

Key Chapter Takeaways

✓ A critical thinker is rational. But this is not by chance. Instead, it comes down to the ability to observe a situation or person, assess and analyze the data available, make conclusions based on data and their knowledge and experiences, communicate their results, and work with others to get an objective outcome.

✓ Elements of thought add to the critical thinking process and enable critical thinkers to be more objective in their decision-making. These are purpose, point of view, information, concepts, assumptions, inferences, and implications.

✓ While critical thinking is beneficial, it is subject to misconceptions that critical thinkers must be wary of. These include notions that critical thinking is negative, innate to some people, only for academics and professionals, neutral, and only relies on facts.

✓ For critical thinkers to avoid sinking into cynicism or making biased decisions, they must embrace curiosity, learn to be skeptical, become more open-minded, and be willing to practice intellectual humility.

In the next chapters, I will delve into these concepts in greater detail to help you elevate your decision-making skills.

Chapter 2:
Why Critical Thinking Is Important And How It Can Help

"When your mind is full of assumptions, conclusions, and beliefs, it has no penetration, it just repeats past impressions."

- SADHGURU JAGGI VASUDEV.

Herd mentality is one of the most interesting and dangerous concepts in this world. Per a University of Leeds study highlighted by Nauert (2017), it takes just 5% of a crowd to influence the rest of the 95% to do something. So, why is it dangerous? The 5% of influential people have the reins and can decide to use their power for good or bad. If they use their powers for good, they can revolutionize thinking, e.g., getting people to advocate for better healthcare. But on the downside, herd thinking replaces critical thinking skills and our consciences, which can result in poor decision-making. Such thinking also suppresses curiosity, creativity, and good judgment. Think MLM marketing - it works so effectively because people want to be in with the crowd. By the time they look up and realize how deep they are into the schemes, they've already made several poor decisions.

Let's look at how critical thinking can help you avoid such thinking by equipping you with the skills to be an independent thinker who can see beyond biases and misinformation.

Section 1: The Importance of Critical Thinking in Today's Society

Do you know what gives power to politicians and news outlets? - People's lack of critical thinking. Here's an example. My daughter's high school class had an election the other day, and her friend came over to prepare her campaign. She had fantastic ideas about changing the policies in school, and I could tell she was a strong candidate. However, the campaign did not center on these intellectual ideas. Instead, it required a ring light, a few dance moves, and a catchy song. "Why?" I asked. She had a solid campaign - she could win without putting on a show. My daughter responded, *"People don't care about that, dad. They want to vote for someone who's like them, not the nerd."* And as much as I wanted to counter, she was right - that's politics!

Of Fake News and Cognitive Biases

My daughter's class is not alone in its thinking. How many times have you supported someone just because of an Instagram post they made? Or a news article that highlighted their successes? We live in a world where we are subject to media that influences our thinking. It is thus vital to be wary of the following:

a. **Fake news**: Every day, we get bombarded with different information, and it can be hard to tell what is true and what is not. In the past, fake news was limited as it was mainly used to push political agendas. But now? Anyone with a smartphone can post information online, making it seem the ultimate truth. So, how can you address fake news? First, you need to understand that it comes in three forms, as follows:

    → *Misinformation*: This is false information shared by well-meaning people who think it's true. For example, when people shared the cabbage soup diet in the 20th century, they thought they were helping others lose weight!

    → *Disinformation*: This is false information used to manipulate others. Take the example of a realtor who lies to a potential buyer that the property values will increase in the next decade due to an alleged mall being put up in the area.

    → *Mal-information*: This is factual information shared with malicious intent. For example, if someone notifies the public that a beauty influencer had cosmetic surgery, this information can decrease the influencer's ratings. It's accurate information but has not been used with good intentions.

    In later sections, I will show you how to spot fake news and avoid being swayed by news or media outlets, friends, or even well-meaning neighbors.

b. **Cognitive bias**: Do you know what helps fake news spread like wildfire? Cognitive bias - we all have it. And in the case of fake news, you might find that you only pay attention to stories that confirm your beliefs. For example, if a story highlights someone as corrupt and you think they have shady dealings, you will likely believe it. Cognitive bias also shows in the following ways:

→ The inability to be accountable for your wrongs and instead blaming others and outside factors,

→ The notion that other people are lucky, yet you have to work hard for all the things you have accumulated,

→ The assumption that everyone else thinks the same way you do and

→ The confidence that you know everything about a topic even if you have barely read it or have only skimmed it.

So, how do we get this bias? It stems from our emotions, motivations, social settings, and ability to process information. While some biases are good, many result in subjective thinking that hurts us and others. For example, if you believe that all fat people are lazy, you may fail to hire a plus-size job candidate despite their high qualifications. Not only will you rob yourself of a good employee, but you will also deny another person the chance to work. In a later chapter, I will break down biases and explain how you can address them to improve your decision-making.

Can Critical Thinking Help?

"I don't want people to say, 'Something is true because Tyson says it is true.' That's not critical thinking."

- Neil deGrasse Tyson

It's easy to downplay the significance of cognitive biases and fake news. After all, who are you hurting if you choose to look the other way? Well, a lack of critical thinking seeps into significant issues like healthcare, global conflicts, climate change, and political leadership. We don't have to look far into our history to find a good example. *Remember when COVID-19 was ravaging the world, and some people still thought it was a hoax and would not wear masks or maintain social distancing? Was that critical thinking, or did they just support leaders who told them what they wanted to hear? Were they buying into the fake news?* That's just one example that proves that when people fail to think critically, they pose a danger to themselves and others.

Let's consider the following circumstances:

1. **Democratic responsibility**: Our leadership choices affect everything - our healthcare systems, the state of our economies, our schools, and our legal protections. Yet, even with all this on the line, many people base their candidate choices on their ideologies, e.g., a liberal candidate attracts votes from people who have the same disposition. A Miller and Shanks (1997) book shows as much. But we can all agree that this is not a critical thinking approach - there's no telling that a candidate will stick to their ideologies once they take office. Moreover, without the candidate *actually* breaking down their strategic plans, voters cannot get the assurance that the candidate will act as they would have in the same position. Critical thinking requires voters to weigh the arguments presented by candidates, sift through the fake news and find the truth, have objective discussions with other voters from all sides, and hold politicians accountable. The more people do this, the more people can have faith in the system and challenge authorities by demanding better.

2. **Social responsibility**: Human beings have ethical, economic, and environmental duties. Let's take the last one as an example. A Uteuova (2024) report based on a University of Michigan study showed that almost 15% of Americans do not believe climate change exists. The reason? - Most people base their decisions on influential persons. So, if their leaders deny climate change, so do they. Can you see the issue here? The same happens in international conflicts. At a barbecue the other day, someone brought up the Ukraine versus Russia war. From the stories, I could gather that most people only watched the news stories in passing and supported the country that people around them supported. None of them had enough justification to support the bloodshed in these countries. Yet these are the voices expected to spearhead change - can you see the glaring problem?

To be a better critical thinker and make this world better for yourself and others, you will thus need to challenge your bias and assess your news sources continually. *Is your aunt Ramona right about that war? Does your friend Kevin have the facts about the presidential candidate, or is he assuming things?* It goes back to the first chapter on cultivating a critical mindset - keep asking questions and don't just assume that people know everything or have the right intentions.

Section 2: Benefits of Mastering Critical Thinking

If you were alone in a dark room with one match, an oil lamp, a fireplace, and a candle, which would you light first?

The match!

Critical thinking shapes even the simplest decisions we make. Yet, people often hold the misconception that it's only practical for academics and professionals. Let's debunk this by looking at different ways critical thinking can better your life:

1. **Better decision-making:** We can all use a little help with our decisions, no matter how big or small they are. Critical thinking helps you assess your choices and determine the best ones once you have considered all the elements of choice. You might even enjoy your meals more if you use critical thinking to choose restaurants instead of going with what's trendy in your circles!

2. **Improved happiness**: The common notion is that teens and tweens have the highest rates of low self-esteem. However, a Guttman (2019) compilation study points out that over 85% of people (including adults) have low self-esteem. Critical thinking has been shown to help people understand themselves better and address their limiting beliefs, which translates to better decisions and improved confidence, hence enhanced quality of life!

3. **Enhanced problem-solving skills**: Problems will always be a part of our lives. We can choose to find solutions to them or complain about our circumstances. Critical thinkers choose the former option - they assess their challenges, consider different ways to address them, and choose the most reasonable approach.

4. **Better relationships:** Mind-reading, passive aggression, lack of communication, and unrealistic expectations are some of the biggest issues in relationships. *For example, if a friend fails to text back within minutes, you might assume they are ignoring you. But they could be dealing with an emergency, and you'd only know that if you waited for their response.* Critical thinking teaches you to look at situations from other people's perspectives so you can be a better friend, family member, spouse, parent, child, colleague, or neighbor.

5. **Refined research skills**: When you embrace curiosity, learn how to differentiate credible information from fake news, and how to analyze data for decision-making, your research skills improve. Making decisions, predicting future outcomes, and achieving independence in your

thinking becomes easy. So, when someone presents you with a claim, *e.g., this investment will pay you 20% yearly,* you can do a deep-dive and get the hard facts yourself.

6. **A boost in your career:** With more companies looking for people who apply strategic problem-solving, being a critical thinker is a plus. Being innovative helps you carve out a niche for yourself, regardless of your career choice. So, whether you are a doctor in the ER or a news reporter, your critical thinking skills can get you to the next level.

With all these benefits, one would assume that critical thinking would be ingrained in our schools. But the truth is that most people don't get critical thinking teaching early in their lives. A Paul (2019) study on critical thinking in college classrooms found that 77% of instructors had limited ideas on incorporating this skill into their sessions. Worse still, only 19% could define what critical thinking entailed.

But all is not lost. While you may not have learned critical thinking at a young age or even in school, you can always develop this much-needed skill by relying on the elements of thought in all your decisions. Over time, it becomes like second nature. I'll illustrate this in the next section for some context.

Section 3: Real-World Applications of Critical Thinking

Employer: *We need someone responsible for the job.*

Job Applicant: *Sir, your search ends here! In my previous job, whenever something went wrong, everybody said I was responsible!*

Bad decisions often serve as funny jokes and great life lessons. But each time you make a bad decision, you rob yourself of better opportunities. For example, if you decide to marry someone you do not love just to spite an ex, that's a decision that keeps you from finding the right partner. It's thus essential to be critical in our thinking, even in simple things like choosing beach attire! Here are some practical critical thinking illustrations to consider:

a. **Workplaces**: According to Sharma (2023), the need for critical thinking skills has increased by 150% in the last three years. And it's easy to see why. Critical thinkers are open to new ways of doing things, know how to communicate their ideas, are great at research, and always strive to foster a favorable working environment. *I'll use my example. I handled customer queries about a decade ago when I worked in the banking industry. Customers would come to me, frustrated about their financial statuses. And I, having worked long hours with a poor work-life balance, would take out my burnout on them. Of course, this was not productive - I was acting like a victim yet it was my* *responsibility to help them. Once I saw the error in my ways after digging into Stoicism, I realized I was more pleasant and objective in my customer service. People started seeking me out to help them with challenging customers. I became an asset!*

b. **Social interactions**: Human emotions are complex - psychologists spend their lives trying to help people understand their feelings and actions. But guess what? Critical thinking can also help you navigate social situations with ease. I'll use a common example - passive aggression. Many people use this tactic to communicate displeasure with people in their lives and try to get back at them. For instance, if someone fails to invite you to their party, you may take offense and host a party just to leave them out. But a better way of dealing with the situation would be to communicate your feelings - perhaps your invite got lost in the mail, and the host is angry that you didn't show up!

You can apply critical thinking in many aspects of your life - guiding your children, interacting with your in-laws, chairing the HOA, or even sending back an order at the restaurant. So, how do you become a better critical thinker? It comes down to the following:

1. Consider your sources of information - are they credible?

2. Ask questions - get more information and satisfy your curiosity. For example, if John wants your vote, what makes him different from the other candidates?

3. Assess your bias - do you have justification for your assumptions?

4. Think before you act - use the elements of thought. It also helps to regulate your emotions and avoid making decisions when angry or sad.

5. Seek help - we don't always have the answers, even when the facts are right in front of us. It's okay to ask for help.

Suppose you want to quit your job after a stressful day at work. After assessing your reasons and managing your emotions, you may find that the true motivation behind quitting is your urge to spend more time with your kids, and your work-life balance is off. In such a case, you can consider practical solutions, e.g., negotiating a hybrid working arrangement with your boss. Doesn't that seem more reasonable than throwing in the towel due to frustration?

Key Chapter Takeaways

✓ Herd mentality sways people's thinking and can have positive or negative effects. It's important to assess the factors influencing your decision to avoid getting swept up by such thinking.

✓ Fake news and cognitive biases weaken people's critical thinking, paving the way for herd mentality, which limits good judgment.

✓ Fake news can result from misinformation, disinformation, and mal-information, which we can get from social media, conventional media, and even the people close to us. Cognitive biases hinge on our social setups, emotions, motivations, and ability to process information.

✓ We must assess our news sources and address our biases to rise above herd mentality, as this helps us in our democratic and social responsibilities, e.g., our contributions to leadership, our efforts in climate change advocacy, etc.

✓ Besides global impact, critical thinking is essential in bettering our life satisfaction, helping us make better decisions, improving our social relationships, boosting our careers, refining our research skills, and enhancing our problem-solving.

✓ Being a critical thinker comes down to cultivating a critical mindset and following the elements of thought, as explained in Chapter 1. Later chapters will discuss these elements to a bigger extent.

BONUS OFFER:
ENHANCE YOUR CRITICAL THINKING JOURNEY

As you're delving into the art of critical thinking, I wanted to share some additional resources to further support your journey. These exclusive bonuses are designed to deepen your understanding and application of critical thinking in various aspects of life.

1. How to Teach Kids Critical Thinking

   - Effective strategies and practical tips for instilling critical thinking skills in children. Includes a special exercise to foster inquiry and curiosity.

2. Applying Critical Thinking Skills in Everyday Life

   - Practical tips for integrating critical thinking into daily routines, enhancing problem-solving and decision-making skills.

3. History of Critical Thinking

   - Explore the evolution of critical thinking and its impact on society, featuring a Socratic questioning exercise.

4. The Resilience Handbook

   - Principles from Stoicism and Emotional Intelligence to cultivate resilience and emotional strength.

These bonuses are my way of saying thank you for investing in your cognitive potential. Simply scan the QR code or follow the link provided to access these free resources.

https://personalgrowthpages.com/winston-free-gift

PART 2:
CRITICAL THINKING AS AN INSTRUMENT FOR A BETTER LIFE

Have you ever had road rage? I know that I was once that annoying driver yelling at pedestrians and honking at other drivers in frustration. And I am not alone. Road rage is a common occurrence in most countries, especially in cities. Take the US as an example. According to a Consumer Affairs Report (2023), 92% of Americans witness road rage at least once a year. Of these incidents, honking and gestures account for 32%, cutting other cars off comes at 22%, aggressive driving caters to 26% of incidents, and tailgating averages 34%! And the causes? - stress (38.06%), anger (32.49%), and fatigue (26.86%). The study also found that responding to aggression with more aggression only worsened the incidents.

Is it safe to say that critical thinking would positively impact these statistics? Of course! A critical thinker would care about the safety of other drivers, give way where needed, and remain calm when faced with aggression. And that is just one example of how critical thinking enhances our lives and that of others, which is the key focus of the chapters in this part of the book.

Chapter 3:
Critical Thinking Is A Skill, Not A Talent

"Contrary to popular belief, critical thinking is not an innate gift bestowed upon a select few. Instead, it is a skill that can be cultivated and honed through deliberate practice and education. But how do we debunk the myth of talent and empower individuals to develop their critical thinking abilities?"

A*re leaders born or made?* This essay is so common in colleges everywhere that anyone pursuing a leadership or management course can expect to work on it at some point. I know I did! And while it is a common debate, people disagree on the answer. Some believe that some people are born with natural abilities to lead - but if you follow their lives, you can tell that they had the abilities and opportunities to develop these skills. Think about that kid in class whose parents encouraged them to do everything and take up leadership positions - is it a surprise that they ended up as a CEO? Not quite. In the same way, while some people argue that critical thinking is innate, enough studies have shown that people learn how to be critical thinkers. How about we settle this debate and craft a path that allows us to discover the best versions of ourselves?

Section 1: Dispelling the Myth of Innate Talent

In the *"Are leaders born or made?"* question, the emphasis always comes back to the fact that human beings are the result of their circumstances. Critical thinking is no different - consider the following key influences on people as they grow up:

1. **Teachers**: Many people expect children to learn how to be critical thinkers in school settings. But here's the thing. For teachers to transfer such skills, they must have them and know how to apply them beyond school essays. But that's not all - teachers must remain unbiased. Is this the case? Several studies have proven that teachers not only lack the skills to impart critical thinking to their students but also have biases. Yuan (2023) highlights this and also breaks down how teachers are unable to incorporate critical thinking in their lessons and instead treat it like a separate matter. As such, students cannot contextualize using these skills beyond the classroom. Also on this, a Reboot Foundation Study (2020) shows that most educators lack the training to incorporate critical thinking in their classes. Moreover, there is bias, with teachers believing critical thinking only suits students with great abilities!

2. **Parents**: Have you ever noticed that you often tend to lean on the beliefs your parents had when you were growing up? For example, if your parents believed in charity, you might invest a lot in the community. Parental rearing styles don't just influence your life-style - they also affect your cognitive thinking skills. Wang (2020) explores this in a study that shows that learners who come from negative home environments (e.g., controlling parents) often suffer low self-esteem, which translates into a fear of veering from the norm. Yet those raised in loving homes with optimal bonding show more self-awareness and are more likely to think critically. A Huang (2015) study also proved the need for more positive parenting relationships.

Now, to answer our question: ***Is critical thinking innate or taught?*** I will use two illustrations for this.

☆ Mary is born into a loving family where both parents are present and are always keen to help her discover her preferences. From a young age, she learns that she can make good decisions, trust herself to make mistakes, and learn from them. This knowledge increases her confidence, which gets boosted in school, where her teachers encourage her to color outside the box. As you may have guessed, she grows into a critical thinker.

☆ Jane is born into a chaotic family where her father is mostly absent, and her mother is cold and distant. She quickly learns not to make mistakes, as these result in punishments, silent treatment, and getting yelled at. As Jane perfects walking on eggshells at home, her school life is no different. Her teachers are intent on proving their exceptional knowledge and do not allow students to bring up debates where the educators might look unknowledgeable. Unable to confront authorities at home or school, Jane learns to color within the lines and grows up to follow the rules always to be safe.

Of course, other outcomes can result from this, e.g., Jane can have teachers who are critical thinkers who can help her steer her life in another direction. Or Mary could have teachers who work to subdue her curiosity and transform her into another standard student. But no matter how you look at it, these examples and previous research prove that critical thinking is not innate - we learn to be critical thinkers!

So, what happens if you miss out on school and home opportunities to develop critical thinking skills? Here's the fun part: **you can learn to think critically at any age**. While it's challenging to break away from habits as we get older, you can always change the trajectory of your life. You only need the determination to keep learning instead of getting stuck in your ways.

I'll share a close example.

My friend, Bob, worked in the investments section of the bank. He had always wanted this job, having moved from the reception side where he had always complained about the long customer queues and short lunch breaks. So, as much as he described himself as a people person, there was more potential in the investments department as he could rise on the ladder. One would think he'd be over the moon (longer lunch breaks and all), but the joy only lasted a few days. He was soon singing another song - his boss was overwhelming him, the work was too much, and the commute was a challenge. It seemed that no matter what position Bob had, something would always be amiss.

But that was not the only issue - he often ranted on social media about his work, relationships, friends, etc. I eventually talked him into Stoicism. While he was highly reluctant at fast, the self-awareness slowly crept in, and he started holding himself back when he felt like lashing out. He learned to pause and think, question his beliefs and actions, be objective instead of subjective, and consider the impacts of his decisions. Fast forward to today: Bob has made many new friends, is happy about his work position, is back on the dating scene, and is a calming presence to those around him. By thinking critically, he realized that he was accountable for his decisions and that people did not wield as much power over him as he thought - he now has the reins, and it shows!

Did Bob just transform overnight? Not even close. It took him a long time to accept his role in his life's outcomes. But he did - and so can you, as this book will show you!

Section 2: The Science of Skill Acquisition

"Intelligence is what we learn. Wisdom is what we unlearn."

   - J.R. RIM

Here are two words I want you to focus on: **Unlearning** and **Transferability**. Let's start with the latter. Many people learn how to be critical thinkers in the professional or academic spheres.

For example, if you ask a scientist to test a hypothesis, they can do it quite well. But task them with resolving a dispute between two friends, and they are at a loss for what to do. To be a good critical thinker, you must understand how to transfer your skills to different settings - at home, at work, in school, in traffic, at a restaurant, etc. When you think of critical thinking along this line, it becomes easier to conceptualize it in your life.

What about unlearning? Critical thinking requires you to develop intellectual humility, as discussed in Chapter 1. Forget what you think you know and instead question your beliefs, news sources, biases, and more. Only then can you be a critical thinker. For example, if you have always believed that fat-reduced yogurt is the healthiest snack, question this belief. You may find that you only think that because your favorite influencer told you so.

Critical thinking is not something you will learn in a class. Even if a teacher wants to transfer these skills, they can only guide you with scientific facts and processes. The rest of the work will always be up to you as you must get into the habit of pausing, questioning, analyzing, and deciding. So, what's your part?

   a. ***Understand the learning process:*** The basics of learning require you to adopt a new slate and admit that you may not even know what you think you know. Once you get to this point, learning will make sense. After all, why would you learn if you already have the knowledge? Embracing this new slate will allow you to adopt critical thinking and start practicing it so that thinking along this line will feel natural. Of course, it takes a while to move past these stages.

   b. ***Set goals for your learning process:*** As we covered in Chapter 1, critical thinking comprises elements of thought that culminate into sound decisions. You cannot master them at once. Instead, you need to determine what to learn. For example, you may decide to focus on your biases. In such a case, your goals may look like uncovering your biases in week 1, investigating the sources of your biases in week 2, and addressing your biases in week 3. Your goals should be SMART (specific, measurable, achievable, realistic, and timed). For instance, "I will conduct two SWOT analyses per week" is a much more practical goal than "I will become a more analytical thinker." Use exercise 3 in the exercise section to set your goals to help you be more intentional with your skill development.

c. ***Be deliberate with your efforts:*** Setting goals is just one part of the process. You must also invest time to develop the skills. For example, if your goal is to become better at assessing fake news, you will likely need to read more papers and review more social media posts. Continuously doing this creates the habits that eventually allow you to master even more complex critical thinking skills.

d. ***Be open to mistakes:*** Many people confuse criticism for conflict. Others consider mistakes to be tied to their identities. A huge part of critical thinking is self-compassion and allowing yourself to venture into different ways of thinking without worrying about failing. Sometimes, someone will point out the error in your logic - consider their arguments and use the elements of thought to assess them. If they are correct, accept the valuable feedback and use it to broaden your learning process.

Can anyone become a critical thinker? We've already covered the "Are leaders born or made?" debate. But what about chess players? Are they naturally talented, or do they put in the work to become good at the game? Many people have always thought that this is a game that requires innate talent. However, per an Allen (2014) study, László and Klara Polgár did not - at a time when society deemed women as limited in spatial thinking, they believed they could teach their daughters to be good players. Polgár, a psychologist, had studied geniuses and was convinced that talent did not exist. Instead, he believed in ***education and training***. Together with Klara, he worked on unlocking the potential in his children by taking on something many people thought was impossible - excelling in chess. Their work paid off as all their daughters ended up ranking among the top female chess players in the world, with one earning the grandmaster title by age 15!

In the same way, you can learn to be a critical thinker if you trust the process and put in the work. The rest of the book will now focus on the elements of thought, guiding you through each process to help you be more deliberate in your learning so you can unlearn the impediments to critical thinking and open your mind to more rational approaches.

Key Chapter Takeaways

✓ Critical thinking is not an innate skill, as many people may think. Instead, it stems from our conditioning from our experiences at home and school. Several studies have shown that parents and teachers strongly impact children's critical thinking - learners from positive environments are more likely to think critically.

✓ While you may not have learned critical thinking earlier in your life, you can embrace rational decision-making processes by embracing the critical thinking elements of thought.

✓ To do this, you must be willing to start from the bottom and question even things you thought you knew. You must also be conscious about your goals, determine how to practically learn the elements of thought, and be open to feedback. Doing this enables you to introduce a more rational way of thinking, getting you closer to becoming a great critical thinker.

Chapter 4:
The Art Of Asking Questions

"The important thing is not to stop questioning."

    - ALBERT EINSTEIN.

Studies show that children between the ages of 2 and 5 can ask as many as 300 questions a day. However, once they join a formal school, their curiosity often falls so much that some teachers report that some students ask about one question every two hours. Why does this happen? First, by the time kids start school, they are bombarded with so much information to remember that their brains can barely keep up with more questioning. Secondly, some teachers and parents get so fed up with the questions that they start subduing children who show too much curiosity - let's not forget that some adults are so worried about having their authority questioned that they will not entertain a curious child. And thirdly, children develop a fear of being laughed at. If you've ever had people snicker when you asked a question, you can understand how it can induce anxiety. When all these factors are combined, many people put questioning to the side, eager to fit into the mold that society deems ideal.

But guess what? The question is the answer - every time you hold back on questioning something, you deprive yourself of the chance to acquire knowledge. We look at the importance of asking questions and challenging assumptions and how you can question authorities constructively.

Section 1: The Power of Inquiry

When I was growing up, adults had all the power. My parents drummed this into my siblings and me any way they could - Bible teachings, a few pinches here and there, reprimanding looks - you know, the works. It got to a point where if an adult told you to do something, you'd do it out of fear of getting into trouble, no matter how ridiculous it felt. At some point, I'm sure I was ferrying drugs for a neighbor, but since adults were always right, I could not snitch on her! I am just lucky that none of these adults ever took advantage of me (save for those suspicious neighborly packages).

As a parent, I have taught my children to question everyone, including us, and not just to follow the rules just because someone said so. Even the government is not always right, nor is the church, nor are their teachers - nobody has all the answers. It's up to my children to keep questioning.

But isn't questioning everything exhausting and annoying to the people being questioned? Well, the benefits outweigh the costs. Consider the following upsides with corresponding examples:

1. **It clarifies your thoughts:** Suppose you're curious about your job role and have been juggling various tasks, unsure what applies to you. Asking your boss for a clear breakdown would save you a lot of time.

2. **It improves communication:** Assumptions are some of the biggest impediments to good relationships. Let's assume your friend has been lying low. Do you assume they are ignoring you, or do you call them to find out how they are doing?

3. **It makes you curious**: In Chapter 1, I highlighted the need for questioning to nurture curiosity. If you are always asking questions about things that interest you, curiosity and knowledge will come naturally, enabling you to be more competent in that area.

4. **It eliminates confusion**: Doubt clouds your judgment, and getting concrete answers can help you move forward with many decisions. Say, for example, that you are not sure what pairs well with merlot. You can experiment and shock your guests, or you can ask someone who has the answer.

5. **It makes you a better leader:** In the past, leaders were thought to be all-knowing. But we know better now. Good leaders acknowledge their shortcomings and are always eager to ask questions that can help them explore new ideas - filling in those knowledge gaps is much better than protecting your ego.

6. **It makes you more confident:** You have two choices. You can hope you have the right answers, even though they might be based on bias. Or you can ask questions and get the information you need to make objective decisions.

7. **It streamlines the elements of thought:** Before you can start analyzing data, you must collect it. And how do you do this? How can you calculate the ROI (Return on Investment) of a project when you don't know how much it will cost or the projected income?

8. **It encourages innovation**: When you question, it's easy to see the obvious gaps. For example, when Alexander Fleming found that mold had somehow killed the bacteria in his lab, he questioned the source of the fungus and how it had acted on the bacteria. And without these questions, penicillin would likely still be a dream!

Also, if you never ask questions, you can't learn. And without learning, you cannot unlearn, which is the basis of becoming a critical thinker.

How Should You Ask Questions?

"Why did swear words get invented if we're not allowed to say them?"

- A CHILD SOMEWHERE.

While kids can get away with asking almost anything, critical thinkers need to be more strategic with their questions. Let's consider the types of questions you can ask and why:

a. *Close-ended questions*: These are great for fact-finding as they allow you to get short and concrete answers. E.g., did you enjoy the cocktail?

b. *Open-ended questions*: Unlike close-ended questions that elicit "yes or no" answers, these questions offer more detailed responses, e.g., why did you choose to become a lawyer?

c. *Probing questions:* These are common in research as they allow you to get more thoughtful responses - they are often used after open-ended questions. For example, once you ask someone why they became a lawyer, they might answer that they wanted to change the judicial system. A probing question would look something like this, "Can you give examples of steps you have taken to achieve this goal?"

d. *Reflective questions:* These allow you to introspect and become more self-aware. For example, when questioning your biases, you may ask, "What aspects of your past influenced these biases?"

It's best to focus on questions, allowing your respondents to share their honest opinions. Your tone also matters, as do your listening skills. Be gentle, show genuine interest, and give people time to reconcile their thoughts. Also, avoid leading questions, e.g., "Don't you think the iPhone is the best phone in the world?" Such questions often guide people to answer in one way by introducing bias.

How to Develop Effective Questioning Strategies

Do bad questions exist? Imagine if someone walked into your convenience store and asked you, "What do you sell?" You'd likely be stumped, unsure if they wanted you to walk them through what you stocked in each aisle. In the same way, you must be strategic with your questioning to get practical answers, as follows:

1. **Determine what you want to know:** Always start with a goal. For example, we will assume you want to buy a house in California and are meeting a realtor. Your questions should align with this goal.

2. **Decide which questions you will ask**: Your goal will influence the categories of questions that will be most impactful. For example, your questions can look like this:

   → How much is a 3 bed 2 bath home in West Covina?

   → What are the square footage ranges, and how do these relate to the prices?

   → How many options do you have in your brokerage?

   → What would you advise a home buyer to do in this market?

   Combining different question categories is the best option in some cases. But, you should limit close-ended questions as they do not encourage dialogue.

3. **Find the right person to answer your questions:** The source of your answers matters as it influences the credibility and objectivity of the information. Consider this: *My friend, who is in her late forties, was curious about IVF treatments, so she set up an appointment with an OBGYN. Right off the bat, the OBGYN was very obvious about her stance on older mothers and tried to dissuade my friend from getting IVF treatments. Interestingly enough, her concerns were about how society feels about older parenting rather than my friend's medical status. And it was not long before my friend realized this was implicit ageism.* My friend is not alone. Ageism, as explained by Cavaliere and Fletcher (2021), is a significant source of bias in the reproductive health sector and

continues to affect people over 35. As such, her choice of OBGYN, who had already chosen a side, was not a reliable respondent. So, how can you ensure your respondents offer unbiased and practical answers? Consider these factors:

- **Knowledgeability:** Does the person understand the subject matter? For instance, an experienced realtor would be a good choice when buying a home in California.

- **Trustworthiness:** It's always good to vet your respondents by getting reviews from people around them. For example, if a realtor is known to focus on commissions rather than helping clients find suitable homes, they will likely have biased answers.

- **Vested interests (motivations):** What does your respondent stand to gain from your interactions? A realtor may want to point you to some homes because of their high commissions or may fail to warn you about a looming market crisis because they want a sale.

- **Values:** Finding someone who shares the same goals as you can help you get more objective answers. For example, if a realtor believes in buying homes that can serve as investment properties and you'd like this, they will be better positioned to help you compared to someone who does not view home ownership in this light.

You can apply the same principles in other situations. *For example, who should you trust if you want to apply for a position in a company? Will the CEO be more likely to give you unbiased answers, or can you get this information from a current employee? What about a former employee who left the company to start their own?* You always have to question your sources.

4. **Pose the questions:** When questioning someone, you should be ready to give them time to consider their answers. Practice active listening and do not rush or interrupt them. Even if you have a follow-up question, wait until they are done talking; otherwise, it appears rude and can negatively impact your discussion. Be open to asking more questions based on the answers. For instance, if the realtor advises you to invest in a home in Pasadena instead, it would be a great idea to get the reasoning behind this.

5. **Assess the answers:** This last part ties in with the third point. As I have emphasized in this book, human beings are subject to bias. As such, you should pay attention to how your respondents react to questions. For example, if the realtor scoffs at the idea of buying a home in West Covina but does not have any facts to back this up, you can identify possible bias. By really listening to what your respondents say and watching their non-verbal cues, you can understand their perspectives and determine if they should play a part in your decisions.

How many people should you question? It depends on the goal. Say you want to buy a home - that is a big deal, and you should get as much data as you can, hence the need to question multiple realtors. But if your goal is to prepare a charcuterie board for three friends, one food enthusiast might be the answer!

Section 2: Questioning Assumptions

"Remember, we see the world not as it is but as we are. Most of us see through the eyes of our fears and our limiting beliefs and our false assumptions."

- ROBIN S. SHARMA

We live in a world where people make assumptions about others. And as I mentioned in the elements of thought, they play a role in our decision-making. Some assumptions are okay as they do not impede critical thinking - but others are not as they are not based on logic and can thus weaken an argument. So, how do you gauge your assumptions?

1. **List your assumptions**: Suppose you are on a weight loss journey. Think about all the things you have assumed and pen them down, e.g., You should avoid dairy because it is high in saturated fat - we will use this in our breakdown.

2. **Analyze your assumptions**: In this assumption, the assumption is that dairy is high in saturated fat, and that's why you should avoid it. Question this reason, e.g.,

   → What happens when people eat saturated fat?

   → How does saturated fat affect weight loss?

   → How much saturated fat does milk contain?

   → What is the saturated fat limit per current studies?

   → Does milk exceed the research quotas?

   → Are you eating other foods that have saturated fat?

   → Should you also avoid them?

3. **Evaluate your reasons**: You must test the strength of your argument. Does research support your argument? Has your doctor raised any concerns over your health status? Are you basing your decision on credible facts? You might find that you only avoid milk because a well-meaning friend told you it was bad for weight loss.

4. **Find conflicting ideas**: We live in a world where information is available at the tap of a button. Look for studies that contradict your assumption. E.g., have any studies pointed out the benefits of saturated fat? Do the benefits of drinking milk outweigh your concerns?

I won't tell you if this assumption is correct and will instead task you to challenge it. As a bonus, exercise 4 in the exercises section helps you identify and challenge your assumptions so you can avoid asking biased questions and instead be critical in your questioning.

Section 3: Questioning Authority

"Nothing strengthens authority so much as silence."

- LEONARDO DA VINCI.

I have always encouraged my children to question those in power. But I do not expect them to be naysayers just for the sake of it. So, what's the correct way to question authority?

1. **Understand the role of authority:** Authority comes in many forms - your boss at work, your research supervisor, your parents, your HOA head, etc. It also comes through professions - for example, a doctor is an authority in a hospital just as much as your mechanic is the authority in the auto shop. These people are in these positions as they are deemed to know what's right. For example, by the time a university places someone as your research supervisor, that person has the qualifications for the job. Approaching authority from this perspective enables you to respect their role.

2. **Review the gap in the authority:** While authority is essential, it's important to ensure that your actions are justifiable. Take the Milgram Experiment, as highlighted by Mcleod (2023). This study followed an interesting case which involved a Nazi war criminal whose defense was *"he was just following orders."* Many scientists sought to find out just how far people would go to conform with their leaders. In Milgram's case, people were actually willing to shock others electrically! Along this line, suppose your boss asks you to pick up their child after school and bring them to the office, yet you are not friends, and your job role is a receptionist. Should you go ahead with the unusual task to please your boss, or should you review the workplace policies?

3. **Fight the fear**: The reason most people don't question authority is because they don't want conflict. Think about questioning your barber or hairdresser - does it feel comfortable? Discomfort

aside, people also fear looking stupid or going through the motions of getting to the gap in the authority's reasoning. For example, if a plumber suggests that you need to change some pipes, you might feel that the cost of the task is so low that you shouldn't bother asking why it's necessary.

4. **Consider your perspective:** People often want to appear knowledgeable, so much so that they may ignore a wrong authority just to fit in with the crowd. In the same way, you may question an authority just because others are doing it. It is thus important to consider the angle from which you are approaching the authority. If you are doing it to provide constructive criticism and spearhead positive changes, you are on the right track. But if you are doing it out of bias or negative emotions, you could be wrong. Take the example of a boss who implements time stamps to allow people to get overtime for extra hours. You might oppose the idea just because you know you don't qualify for the hours or don't like the boss.

5. **Review your approach**: Assume you find a gap in the authority and determine that you have good intentions. How should you present your concerns? Some people go on smear campaigns. E.g., instead of telling your HOA head that a ban on fences might not be practical, you could hold small meetings where you talk ill of them to turn people against the idea. But we all know this only worsens situations as it sets the pace for conflict. The best way to approach someone is to lead with good intentions. Find a suitable time and platform to discuss the issue with them, question their approach, and highlight your concerns. For example, if your boss insists on using the income approach for an appraisal and you think the cost approach is much more suitable, explain this to them respectfully and back up your opinions with research. Allow them to counter, and together, you can come up with a practical solution. That works much better than criticizing their approach with your colleagues.

Is questioning authorities all rainbows and unicorns? Hardly. People in power are often used to getting their way, and your questioning, while respectful, might be met with hostility. In such cases, you should weigh your options. Should you continue with this possibly detrimental trajectory, or should you remove yourself from this position? For example, *if your boss does not take well to criticism and often lashes out at people who offer their two cents, you'd be between a rock and a hard place. Or if the authority in question is a mob leader, do you truly want to stand out as the opposition?* Critical thinking requires you always to assess your decisions' implications, as explained in the elements of thought. We will get more into analytical thinking and decision-making in the next chapters.

Key Chapter Takeaways

✓ Critical thinking requires you to ask questions. Only then can you expand your knowledge, foster your curiosity, improve your relationships, and enhance the quality of your life.

✓ When asking questions, consider the type of question that is ideal. For example, open-ended questions encourage people to share their opinions without feeling limited in what they can say.

✓ Strategic questioning is integral to getting practical answers that can inform our decision-making. To do this, you must determine what you want to learn, figure out the right questions to ask, and find someone qualified to provide you with those answers. Active listening is crucial if you are to create a favorable environment for your respondents.

✓ Assumptions can affect our questioning positively or negatively. It is thus important to identify and challenge them to ensure they benefit our questioning processes and do not close our eyes to biases.

✓ While questioning authority can be daunting, it beats following the crowd. Critical thinkers must assess their intentions behind questioning authorities, how to do it right, and when not to go ahead with questioning.

Chapter 5:
The Power Of Logic

"Logic will get you from A to Z; imagination will get you everywhere."

- ALBERT EINSTEIN.

Years ago, my wife posed a very interesting question in our home. She'd just come from an HOA meeting where members had disagreed about allowing a potential neighbor to move into the neighborhood. The man in question, who I'll refer to as "Nick" for anonymity, was the son of an investor who had just been found guilty of fraud. It was all over the news, and while Nick had a clean record, the HOA chair was against accepting his application. The chair was convinced that since Nick's father was a criminal, so was he! Of course, this had resulted in a rift, with people taking different sides to the issue. Was the HOA chair logical in her approach?

If answering this question feels difficult, you are not alone. Many people have difficulty justifying arguments as they do not know what qualifies as a good argument. This chapter explores the concept of logic, why it is important, and how you can use it when making decisions:

Section 1: Introduction to Logic

Logic is the ability to draw conclusions or make predictions based on existing knowledge. Back to the HOA meeting - *Would you have supported the chair's argument?* Per logical form, she was on a roll. She probably got many people to side with her by showing a relationship between her premise and conclusion. Here is her perspective:

> *Criminal tendencies run in families.*
> *Nick's father is a criminal.*
> *So, Nick is also likely to be a criminal.*

She had drawn a conclusion based on research findings on the heredity of criminality and the news about Nick's father. However, as critical thinking teaches, that is not enough, and critical thinkers must know how to differentiate between good and bad reasons to believe in or support something.

So, what makes a good argument? It must:

- *have good logical form,*

- *be based on a true premise,*

- *reach a correct conclusion, and*

- *be free of fallacies.*

Interestingly, an argument may have a true premise and follow good logical form, yet its conclusion is illogical. In the same way, a conclusion may be logical, yet the premise and form are incorrect. Here is an example:

> *All men love football. Joe is a man.*
> *Therefore, Joe loves football.*

Do all men love football? Not at all. So, while it may turn out that Joe actually loves football, this conclusion is based on an **incorrect premise**. And if we go back to criminal tendencies, it's clear that the supporting research *is not enough to predict criminality* in subsequent generations (Baschetti, 2008). So, when an argument fails in one of the key reasoning aspects, critical thinkers should be wary about accepting it.

But why is assessing arguments so important in critical thinking?

1. *It makes it easier to understand what is likely probable or true.* For example, Nick's father's choices have no bearing on Nick as the effects of criminality genes have often been overshadowed by social environments.

2. *It helps you uncover false beliefs that may be clouding your judgment.* For example, if you have stereotypes about gender, career, etc., logical arguments can help you uncover them.

3. ***It enables you to realize when someone is trying to manipulate you through faulty arguments*** - I will cover this under fallacies.

We've already covered how to assess premises. But how can you judge **logical flow**? You'd first need to understand how different types of reasoning work, as follows:

a. **Deductive reasoning**: This type of reasoning follows a top-down approach and relies on general assumptions. From here, you must apply logic to reach a conclusion such that ***if the premise is correct, the conclusion will be logical***. However, the conclusion will be invalid or illogical if the premise is incorrect. Here are two examples showing logical and illogical conclusions based on this approach.

   - *All dogs have ears. Bulldogs are dogs. Therefore, bulldogs have ears.* This conclusion is correct as the premise is also correct.

   - *Snakes are poisonous. The milk snake is a snake. Therefore, the milk snake is poisonous.* While the conclusion follows the correct inferential process, it is illogical as the premise is false - ***not all snakes are poisonous***.

Since deductive reasoning starts with assumptions, it is not foolproof, as people can make wrong assumptions.

b. **Inductive reasoning**: While deductive reasoning starts with general assumptions to reach a conclusion, inductive reasoning starts with a specific assumption and expands its scope to reach a general conclusion. To do this, you must choose one observation, find patterns that support this observation, and reach a decision. Here are examples.

   - Gary is a brown dog that barks loudly. The brown dogs I have met bark loudly. So, all brown dogs bark loudly.

   - Jane gets tired when she does not drink coffee. Coffee is an addictive drink. Jane is addicted to coffee.

While the premises may be true in inductive reasoning, ***the conclusions can still be false***. For example, Jane being tired does not mean she has developed a coffee addiction - she could have an ailment affecting her energy levels. As such, ***the observations must be complete*** for inductive conclusions to be correct.

Abductive reasoning: This kind of reasoning requires you to reach a conclusion with incomplete information. Here are examples:

- My shirt feels tight on my skin. It was not this tight last month. I must have gained weight.

- My daughter is usually home by 6 pm. It is now 7 pm. She must be in traffic.

This kind of reasoning thus relies on your best guess based on the information available. Doctors often use this reasoning when they have limited data about a patient's symptoms.

Here's a breakdown of how these types of reasoning work:

- *Deductive*: *All dogs have ears. A bulldog is a dog. A bulldog has ears.*

- *Inductive*: *A bulldog is a dog. A bulldog has ears. All dogs have ears.*

- *Abductive*: *All dogs have ears. A bulldog has ears. A bulldog is a dog.*

Do you see the difference? When you understand how logical arguments should flow, it will be much easier to identify when someone is on the wrong track, whether they are doing so intentionally or unintentionally. But that's not all - as explained in the next section, you must also know how to *recognize fallacious arguments*.

Section 2: Logical Fallacies: Pitfalls to Avoid

The HOA chair had good logical form. However, her argument had the following glaring issues - *the premise was questionable, the conclusion was also questionable due to the premise's questionability, and her argument had* an evident *correlation/ causation fallacy*. Let's discuss that last part. She believed that Nick was automatically a criminal because he was a direct descendant of a fraudster. However, correlation does *not always* equal causation, and there lay the weakness in her argument.

A logical fallacy is an error in reasoning that can weaken or invalidate an argument with logical form and a strong premise. In the HOA chair's case, this weakness was enough for Nick to argue his way into our neighborhood, and he did! After all, children should not be to blame for their parent's mistakes - he got a lot of support from his new neighbors and escaped his father's looming shadow. Of course, this did not bode well for the HOA chair, who had to step down later.

Making logical fallacies during arguments is quite easy, and it is thus essential to understand what they are so you can avoid them and present sound arguments. Here are some common examples:

☆ **The bandwagon fallacy** is the idea that if many people believe something, it must be true. It ties to the herd mentality I covered in Chapter 2. Here's an example: *Many people want to lose weight. Losing weight is a great goal.*

☆ **The anecdotal or empirical fallacy** is when people base arguments on their experiences and assume they apply to everyone. Example: *My girlfriend never eats fruits and is in great health. Fruits are overrated.*

☆ **The false dilemma fallacy** is where someone offers only two options. Yet, more options exist, making it seem like supporting one option results in rejecting the other. As such, it results in black-and-white thinking and can be misleading. Consider this example: *You can either be successful or happy.* It implies that people only have two options, which can be used to manipulate their thinking. Yet it's possible for people to be happy and successful!

☆ **The straw man fallacy** is where someone counters your argument with an unrelated point and avoids your initial argument. Usually, the person doing this does not have a strong counter-argument and thus distorts what you have said and counters that instead. Let's use an example:

- Receptionist: The restaurant has an adult-only setting from 9 pm.

- Visitor: Why are you discriminating against my children?

☆ **The ad hominem fallacy** occurs when someone opposes someone's argument by attacking their personality rather than their argument. This fallacy can be valid where the attack has a bearing on the argument. But where it has no relationship with the initial argument, it is invalid. Here's an example:

- Person 1: We need to encourage carpooling to reduce our carbon footprints.

- Person 2: You are an accountant. What would you know about the environment?

While person 1 has a valid point, person 2's attack has nothing to do with the argument's validity and instead focuses on person 1's career. But what if person 2 answered, *"You live in a big house and fly in a private jet. How can you lead by example?"* In this case, the counterargument would tie to the initial argument even if it centered on person 1's life choices!

Other fallacies include:

☆ *The hasty generalization fallacy* is where people base their arguments on weak evidence that fits their position.

☆ *The burden of proof fallacy* - where people think something is true because there is no opposing evidence.

☆ *The middle ground fallacy* - is where people think the only solution to a problem is the middle ground between two opposing arguments without considering alternative arguments.

☆ *The Texas sharpshooter fallacy* - where people pick evidence that supports their claim and ignore opposing data to justify their premise.

And, of course, there is the *fallacy fallacy*, where someone discredits a claim just because the argument comprises a fallacy. So, how can you identify and counter fallacious reasoning?

1. **Consider the premise**: Does it appeal to facts or emotions? Is the data sufficient and accurate to support the reasoning? Is the argument trying to divert your attention from the real issues? Can you verify the findings? Are the sources credible?

   Take this argument as an example. *If you don't get home insurance, you could end up broke and homeless.* It appeals to fear and is thus not focusing on facts but rather your emotions.

2. **Review the choices**: Does the argument limit the number of options? Could there be alternatives to this argument? Is the comparison correct?

   Look at this argument: *Either we pass this bill, or people will riot in the street.* It creates a false dilemma by presenting two options, yet other choices exist.

3. **Consider the logic flow**: The proof and the conclusion should be directly linked. Can you find it? Is it justifiable?

   Example: *My husband developed the flu after getting a yellow fever vaccination. So, the vaccine is to blame.* This argument does not consider other possible causes of flu and confuses correlation with causation.

If you spot such gaps in arguments, the best option is to explain the fallacy using another example to help the audience understand this shortcoming. You must also present sufficient and credible data highlighting your stance. For example, *suppose someone argues that all American Indians are great spellers because 5 out of the 7 winners in the last competition were American Indians.* In that case, you can point out the hasty generalization by using a similar example. But you'd also need to explain what this fallacy entails and why basing an argument on one competition would be illogical.

Exercise 5 helps you become a great fallacy detective so you can point them out more easily in arguments.

Section 3: Constructing Valid Arguments

Logic focuses on reaching a conclusion or predicting an outcome based on existing knowledge. For example, *Coffee contains caffeine. Caffeine is a stimulant. So, drinking coffee can have stimulating effects.* On the other hand, arguments focus more on compelling people to accept an idea. To do this, an argument must comprise the following:

1. **The claim**: This is the statement regarding what you think people should do.

2. **The reason:** This is the justification for the statement.

3. **The support** is the evidence behind the claim, e.g., testimonies and statistics.

4. **Warrants**: This is the inference that links the support and the claim and is usually assumed.

Without evidence, an argument becomes an opinion. As such, you must introduce credible evidence compelling enough for the audience to consider. Let's see this as an example.

- *Claim*: *People who want to lose weight should eat less food.*

- *Reason*: *Eating less food results in a calorie deficit, which forces the body to use stored energy sources, resulting in weight loss.*

- *Support*: *Statistics show that people who reduce their calorie intake by 3500 calories a week lose up to one pound of fat per week. (Kim, 2020)*

With this structure, it's easy for people to understand your premise (as it has credible support), logical flow, and conclusion, which helps them consider your argument. So, how can you present such sound arguments?

1. **Research the topic you want to cover and ensure you understand it well enough**. Focus on all sides of the argument and review credible sources of information. Doing this prepares you for opposing arguments and helps you understand how to counter them. *For example, if you want to convince your partner to move to a better school district, you would research the benefits of such a move and the best options.*

2. **Present your claim to your audience**. Compile strong supporting points and communicate them to your audience. Back to our example, *you can outline the statistics in good school districts and how these compare to your current neighborhood.* Start with your premise and bolster it with

relevant and credible sources that can support your claim. Doing this shows you have taken the time to review the issue.

3. **Focus on a shared concern**: Why should your audience care about what you're saying? *Take the example of moving to a better school district - think of good reasons that can resonate with your partner.* Show them how this issue impacts them by introducing emotional benefits or factual information. For example, *moving to this better district also helps your partner get nearer to their favorite gym.*

4. **Allow feedback**: Even if you have researched and presented a valid argument, you should not expect people to agree flat-out. Allow people to counter your argument. If they do so with fallacies, be prepared to identify and explain the gaps in their arguments. Also, be ready for opposing arguments or alternatives you may not have considered - be open to them and consider whether they are good arguments by reviewing their premises, flows, and conclusions. Doing this allows you to qualify your argument and foster a good relationship with your audience.

Are you ready to practice? Use the above steps to formulate an argument and present it to someone in your circle. Do they find it compelling? Can they spot gaps in your reasoning? Can you defend your position? It takes a while to become great at this. But by continuously backing your reasoning with facts, you can become a compelling speaker who people can turn to for rational discussions.

You also need to be aware of cognitive biases, which can creep into our arguments. The next chapter will cover these, showing you how to remain objective even when you are invested in the outcome of an argument.

Key Chapter Takeaways

- ✓ Logic is the ability to review existing knowledge and base conclusions or predictions on it. For an argument to qualify as good, it must be based on a true premise, have good logical form, be free of fallacies, and reach a correct conclusion.

- ✓ The correctness of a premise relies on the data on which it is based. For example, if a premise is based on a stereotype, the conclusion will likely be false, e.g., all Italians eat pasta daily.

- ✓ Logical form follows different approaches, with the fundamental options being deductive, inductive, and abductive. For example, deductive reasoning starts with an assumption and uses logical flow to reach a conclusion. Example: All female birds lay eggs. Peahens are female birds. So, peahens lay eggs.

✓ Fallacies are errors in reasoning that can result from generalizations, insufficient data, cognitive biases, emotional reasoning, and other factors that invalidate or weaken arguments. For example, someone can argue that all girls like poetry, which is a bandwagon fallacy.

✓ Critical thinkers must understand how to assess arguments based on these individual aspects. Doing so enables them to uncover false beliefs, separate what's true from what's not, and realize when someone is trying to manipulate their thinking. They must also know how to construct sound arguments with credible claims, adequate verifiable support, and justifications.

✓ In the next chapter, we will focus on cognitive biases and how these, too, play a part in logical arguments.

Chapter 6:
Recognizing And Overcoming Cognitive Biases

"It's not at all hard to understand a person; it's only hard to listen without bias."

- Criss Jami.

In Chapter 4, I broke down the components of a logical argument. It seems easy enough, does it not? After all, you only need to review the credibility of the premise, the flow of logic, the justification, and the conclusion. But that's not enough. Even when the facts are right before you, refuting them *only* because of underlying bias is possible.

Bias, a distortion in judgment, is not an individual problem - it affects everyone! In 2015, scientists from Okayama University released a study highlighting the impact of cognitive biases on crucial industry accidents. From their analyses, they could gauge that optimistic bias and loss aversion accounted for irrational behavior (despite adequate training) that often resulted in accidents. They thus argued for an emphasis on cognitive bias awareness (Murata et al., 2015). In another study by Berthet (2022), research findings showed that cognitive biases influenced decision-making in management, finance, law, and medicine. Of the key biases, overconfidence ranked high, especially among managers and CEOs who often took risks based on self-importance. Many other studies have also highlighted the influence of cognitive biases on our decisions, showing that our minds are not as rational as we think.

But here is the thing - bias is not inherently good or bad. What it influences is what informs its suitability in decision-making. For example, if you have an adaptive bias that makes you prefer sandwiches over burgers, that does not harm anyone and is just a preference that makes eating out easier. But if you have a maladaptive bias that pushes you to accept people similar to you and shun different people, this thinking is logically fallacious.

This chapter will explore why we develop cognitive biases, some of the most common biases, how we can be aware of our biases, and ways to mitigate their impact. Does this mean you will finally be *free of bias?* Not at all. We can never eliminate all our biases as we have developed them due to natural selection. The best we can do as critical thinkers is understanding what may distort our thinking and learn how to manage these barriers to logic.

Section 1: Understanding Cognitive Biases

Sometimes, people confuse cognitive biases with logical fallacies, but they are different. —A logical fallacy, as covered in Chapter 5, results from an error in a logical argument. However, cognitive bias is an error in our thinking that results from our brain's need to simplify information.

Think about it like this. Every day, an adult makes about 35,000 decisions (Reill, 2023). It's thus natural that the brain would try to simplify decision-making by developing rules of thumb that speed up the process, e.g., *pizzas taste better than burgers.* Unfortunately, this can lead to cognitive biases - consider some examples:

☆ **Action bias** is the tendency to prefer action over inaction even when there is no rationale for this or even when the better option is to do nothing or wait. For example, *an investor may sell all their stock when the price starts falling instead of researching the reasons for the dips and waiting to see what will happen.*

☆ **Anchoring bias** is the tendency to rely on the initial information we get and use it as an anchor for our decisions, even when exposed to new information. *Suppose a fitness trainer starts by showing you all the hard fitness plans that seem impossible to follow. Then they show you moderate ones. The moderate ones will seem doable since you will use the hard plans as an anchor.*

☆ **Attentional bias** happens when we focus on some elements and ignore others - it results from our limited attention capacity such that we pick what applies to our needs and beliefs. *For example, when you are hungry, you will likely focus more on food-related words and images than* *other topics.* In the same way, a scent or sound can remind you of an emotion you felt, e.g., sadness, and influence how you respond to a situation.

☆ **Confirmation bias** is the drive to focus on information that aligns with our beliefs and avoid or ignore what does not. People often do this to confirm their opinions and protect themselves from opposing views. *For instance, if you think that a keto diet is the best option for weight loss, you might only follow social media accounts that reiterate this thinking.*

☆ **Extrinsic incentive bias** is where we think other people are out to benefit themselves rather than help others or gain self-development skills. It hinges on cynicism and general mistrust. Example: *A social media user may assume that a social media influencer is only in it for the money and likes rather than to forge social connections with others.*

☆ **Hindsight bias**, also known as the "knew-it-all-along" effect, is the tendency to assume that we could have predicted an unpredictable event. It results from misremembering the past, assuming the past event was inevitable, and assuming we could have foreseen it. Take the example of *investors saying they could have predicted that a company's stocks would increase in value after the effect.*

☆ **Negativity bias** stems from the push to focus on negative rather than good things. Scientists have shown that this results from the significant impact of negative things. For example, *many people often consider the news to be full of negative stories as they have developed biases due to their experiences with dark stories.*

I could explore more examples. But here is the thing - by 2023, scientists had uncovered over 200 cognitive biases (Reill, 2023)! So, rather than explore all of them, I will use the common ones in the examples, underpin their sources, and show you how you can better identify them and mitigate their effects.

How Did We Become Biased?

"If there's something you really want to believe, that's what you should question the most."

- Penn Jillette.

Biases make our lives easier to a large extent. Take the ***actor-observer bias*** as an example. In this reasoning, people blame others for their shortcomings, e.g., *"I was late for a meeting because my wife forgot to wake me up."* And when accountability is off the table, justifying the wrongdoing becomes easy.

Well, biases like these don't just pop up. They result from the following influences:

a. **Our limited capacity to process information**: Since our brains process a lot of information, they make it easier to draw inferences by presenting subsets of all the information. Take the *false consensus effect* as an example, where people think that most of the population agrees with them on controversial topics. *E.g., you may think a certain politician is popular because you often interact with friends and family with similar beliefs, and your brain will use these discussions to inform this bias.*

b. **Our relationships with others:** We tend to favor people we connect with, e.g., our friends and families. Consider *in-group bias*, aka in-group favoritism, where people treat those in their group better than those who are not. This reasoning stems from social identity theory, which states that people identify more with their group members even if the grouping is random. *For example, you may feel more inclined to befriend someone who supports your favorite football team than someone who supports an opposing team.*

c. **Our motivations**: What we believe informs our decisions often and can result in bias. **Belief perseverance**, also called conceptual conservatism or the backfire effect, is a good example. It shows that some people rely on their initial information to make decisions, even when exposed to opposing credible information. It relates to confirmation bias and the need to defend our egos. *Take the Royal Mail Ship (RMS) Titanic, for instance. Many people thought this ship was unsinkable. So, when evidence of potential structural vulnerabilities emerged, they ignored it as it did not align with their beliefs.*

d. **Our need to conform**: We are back to herd mentality yet again. Remember the bandwagon fallacy from Chapter 5? There is a **bandwagon effect** in cognitive biases, which is our urge to adopt behaviors that many other people have. People do this to fit in and to be on the winning side. *For example, assume all your friends join the local gym to get fitter. You might feel the need to also join the gym without fully thinking about why you're doing it and how it aligns with your goals.* Oh, and here's an interesting one - *most doctors started using tonsillectomies on their patients due to the popularity of the procedures despite the lack of adequate scientific support for this move!*

And finally, there is the issue of our age. I strive to avoid the *"you can't teach old dogs new tricks"* thinking. However, as science has shown, aging reduces cognitive flexibility, which pushes people to get stuck in their ways. But that's not to say you cannot learn new things - you just need to unlearn your biases. Why, though?

Section 2: The Effects of Cognitive Biases

Do cognitive biases have considerable effects? Let's use **social norms** as an example - this bias pushes us to conform to societal norms. E.g., *if people often welcome neighbors with fruit baskets in your neighborhood, you might find yourself curating such a basket when someone moves in next door.* It seems harmless enough. But here is the thing - our tendency to conform can hold us back from taking action when we should. For instance, *if people are often mean to one of your colleagues for no reason, you might hold back from defending them even when you think it's the right thing to do.*

Let's consider other ways cognitive biases affect our worlds and the lives of the people around us:

1. **Decision-making**: Critical thinking hinges on reviewing the information available to us as we follow the elements of thought to make a decision. However, biases affect how receptive we are to the information. Take the **ambiguity effect** as an example - it pushes us to prefer the options we know such that we oppose new information. Or **authority bias**, which encourages us to trust people with authority even when they could be wrong. We can ignore credible information without being aware of our biases because it does not align with our beliefs.

2. **Problem-solving**: To address the challenges we face in life, we must be able to recall incidents well, focus on all sides of the coin, and remain objective. Is this possible with bias? Hardly. Consider **optimism and pessimism biases**. With optimism bias, you automatically think your approach will be successful. And with pessimism bias, you think you are destined to fail. With such thinking, it's difficult to objectively solve a problem as you will already have predicted the outcome and aligned your actions with it. For example, if you think you will fail, you'll likely avoid doing anything to avert a bad outcome, as you will consider your efforts pointless.

3. **Our relationships**: Have you ever met someone and immediately decided how you felt about them even before they said or did anything? You can hold your biases responsible for that, whether positive or negative. For example, the **Benjamin Franklin effect** results in liking someone more after you do them a favor. On the other hand, with the **messenger effect**, you might think that some people are more credible than others based on your perception. By understanding your bias, you can better judge social situations and make more objective decisions rather than letting your biases take the lead.

Unfortunately, these effects trickle down to all aspects of our lives. Consider these examples:

- An interviewee subject to **social desirability bias** (under **response bias**) might offer answers they think will make the interviewer happy, even if they are false.

- An HR manager may refuse to hire someone due to *status quo bias*, insisting on retaining things as they are.

- A new neighbor might misjudge everyone in the neighborhood after experiences with some neighbors due to *survivorship bias*.

- An investor may hold on to a bad investment due to the *sunk cost fallacy* related to loss aversion.

Cognitive biases affect our ability to understand events, people, and information, which impacts our behavior and can get in the way of our critical thinking. It is thus important to identify and assess them whenever they present themselves.

Section 3: Strategies for Overcoming Cognitive Biases

"If you are wearing yellow goggles, every blue thing will appear green to you. It is your perception, and it is your reality."

- NAVED ABDALI.

Not all cognitive biases are bad. In fact, scientists have shown that some biases have positive effects. Consider the *Pygmalion effect,* which occurs when someone expects you to perform well, pushing you to work hard to achieve their expectations. *For example, if your boss thinks you will excel in a presentation, you will likely do so to please them.* On the downside, the Pygmalion effect can overshadow your colleagues, who may react negatively to the differential treatment and feel discouraged from putting in hard work.

Since this can be a double-edged sword, how can we monitor our decision-making biases?

1. **Be aware of your bias:** Nobody is free of bias. As such, no matter how logical you are in your arguments, you must consider that you may have introduced bias in your premise, justification, and conclusion. Unfortunately, identifying bias is not easy as it is not usually evident. You must thus consider the following:

   - How have you chosen your information sources?

   - Are they credible? What makes them credible?

   - Have you ignored some information sources? If so, why?

- What's the basis for your decision? E.g., you might find that you are biased against a researcher because their findings don't align with your beliefs.

2. **Challenge your biases:** Reviewing your information sources and justifications for your arguments will help you understand the basis of your decision. Now is the time to challenge it, as follows:

   - What factors have you considered the most? Why?

   - Which factors have you ignored? Why have you ignored them?

   - Do your justifications hinge on objectivity, or have you introduced bias?

   - For example, you may have focused more on information supporting your thinking, introducing *confirmation bias*.

3. **Get more opinions:** You can seek different approaches from other people or information sources. Note that *groupthink* is also a type of bias, and you should thus ensure you're not just seeking people who agree with you. Aim for diversity and use the questioning techniques we covered in Chapter 4 to get objective and practical answers.

4. **Take your time:** If you have to make a fast decision, your brain will usually rely on cognitive biases, as this is easy. To avoid going down this route, do not rush your decisions. Start by evaluating your information sources before challenging your biases and involving others. Doing this minimizes bias and enables you to make much more practical decisions.

Cognitive bias modification does not happen overnight. Instead, it requires you to keep questioning your motivations and decisions. Exercise 6 in the exercise section helps you continuously critique yourself and learn more about your biases. Use it whenever you have a few minutes to introspect.

Now that you understand the role of biases, the next chapter will focus on objective decision-making to help you be more creative with solutions.

Key Chapter Takeaways

✓ While logical fallacies relate to errors in logical arguments, cognitive biases are errors in our thinking that affect our decision-making.

✓ Cognitive biases affect everyone and result from our limited information processing capacities, relationships with others, motivations, and need to conform.

✓ By 2023, scientists had discovered over 200 cognitive biases! Common ones include action, anchoring, attentional, confirmation, hindsight, negativity, and authority biases.

✓ These biases affect our decision-making, relationships with other people, and problem-solving skills. They can thus affect us in different aspects of our lives, including at home and work, robbing us of opportunities, e.g., where you fail to apply for a good job just because you have a pessimism bias.

✓ Identifying and challenging our biases helps us be more effective when going through the elements of thought and enables us to accept logical arguments even when they don't align with our beliefs. Exercise 6 sheds more insights on how you can do this to get ahead of your biases.

Chapter 7:
Solve Any Problem With Reason

"Every problem is a gift — without problems, we would not grow."

- TONY ROBBINS.

Most innovations we have today started as problems. Take paper currency as an example. Before people started exchanging notes for goods, they relied on barter trade. A person would come with vegetables and trade them for precious coins, metals, or even livestock. But it wasn't all rosy. Coin shortages and challenges in determining raw material values often deterred efficient trades. Then, someone had the bright idea of paper currency, which not only eased trade but also enabled governments to regulate money. Plus, it paved the way for efficient electronic banking systems today!

This chapter focuses on helping you use your problems to elevate your life. Sure, these stumbling blocks might seem like daunting mountains. But with reasonable problem-solving strategies (free of biases), you can get to the other side. Who knows? Your problem could be the catalyst of yet another incredible innovation!

Sub-section 1: Understanding the Problem

A man says to his boss, "Can we talk? I have a problem."

Boss: "Problem? No such thing; we call it an opportunity!"

Man: "Ok, I have a serious drinking opportunity."

A SPANA (2015) survey, which featured 2,000 adults in Britain, found that 90% of the respondents believed that being concerned about small problems was innate in human nature. When asked what problems they faced, many cited runny noses, lack of WIFI access, poor phone signals, late online deliveries, blisters from new shoes, running out of hot water, and forgetting their phone chargers at home. Some even stated that dunking a biscuit in tea and losing part of it was a problem! The survey showed that problems are not the same, and people encounter different life challenges. While one person struggles to pay rent, the other can't find the other end of the cello tape!

As problems are ingrained in our lives, problem-solving skills are integral in critical thinking. When you have these skills, you can:

- Approach the problem logically to assess what's wrong.

- Determine what you should do next based on the cause of the problem.

- Follow through with the decision and assess its effectiveness in addressing the problem. For example, if your problem was a late delivery, you can follow up with the delivery company to understand the delivery status.

- Learn from your decision-making mistakes so you can modify your behavior when a similar problem arises.

Problem-solving thus involves the following steps:

1. Understanding what constitutes a problem.
2. Defining the problem you're facing.
3. Reviewing alternative solutions.
4. Determining the best solution.
5. Implementing the solution.
6. Monitoring the solution's effectiveness. You keep what works and revise what does not.

Problem-solving skills are thus broad and involve analytical and creative thinking. You must be willing to objectively analyze the situation to determine possible solutions, think outside the box for other effective solutions, and confidently implement the strategies you think best suit the problem.

Problems Are Not the Same

Have you ever heard about the Cynefin framework? This model, developed by Snowden & Boone (2007), allows you to categorize your problems and determine the best approach easily. Consider these categories:

1. ***The simple problem (known known):*** This problem has a known solution because the cause and effect are evident. For example, *if your tea gets cold, you can microwave it to warm it.* Such problems are usually easy to solve as they follow a standard process. Even so, you should still analyze the problem to ensure it has not veered from the norm - if the situation has changed, the solution may also need to change. Otherwise, you could approach it with an optimistic bias that could worsen the problem and push it into the disorder or chaotic category.

2. ***The complicated problem (known unknown):*** This problem requires expertise. *For example, when you fall ill, you go to the doctor. They don't know why you are sick but know they can run tests to figure it out and prescribe medication to help you get better.* While experts usually rely on principles and experience, they are also subject to bias, e.g., overconfidence, that can bar them from considering alternative solutions to problems.

3. ***The complex problem (unknown unknown):*** This problem has no known causes or effects. As such, there is no previous process you can rely on, nor do you have expertise in the matter. *Take raising a child as an example. I have three. Sure, I had some experience after raising my first child. However, that did not guarantee success in raising any of them as they are all highly unique individuals.* When dealing with a problem in a dynamic environment where things are always changing, you must be ***creative and try new solutions until you find the one that works***. I have covered this in subsection 4.

4. **The chaotic problem (crisis):** With complex problems, you have time to figure things out. *For example, if your startup is failing, you can always try new ways to boost your revenue, as time might be on your side.* However, with the chaotic problem, you have no time to plan and implement solutions. Take the example of an accident on the highway or a burning building. Such issues escalate so fast that failing to take action can result in drastic effects. In such a case, you must do your best to stay calm and figure out how to transform the chaos into complexity. *For*

example, in an accident, you can call an ambulance as you try to divert the traffic so that nobody else gets hurt. You'd also need to follow the medical team's instructions on handling the injured people before the medics come.

And the last one - **disorder**. This is not exactly a problem. Instead, it refers to a state where you are unsure if a problem exists. If this happens, you must go back to the drawing board (restart the process), review the data, and understand the issue. You might find that it comprises several different aspects, e.g., complex and simple issues. By breaking the problem down, you can solve it gradually and finally address it.

Defining Your Problem

When you know your faucet is leaking, you can fix it or find someone who can fix it. But what if you have no idea why there is water on your floor? You'd likely keep mopping it and get tired without uncovering the cause! So, understanding your problem is **half the solution**.

But how do you do this? Let's use the example of someone gaining a lot of weight.

1. **Get on the "why" train and break down the problem**: To know your problem, you must get to the why. For example, *if you are gaining weight, you'd ask, "Why am I gaining weight?"* If the answer is because you are eating out a lot, you can ask, *"Why am I eating out a lot?"* You'd continue down this path until you got to the root cause. To get better at this, refer to Exercise 7 on the 5 Whys Technique.

2. **Pick out what you know:** Having enough information about a topic is important when defining a problem. *For example, you may compare your average meals to a partner's and realize you eat 1,000 extra calories more than them,* explaining the variation in weight gain. So, what do you know about your problem?

3. **Research what you don't know:** Once you have your opinion and review the knowledge, you must consider what you don't know. You can research credible sources or consult with people who understand the issue. *For example, you may talk to a dietician who can help you understand how your food choices affect your weight.* Chapter 8 discusses analytical thinking to a greater extent and can help you analyze your data to make informed decisions.

You can define your problem from the results, e.g., *"I am gaining weight because I have been so busy at work that I have been eating out most days. Per TDEE (total daily energy expenditure) calculations, my maintenance calories should be about 1,700. But further analysis shows that I consume at least 2,400 calories a day."* Once you do this, you can figure out how to address your problem, as covered in the next section.

Sub-section 2: Problem-Solving Strategies

Since problems differ in complexity, you must review the available solutions and determine what best suits your situation. Consider the strategies below:

a. **Heuristics**: You can solve some problems with formulas, e.g., equations and algorithms. *For example, if you have a cake recipe that serves 4, you can use an equation to determine how to use the same recipe to serve 40 people!* But you cannot use heuristics to determine how to apologize to a friend as there is no standard formula for this.

b. **Trial and error:** Sometimes, the solution to a problem is unclear, and you must try different options to see what works. *For example, if your washing machine won't work and you don't know the cause, you can try plugging it into another socket, checking the drainage, reading the manual for troubleshooting, etc.* Trial and error is a good option when the number of solutions is limited. But if you have many choices, using another problem-solving strategy is the better option.

c. **Means-end analysis**: In this strategy, you compare where you are and where you want to be. *Say you want to launch a website in one month and don't even have a domain name. You'd need to consider what you need to do to get what you want, e.g., find a good hosting site, figure out a name, determine a theme, work on your blog, etc.* Doing this also helps you understand the obstacles you will face and figure out ways you will address them, e.g., what happens if someone else owns the domain name you pick?

d. **Working backward:** Instead of starting with the solution, you start with the desired result. *For example, if guests arrive at 6 pm, you will work backward to determine when to start preparing the food.* It works for different scenarios, including work. For example, how soon must you begin working on a presentation due in three days?

e. **Insight**: Have you ever faced a problem and knew exactly what to do? This problem-solving strategy is also known as gut instincts and usually relates to problems you have faced or seen people face. *For example, you may need extra cash but do not know how to get it. Then, out of nowhere, you remember you have a collectible you can sell. And on further analysis, you remember that your aunt once did the same thing to get out of a tight financial situation!*

f. **Seeking help**: While the above methods often work, sometimes, the skills, knowledge, or experience needed to deal with a problem are beyond your scope, and external help is the only way out. *For example, if your business has been continuously making losses due to poor lead generation, you may want to hire a marketing expert.*

Sleeping on it also helps. We are much more likely to be objective when we have had time to review the problem. *Today, you may want to fire an employee because of low performance.*

But come tomorrow, you may realize the problem is not just with employees but also with the company, and you need to consider altering the organizational structure!

So, how do you determine the best problem-solving strategy? It starts with asking yourself questions:

I.   ***Have you faced this problem before?*** Past solutions can inform the best approach.

II. ***Does it have a known solution?*** E.g., mathematical problems often have mathematical formulas. However, complex problems require creative solutions, as covered in subsection 4.

III. ***How many alternative solutions do you have?*** For instance, a few solutions align with the trial and error method. Still, many solutions might work better with means-end analyses.

IV. ***Do you have the expertise to solve the problem?*** For example, if you are sick, a doctor is better positioned to help you figure out what's wrong.

Once you have figured out the best way to solve a problem, implement it and monitor its effect to help you figure out what solutions can apply to specific problems in the future. *For example, I know that adding milk to overnight oats makes them less thick, which I learned from months of trial and error and referring to social media posts about oats!*

Sub-section 3: Improving Problem-Solving Skills

The furniture store salesman told me, "This sofa will seat 5 people without any problems."

I asked, "Where will I find 5 people without any problems?"

Problem-solving is something you will do for the rest of your life. Today, the issue will be a recipe gone wrong. Tomorrow, it will be a flight cancellation. So, since you cannot escape these challenges, becoming a better problem-solver can help you get more out of your life. But how do you better your skills?

1.   **Become better at defining and analyzing problems:** The 5 whys technique in Exercise 7 helps you understand how to get to the root cause of the problem by breaking it into smaller parts. Often, people spend a lot of time agonizing over a problem instead of understanding why it happened. You are halfway to the solution if you can get to the cause. *E.g., instead of focusing on how often you get the flu, ask yourself why you get it. It might be because you work around children a lot. And in such a case, getting a flu vaccine can help you avert these frequent ailments.*

2. **Be open to alternative solutions:** Biases are common in problem-solving. For example, you may want to do things one way because that's what you have always done. But unless you're dealing with a crisis, there is always time to consider different problem-solving approaches. *Say your cat is lost; what options can you use to get him home?* Write down the different options even if you think hanging a poster is the only effective way.

3. **Involve other people:** Brainstorming is one of the best ways to deal with complex or complicated problems, as it allows you to get varied insights on the best strategies. *For example, you may think the best way to celebrate your spouse, who has been working long hours, is to buy them flowers. But after getting objective insights from your friends, you may realize that a vacation might be the better option!*

4. **Be objective in evaluating solutions**: Sometimes, we brush things off because they are unfamiliar. Remember the biases in Chapter 6? It's important to assess your reasons for choosing one problem-solving strategy over the other. *Say, for example, that you often wake up late. You have several options to address this, including setting several alarms, sleeping early, getting someone else to wake you, etc. Yet, because of cognitive bias, you may consider just one option.* It is important to review your options and determine their suitability without allowing bias to cloud your judgment.

5. **Implement action plans**: Finding a solution is just one part of the problem. *For example, if you've been stressed, you may figure that meditation is a good way to deal with the stress.* But without implementing it as a solution, you cannot address the problem, can you? Make the habit of following through with your plans.

6. **Evaluate the effectiveness of your solutions**. Just because you chose the best option does not mean it will work. If it fails, use this as a lesson and consider alternative ways to deal with the problem. If it works, add this to your problem-solving approaches that you can rely on when time is not on your side.

Problem-solving is a journey you will be on for a lifetime - be patient with yourself as you learn the ropes.

Sub-section 4: Creative Problem Solving

I told my doctor I was having problems with my memory. He made me pay in advance.

Analytical problem-solving breaks down a problem to identify its cause before evaluating solutions and implementing the best one. This approach works like a charm when the problem is well-defined and has an evident answer. *For example, if you want to level up professionally, you can use a SWOT analysis to understand your weaknesses and find solutions to them.* But what if the problem is vague or has too many or no answers? In such a case, you must think beyond the standard solutions and determine what can work. *Take the example of raising a genius. Not many people know how to do it. Children are already different enough without throwing in a heightened IQ.* When faced with a complex problem (as addressed in subsection 1), you cannot afford to rely on the same old strategies.

So, what do you do?

1. **Identify and analyze the problem**: Refer to Subsection 1 on defining your problem using the Why Technique, reviewing data, and referring to external and credible sources.

2. **Pose questions**: Instead of having the problem as a statement, write it down in questions. Say, for example, that your business is not doing well on social media. You can reframe your problem as questions.

   How can we attract more followers?

   How can we get more people to engage with our content?

   How can we get more likes?

   How can we get more people to follow our website link?

   Think of as many questions as you can to reframe your problem so that you open it up to evaluation.

3. **Generate ideas for each question**: Consider all the questions you have posed. What ideas can you generate? Tackle each question at a time. For example, ***how can we get more likes***? Possible ideas include collaborating with influencers, posting entertaining videos, using infographics, scheduling posts to align with traffic, etc. Keep doing this for all the questions.

Here are some ways to get creative:

- ***Create a positive environment where anything is possible*** - throw out everything you think you know. E.g., if you are a social media expert, forget what you learned and instead think on your feet.

- ***Aim for many ideas***, e.g., try to generate 10 ideas in 2 minutes. Don't worry about their sensibility - just throw them out there!

- ***Use these ideas to build on others***, encouraging your brain to keep going.

- Think of wild ideas you would never have considered and include them, even if they are out of this world. ***Aliens?*** Write it all down!

4. **Don't brush off ideas:** The ideation stage requires you to be open to new ideas, no matter how unreasonable they sound. Being open paves the way for creativity, allowing you to explore more ideas without fearing judgment. Now is the time to let go of biases and consider all ideas equally. So, instead of "no, but," go with "yes, and." Think of it like improv.

5. **Introduce convergent thinking:** Creative thinking is divergent; it allows you to explore all sorts of ideas, which is great for the ideation stage. However, when evaluating solutions, you must be stricter about what you consider. Now is the time to back your ideas with efficacy. *For example, is it truly possible to create 1,000 posts a day to increase engagement? Would this work? Do you have the capacity to do it?* Convergent thinking enables you to narrow down to the most plausible ideas based on their ease of implementation and potential effectiveness.

6. **Refine your ideas so that they are best suited for the problem**. And, of course, implement them and monitor their efficacy! With complex problems, you'll likely need to return to the drawing board (restart the process) if the first solution does not work. Don't let this discourage you - keep throwing ideas out there and evaluating them - you will get it right somehow.

Creative problem-solving encourages experimenting with different ideas and forces you to step outside your comfort zone. By considering various solutions you never would have you can pave the way for innovative solutions at home and work.

Key Chapter Takeaways

✓ Problems are part of the human experience. Critical thinkers cannot escape problems and so, must learn how to deal with them.

✓ To be a good problem-solver, you must know how to identify and define the problem, seek alternative ways to solve it, determine the best approach, implement the solution, and check its efficacy.

✓ Problems differ in their causes and effects. They fall into the following categories: simple, complicated, complex, chaotic, and disordered. The strategies used to deal with each problem differ; for example, in chaotic problems (crises), urgency is of the essence, and the immediate response should target minimizing the adverse effects of the problem.

✓ Defining a problem is half of the solution. Besides knowing a problem's category, you should be able to get to the root cause by asking yourself what has caused the issue and comparing this to what you know and what you can get from credible sources.

✓ You can solve problems in different ways, including Heuristics, trial and error, means-end analysis, insight, working backward, and seeking help. Your choice depends on whether you have faced the problem before, if it has a known solution, the number of options that exist, your expertise, and the amount of time you have.

✓ Complex problems require creative solutions. In such a case, you must be willing to think outside the box and experiment with different ideas. You do this by identifying the problem and posing questions, which you answer with out-of-the-box ideas. It's important to narrow your options using convergent thinking to help you determine what best suits your problem.

✓ Implementation and monitoring are central to problem-solving as they help you assess the effectiveness of a solution. Whether the solution works or fails, you learn from the experience.

SPECIAL OFFER:
FREE BONUSES TO SUPPORT YOUR LEARNING

As you work through this book, I want to offer you some additional resources to help you get the most out of your critical thinking practice. These bonuses are designed to provide further insights and practical exercises to enhance your skills.

1. How to Teach Kids Critical Thinking

    • Learn how to effectively teach critical thinking to children, with a special exercise to encourage their curiosity.

2. Applying Critical Thinking Skills in Everyday Life

    • Practical advice for incorporating critical thinking into your daily life, boosting your decision-making abilities.

3. History of Critical Thinking

    • A journey through the history of critical thinking, featuring an exercise in Socratic questioning.

4. The Resilience Handbook

    • Utilize principles from Stoicism and Emotional Intelligence to develop resilience and emotional fortitude.

These bonuses are free and easy to access. Just scan the QR code or follow the link to get them.

https://personalgrowthpages.com/winston-free-gift

Chapter 8:
Analytical Thinking And Data Interpretation

"Think left and think right and think low and think high.
Oh, the thinks you can think up if only you try!"

- DR. SEUSS.

Section 1: Introduction to Analytical Thinking

Is analytical thinking synonymous with critical thinking? Not quite. Critical thinking requires you to question your assumptions and biases, review credible information, consider different approaches, look out for fallacies, and make objective decisions supported by logical arguments. *For example, a doctor must review a patient's medical history, note their symptoms, ensure they are not biased against possible ailments, and determine the best tests based on all this data.* On the other hand, analytical thinking focuses on gaining insights about problems. As such, you must break down the problem, review the data available, rely on proven analytical methods to look for patterns, and solve the problem using the evidence. *Take the example of an accountant reviewing your financial information to help you develop a sound savings plan. They will use the data available and rely on accurate formulas to determine what will work for you.*

As such, critical thinking and analytical thinking have a strong relation. Analytical thinking helps you uncover insights you can rely on for effective critical thinking. *E.g., a CEO can rely on an accountant's findings to determine the best corporate decision to make.* In the same way, critical thinking can help you gauge the validity of analytical findings. *For example, a psychiatrist can review research by scientists when reviewing a patient to determine the most effective treatment plan.*

In most cases and in life, we rely on a mix of critical and analytical thinking. *Take a judge as an example. They rely on critical thinking when reviewing case files, which helps them remain unbiased and objectively evaluate the cases. Once they have done so, they use analytical thinking that hinges on precedence to deliver their judgment.* You can thus think of the two as complementary.

Do you need to be a good analytical thinker to be great at critical thinking? Of course! Analytical thinking influences your critical thinking in the following ways:

1. ***It helps you get to the heart of problems:*** Rather than using generalized solutions, analytical thinking helps you break down problems and identify their root causes. Doing this can help you choose more practical problem-solving strategies and can even help you be more innovative.

2. ***It informs objective decisions:*** Say you want to leave your partner. Analytical thinking helps you evaluate your choices based on their advantages, risks, and disadvantages, which allows you to be more logical than you would if you relied on just your feelings. Over time, you become better at avoiding costly mistakes.

3. ***It helps you filter data:*** Critical thinking requires you to review credible sources of information before making a decision. However, sifting through a lot of data is time-consuming. Analytical thinking helps you easily filter what you need to identify trends and project potential outcomes.

4. ***It supports critical thinking:*** When you learn to analyze data before making a decision, you learn to stop and think about problems from different angles. This approach is especially useful in cultivating curiosity as you will always question your alternatives to a problem. *For example, should you buy that Toyota without considering what other cars at that price point can offer? What makes it a good choice?*

Best of all, analytical thinking makes you more productive in life. You will be a gem everywhere since you can identify the most suitable ways to approach problems, e.g., *if your neighbors need help with the city council, they will know they can count on you to develop efficient solutions. Or if your child has a relationship problem, they will know they can come to you, and you can help them figure out the most reasonable approach!*

Common Analytical Thinking Pitfalls

Working with data is fun - even if you are not a geek, you'll enjoy deriving results from raw data. For example, if you learn to decide where to vacation based on pros and cons lists, you might find yourself doing that in your free time! But here are some challenges you should be wary of as you go down this exciting road:

I. **Logical fallacies:** When working with data, you should be careful not to develop bad arguments, e.g., assuming correlation equals causation. (We have discussed this in Chapter 5).

II. **Overfitting and underfitting:** Your data should be enough to inform your decision but not so much that it becomes specific to the problem and veers from objectivity. It should also not be so limited that you cannot capture trends.

III. **Poor data quality:** Where are you getting your data? For analytical thinking to be objective, the data informing the decisions should be accurate, complete, and consistent. You must also handle the data with integrity, ensuring you collect, analyze, and store it correctly per data protection policies.

IV. **Complex communication:** Your findings should be easy to interpret. For example, if you calculate the ROI of a project as 10%, it should be easy for a third party to understand the process and the results. Otherwise, if the findings and recommendations are not easily understandable, you will have a problem explaining the reasoning behind your analysis. I will cover more on communication in Chapter 10.

It's also important to realize that data alone is not enough. Critical thinking requires you to dig beyond the numbers and understand the reasons behind the data. *For example, if data shows that 5 in every 10 people in your organization prefer emails over meetings, the next step would be to uncover the cause. The reason might not be a simple email-over-meeting issue. It could instead point to a more significant issue in the company.*

Section 2: Analytical Tools and Techniques

Data is like people – interrogate it hard enough, and it will tell you whatever you want to hear.

- Joke.

To be a good data analyst, you must approach data objectively. For example, if you want the data to tell you that buying a new home is a good idea, you can skew it to do so. But if you want the truth, you must use the correct data collection and analysis techniques. Only then can you have enough credible information to base your decision on - Let's consider your options:

Data Collection Methods

Patient: *"Will I survive this risky operation?"*

Surgeon: *"Yes, I'm absolutely sure that you will survive the operation."*

Patient: *"How can you be so sure?"*

Surgeon: *"9 out of 10 patients die in this operation, and yesterday, my ninth patient died."*

Data can be quantitative, qualitative, or both. The data collection method you choose hinges on the type of data you need and influences the data's accuracy, relevance, and quality. *For example, anonymous surveys might be better than interviews for large organizations due to ease of distribution and privacy.* So, what options do you have?

1. **Primary data collection** relies on first-hand experience, making it highly specific to the problem. Possible options include surveys, polls, interviews, focus groups, questionnaires, and the Delphi technique for qualitative data. *Take a focus group as an example. You can use this with up to 10 people to discuss a common problem, e.g., what can you do about the noise problem in the neighborhood?* The idea is to get unbiased opinions from everyone and reach a consensus. On the quantitative side, barometric methods and smoothing techniques are good examples.

2. **Secondary data collection** is available in existing sources, e.g., books, journals, financial reports, the Internet, press releases, executive summaries, and health records. *For example, if you want to figure out how to make extra money, you can get this information from published records.* It's important to vet the credibility of your sources, as verifying secondary data can be challenging.

So, how do you determine the best data collection method?

→ **Define the problem as discussed in Chapter 7**, as this will help you determine your research question. For example, if you want to lose weight through intermittent fasting, you will collect data related to this problem.

→ **Consider the best data sources per your problem**. Where can you get reliable and high-quality data? Assuming an intermittent fasting plan, you can get information from health journals, dieticians, friends who have tried this approach, etc.

→ **Evaluate the collection options:** Consider factors such as cost, time, reliability, and validity when choosing a collection method. *For example, can a survey work for an intermittent fasting study? Would interviews be better? Do you have time to collect data this way?* Once you have decided on the best options, test them to identify any glitches you should fix before starting data collection. For example, your questionnaire may be too open-ended to get data from which you can draw patterns.

Often, it's best to combine secondary and primary data collection methods. *Say you're having marital problems and want to better your relationship. You can use primary data collection methods like interviews with marriage counselors and read more about the topic in journals, books, and other reliable secondary data sources.*

Data Analysis Methods

Your data collection will leave you with a lot of data, some of which may not be necessary. It's thus best to analyze it and extract insights to inform your decision, i.e., make sense of the data. Analysts use different methods to do this, including descriptive, exploratory, diagnostic, predictive, and prescriptive analyses. Take descriptive analysis as an example - it helps you identify patterns such as frequency, central tendency measures, dispersion measures, and position. *For example, you may analyze your business income based on your yearly reports and realize your mean monthly income is $7,000.*

While highly analytical methods may be a tad too complex for everyday issues, here are simple analyses you can use for most problems even if you don't have a statistical background:

1. **SWOT analysis**: Companies often use this analysis to strengthen their internal processes. But it also works for personal problems too. *Consider Lucy, a marketer who wants to apply for a promotion at work.* Here's what her SWOT analysis may look like:

    *   *Strengths*: *10 years of marketing experience. Master's degree in marketing. Excited about new marketing trends.*

    *   *Weaknesses*: *Difficulty dealing with failures. Easily overwhelmed. Poor time management.*

    *   *Opportunities*: *Attend a time management workshop. Invest more in marketing courses.*

    *   *Threats*: *Competition from other marketers with more experience or confidence.*

Let's consider this in a visual chart:

SWOT ANALYSIS FOR LUCY

STRENGTHS

Internal characteristics that give you an advantage over others.

- 10 years of marketing experience.
- Master's degree in marketing.
- Enthusiastic about marketing trends.

WEAKNESSES

Internal characteristics that put you at a disadvantage relative to others

- Difficulty dealing with failures.
- Easily overwhelmed.
- Poor time management.

OPPORTUNITIES

External factors that you can capitalize on to improve your performance.

- New marketing courses.
- Online time management workshops.

THREATS

External factors that can harm your performance

- More experienced marketers applying for the promotion.

With this list, Lucy can determine what she can work on to ensure she stands out as a candidate. For example, she can attend more marketing courses to help her position herself as an ideal marketer. In the same way, you can use a SWOT analysis for almost any problem, including how to parent a teenager!

2. **Root cause analysis**: While SWOT analysis helps you figure out how to deal with current problems, root cause analysis enables you to understand why you're facing a problem. Doing this helps you prevent it from happening again. Here is how you do this:

- ***Define the problem*** *as described in Chapter 7. E.g., I have not been sleeping continuously through the night.*

- ***Collect data*** *that proves the problem exists and its likely impact. For example, you can track how much and how often you sleep, review sleep suggestions in health journals, consult a sleep specialist, etc.*

- *Identify the causes of the problem.* *For example, your sleep may have suffered due to a lousy nighttime routine, stress at work, not being active enough, etc. List all possible causes of the problem - dig deep using the 5 Whys Technique in Exercise 7.*

- *Hone down on the root cause.* *E.g., after your assessments, you'll have an easier time figuring out the main reason. For example, you may realize that your sleep quality declines after you start snacking late at night.*

- *Evaluate possible solutions* *and implement the best one based on its advantages and associated risks. For instance, instead of snacking late at night, you can eat a big dinner so you don't get hungry and get up later.*

See? It can be that simple! You can refer to Chapter 7 for a detailed breakdown of problem-solving strategies.

3. **Pareto analysis**: This approach relies on the Pareto Principle, which states that 80% of a project's benefits (or problems) relate to 20% of the work done (or causes). The idea here is thus to figure out the causes of the problems and address them. Here is how you do this:

  - *Identify and list your problems, as shown in Chapter 7.*

  - *Use the root cause analysis method* *described above to find the root cause of each problem. E.g., if you suffer from anxiety, list all the things that make you anxious.*

  - *Assign scores to the problems.* *For example, you can score your work pressure as 8, traffic as 6, and strangers as 9.*

  - *Group the problems together.* *Some of your problems will be related. For example, a strict boss and tight work deadlines can go into the same category.*

  - *Sum up the scores in each group* *to understand the one with the highest priority. For example, you may find that social anxiety scores are the highest.*

  - *Find solutions using the strategies in Chapter 7* *and start by addressing the highest-scoring problems first. As you work through the list, you may find that some problems are less significant than you thought!*

You can apply these analyses to everyday problems and can even teach them to your children to use in and out of school. To practice using this analysis, refer to **Exercise 8.**

Section 3: Making Data-Driven Decisions

"You can have data without information, but you cannot have information without data."

- DANIEL KEYS MORAN

What does your data say? It's possible to identify a problem, conduct a thorough analysis, and still make the wrong decision because you did not make sense of the data. How can you avoid this? You need to consider the steps below:

1. **Visualize the data from the data analysis**: What's easier - evaluating a bar graph or reading the raw data from a form? Most people would argue that visuals are much better at representing data, which enables them to understand what it means. *Say, for example, that you are looking at the popularity of fruits in PTA meetings. Visualizing the data can help you determine which fruits to include more in the next meetings.*

    Here are some easy ways to visualize your data:

    *   Pie charts.

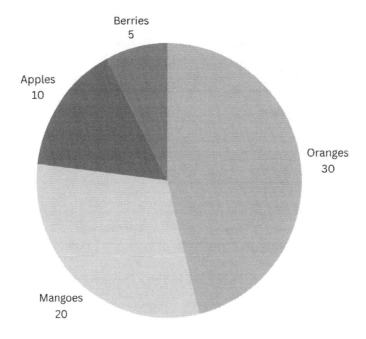

- Bar graphs.

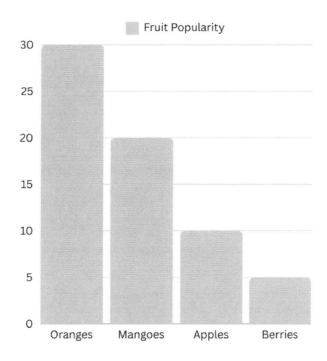

- Line graphs. The following graph indicates the popularity of fruits per month.

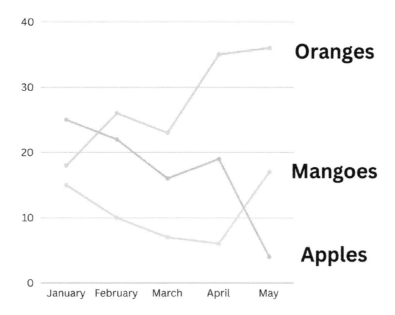

Other great ways to present quantitative data include frequency tables, heat maps, and scatter graphs.

With qualitative data, you don't always need to present it in visuals. Instead, you can relay it as a statement. E.g., "Lack of a timetable accounts is the biggest hurdle towards making healthy meals for my family."

2. **Interpret the data**: The next step is to seek meaning from the data by making conclusions supported by the analysis. With quantitive data, you can focus on the numbers, e.g., *"most fit people exercise at least 3 times a week on average."* And with qualitative data, you can focus on patterns. Once you understand what the figures or patterns convey, you can move on to the decision-making stage. For example, if you want to be fit and the data points to 3 active workouts a week, you can determine how to achieve this goal.

Now that you know how to analyze data, the next chapter will focus on how you can use it for objective decision-making.

Key Chapter Takeaways

✓   Analytical thinking is important in critical thinking as it lets you gain insights into problems to help you make better decisions. For example, accountants use financial data to project incomes and expenses for companies, which can help CEOs determine the best approach to mitigate likely risks.

✓   To conduct a good analysis, you must collect enough data (without overfitting or underfitting), avoid logical fallacies (as detailed in Chapter 5), collect valid and reliable data, and communicate your findings in an understandable way (Chapter 10).

✓   Data collection methods fall into primary and secondary categories. Primary data refers to first-hand experience data, e.g., surveys and interviews. Secondary data refers to data from existing sources, e.g., health journals and financial reports. Your choice of data collection method depends on your problem, the best data sources, and the resources available. E.g., surveys might be cheaper and more practical than interviews when addressing delicate issues.

✓   For collected data to convey meaning, you must analyze it. SWOT analyses, root cause analyses, and Pareto analyses are approaches you can rely on for everyday challenges.

✓   While analyses will help you uncover patterns, the only way to make sense of them is to visualize the data, e.g., with line graphs. These make it easier to interpret the data, note the trends, and make informed decisions. The next chapter will cover decision-making in more detail to help you uncover practical and unbiased ways to do it.

Chapter 9:
Mastering Decision-Making Skills

"In any moment of decision, the best thing you can do is the right thing, the next best thing is the wrong thing, and the worst thing you can do is nothing."

- THEODORE ROOSEVELT.

Section 1: The Art of Effective Decision-Making

Marriage counselor: *Does your partner allow you to make independent decisions?*

Me: **looks at wife**

Wife: **nods**

Me: *Yes, of course!*

Did you know people can make decisions in as little as 0.3 seconds? In a Milosavljevic et al. (2023) study, researchers divided respondents into two groups. The first group was tested for speed and had to choose between differently rated snacks as fast as possible, with the promise that they would eat whatever they had chosen at the end of the trial. Decision-making timelines averaged 0.4 seconds. The second group was tested for accuracy rather than speed. Research findings showed that their responses were 10% more accurate due to the slower decision-making.

In another study by Grabmeier (2022), researchers embarked on three trials. Per the study, respondents were told that they would eat whatever they chose at the end of the trials. The first trial had respondents choose between two highly-rated snacks. Results showed that respondents made fast and accurate decisions in this case. In the second trial, respondents had to choose between two low-rated snacks - the decision-making timelines were longer in this instance. In the third trial, researchers emphasized that participants were deciding between high-value items. While respondents made these decisions fast and accurately in the first trial, this new information slowed down their decision-making, proving that people respond to decision-making processes based on the perceived value of their outcomes.

So, what goes into a decision? Several factors come into play before you go with an ice cream flavor, buy a home, or break up a fight. Consider them as follows:

1. **Your values**: Core to our decisions are the things that matter most to us. *For example, if you must choose between throwing a colleague under the bus or owning up to your mistakes, your values will inform this decision. If you value integrity, you will face the consequences of your wrongdoing, even if that means losing a project.*

2. **Your beliefs (biases):** What you believe can influence your decisions. Say you have authority bias. You may decide to look the other way even when someone in authority is in the wrong. For example, you can let your boss get away with withholding people's salaries. (**For more about biases, refer to Chapter 6.**)

3. **Your emotions**: If you're not assessing your reasoning, your emotions can take over. For example, you may skip a gym class you committed to because you are sad.

4. **Your experiences**: Most of our biases come from our experiences—it's our brain's way of saving time and protecting us. Say you once decided to buy chocolate ice cream and did not enjoy it. You will likely avoid chocolate flavors the next time you buy ice cream.

So, when deciding, all these factors usually come into the picture. Why *usually?* Well, there are two kinds of decision-making processes:

1. The rational decision

In this case, you look at all the possible options and base your final decision on logic and reason. (Chapter 5 explores logic in detail.) For instance, *assume you are choosing between quitting your job or staying at a job you don't enjoy.* In this case, you would weigh the pros of staying versus the cons/ risks of quitting. In addition to these, you would consider your values, biases (beliefs), emotions, and experiences.

- **Example 1:** *You're considering quitting because you have had a bad week.* You'd reason that this was insufficient to warrant such a big change.

- **Example 2:** *You are quitting because the work environment is toxic, and you value your peace of mind and can afford to stay out of a job.* This decision sounds rational.

Beware of bounded rationality.

Would you rather receive $1,000,000 today or $3,000,000 in 12 months? Many people would choose the first option as it allows them to get money today. Bounded rationality, a bias in decision-making, influences people to choose the most satisfactory options at the time of decision-making without thinking far into the future. *For example, buying a cheap weighing scale for $15 today is much easier than saving $100 in 2 months for a durable scale.* As such, you must vet your decision based on your need for immediate gratification, whether you have enough information about the situation, and whether you're aiming for convenience. Are you truly rational?

2. The irrational decision

While many people base their decisions on instincts (gut feelings) or emotions, they are subject to biases and do not rely on credible data. *For example, your intuition may convince you to quit a job because you don't think your new boss likes you.* And without evidence of this, you may call it quits! It's thus beneficial to be wary of these barriers to decision-making by assessing your ability to validate your biases. *For example, what evidence do you have that your boss dislikes you? Does this affect your job? Are there company policies you can review regarding employee protections?*

Interestingly, even when people think they are being rational, some semblances of irrationality still make their way into the final decisions. For example, if you are subject to the bandwagon effect, you may make a bad decision just to fit in with the crowd! Thus, it's vital to assess the rationale behind your decisions. If you allow your emotions, biases, or intuition to lead the way, you'll likely make a subjective decision that hurts you, *e.g., walking out of a marriage because your spouse forgot to take you along to the gym!* Chapters 6, 7, and 9 explore how to lean on logic, address your biases, and analyze the information available for rational decision-making.

Section 2: Making Big Life Decisions

We make big decisions every day. These range from choosing our spouses to adopting pets, pursuing higher education, quitting our jobs, buying homes, walking out of relationships, and cutting off friends. The bigger the decision, the bigger the impact. *For example, if you decide to take on a 20-year mortgage, the consequences could follow you for two decades. And the outcomes range from being a proud homeowner two decades from now or getting foreclosed and losing your equity a few years from now!*

Critical thinking enables you to evaluate all your options to end up with the best option rather than the one that aligns with bounded reality. Here's how you do this:

1. **Understand your values**: Rational thinking builds on the values that underpin your decisions. *For example, someone who believes in fairness will gravitate towards decisions that uphold this value.* Understand what resonates with you, challenge its role in your life, and focus on building an authentic life around it.

2. **Be clear about your decision**: Decisions are not simple "do this" or "do that" dilemmas. Instead, you often have several options. Assume you want to start a daycare center because you want extra income. Alternative options could be:

    •   Stick to your current job and run the business on the side.

    •   Quit your job and run the business full-time.

    •   Pursue a degree in early childhood education, and then start the business.

    •   Find an alternative job with higher pay and forego the business.

    These are just examples. Review your decision and think about all the possible outcomes you could pursue using the **mind mapping technique** in Exercise 9 of the exercises section.

3. **Do your research**: As described in Chapter 8, you will need to gather and analyze credible information to weigh each option while ensuring your biases (explored in Chapter 6) do not get in the way. *For example, even if you'd like to quit your job, don't look for only data confirming your preference.*

4. **Review the consequences of each decision**: Suppose you decide to follow through with a decision; what will happen? Do this for each of the options while referring to your data. *For example, if you stick to your job and run the business full-time, possible advantages include having reliable income and learning the ropes. But on the downside, you'd lack the ability to be on top of operations and would need to delegate.*

Let's consider some of the best ways to evaluate consequences:

a. **The cost-benefit analysis** enables you to assess the benefits and costs of pursuing different actions to choose the most beneficial one. Here is how it works:

- *Outline the cost of following a decision, e.g., buying and maintaining a home could be $400,000.*

- *Consider the benefits of the decision, e.g., not paying rent and instead investing $3,000 a month in equity.*

- *Compare the costs and benefits, i.e., value equals benefits minus costs.*

- *Review the value and determine if the decision is worth your time and money.*

b. **The intuitive decision-making model** relies on instincts when you have to make decisions fast and don't have much information about a subject. It works as follows:

- *Be clear about the goal behind the decision, e.g., choosing a cheap flight.*

- *Consider how people have made such decisions before, e.g., airlines known for cheap and reliable flights.*

- *Address your biases and logical fallacies and consider how they may have affected your decision, e.g., negativity bias against an airline.*

- *Determine the best solution based on the options available and follow through with it.*

5. **Take a beat**: Big decisions do not require you to act fast unless you're dealing with an impending problem. It's best to take your time to consider the impact of your choices. Can you live with the decision? *For example, what if your business fails? What if you can't make money for at least a year?*

6. **Get support**: Some decisions are so heavy that being logical about them can be challenging, and it's thus best to reach out to trustworthy people regarding possible outcomes. *Take the example of a divorce. Certified marriage counselors and therapists may have good insights that may prove invaluable to your decision.*

Support does not always have to be human. In today's digital age, **artificial intelligence** can help you make complex decisions. This technology now features in several apps and websites that are available to businesses as well as individuals. How does it work?

- *Define the decision you need to make. E.g., should I get a German Shepherd or a Golden Retriever?*

- *Enter your options and their pros and cons. For example, German Shepherds are easy to train and are great for security. On the other hand, Golden Retrievers are friendly and do not require much bathing as they have short coats.*

- *Score each pro and con and assign a value to each. You can rate the dogs based on each factor, e.g., grooming needs, friendliness, training needs, etc.*

- *Allow the site or app to run and give you an answer.*

On the upside, ***AI-driven decisions*** will be free of cognitive biases. But on the downside, the lack of human touch may result in logical yet impractical choices. It is wise to ensure you use quality data the app or website can rely on to generate decisions you can implement.

7. **Take the plunge:** Have you heard of choice overload bias? This problem presents when you have several options and can negatively affect your decision-making skills. Once you have reviewed your possible decisions using the strategies in this section, determine and implement what best fits your needs.

Even with logical reasoning and well-thought-out processes, decisions will not always produce the best possible outcomes. And here is where **iterative decision-making** comes into play. It is much like the rational decision-making model. But beyond defining the decision and evaluating outcomes, it also includes the following steps:

- **Develop measurable criteria for assessing the goal's performance.** Website traffic, for example, can inform the suitability of a marketing approach.

- **Assess the viability of the decision:** Implement the preferred decision and measure its impact against the set criteria. *E.g., if you choose to work with an influencer as your marketing, you can measure their engagement for a month.*

- **Implement alternatives when the chosen option fails**. For example, if you have chosen to work with one influencer and don't like the engagement, you can move on to another option and gauge their performance based on the set criteria.

These strategies work great for critical thinking in conditions of certainty. But what if you can't predict the future? Let's find out.

Section 3: Decision-Making Under Uncertainty

Is getting married after two months of dating a good idea? Should you move your family to a new country? Uncertainty will often crop up when you're making life-changing decisions. After all, you can't always tell what lies ahead. It stems from the following conditions:

1. **You don't have enough information or knowledge about the impact of a decision**, *e.g., moving to a new country during an economic crisis.*

2. **You have too much information or knowledge about what a decision entails**, *e.g., marital advice from other people.*

3. **The data you get is conflicting**, *e.g., whether marijuana is addictive.*

And then there is pure uncertainty, where you don't know anything about the future and don't have enough data to predict what will happen. *For example, you can decide to invest in a trust fund for your grandkids even if you have no idea whether your children will want or have children.*

Making decisions in conditions of uncertainty can feel challenging. But you can always push through with these tips:

a. **Gather objective data**: Since uncertainty can result from too little or too much data, gather just enough information to hit that balance. *For example, if you're about to have surgery, look at enough health journals and interview enough trustworthy people, but avoid veering into the deep end of "surgeries gone wrong."* It's important to know when to stop.

b. **Be realistic and clear with your expectations:** Uncertainty makes it hard to predict the future, especially when dealing with many unknowns, and you might find yourself grappling with many questions. **Exercise 9 on mind mapping** in the exercises section helps you to organize your thoughts and ideas so you can be clear about your ideas and assess their impact.

c. **Rely on proven strategies**: While you cannot control uncertainty, some techniques make it easier to arrive at a decision, as follows:

1. **Risk Analysis** helps you identify and manage potential problems that could affect your decision. Here is how it works:

   • **Identify the threats you might face:** Assume you want to move to another country during an economic downturn. *Possible threats include going over your budget and changes in tax policies.* A SWOT analysis, as described in Chapter 8, can also help you uncover threats.

- **Estimate the risk of the threats:** How likely are these threats? Estimate the probability by researching credible sources (as in Chapter 8) and **Baye's Theorem**. Then, multiply this by the cost of the threat. For example, if you might have to spend $200 extra on rent, and there is a 70% chance of this, the risk value will be 200* 0.7 = $140.

- **Avoid, share, or accept the risk:** The first option is to forego the decision. The second one is to involve other people and share the risk, e.g., move with your partner. The third is to accept the risk and find ways to reduce its impact, e.g., you can find ways to cut back on expenses if your budget increases.

2. **The Decision Tree** helps you break down a complex decision by comparing possible outcomes based on different choices. Here is how it works:

- **Write down the primary decision you need to make**, e.g., starting a business. Then, create different options that you could pursue, *e.g., sticking to your current job, retiring, etc.*

- **Include the aspect of probability using Bayes Theorem to expand the tree.** E.g., your business may have a 60% chance of succeeding in the current economic climate.

- **Add outcomes for each decision**. E.g., if you decide to stay in your current job and get promoted, you could earn $80,000 annually.

- **Keep doing this until you have no more choices left.** Then, assign a score or value to the outcome. For example, you can assign a value based on probability for business decisions.

Consider the example below:

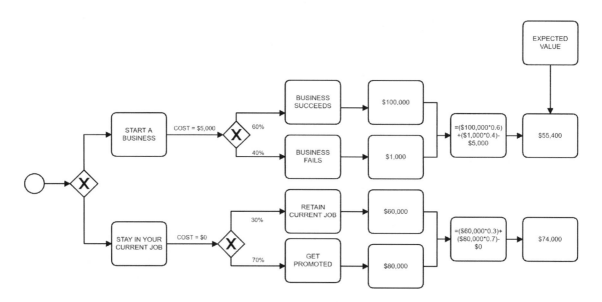

Ambiguous or uncertain situations require assessing the probabilities and risks attached to your choices. You can then evaluate your options logically, basing your final decision on what's most rational, as discussed in Section 1.

Key Chapter Takeaways

✓ Your values, beliefs (biases), emotions, and experiences often impact your decision-making. For example, you're likely to react out of anger when angry.

✓ As a result of these decision-making factors, you can either make a rational or irrational decision. As discussed in previous chapters, a rational decision relies on logic and reason and accounts for influences such as bias. Irrational decisions rely on emotional reactions and gut instincts and do not account for biases.

✓ To make a rational big decision, you need to understand your values, determine your options and their impacts, do extensive research, and rely on trusted processes. Examples include cost-benefit analyses and intuitive decision models.

✓ Given the potential impacts of big decisions, it's advisable to be patient with the process, seek help where necessary, and use iterative decision-making that allows you to review your decisions and tweak what does not work.

✓ When making decisions in conditions of uncertainty, you must gather as much credible data as possible and maintain a realistic overview regarding possible outcomes. Strategies like risk analysis and decision trees can help mitigate possible risks and make more rational decisions even when the future is unpredictable.

Chapter 10:
Effective Communication And Persuasion

"The single biggest problem in communication is the illusion that it has taken place."

- GEORGE BERNARD SHAW.

When communicating with people, it is important to say what you mean and mean what you say. For example, *if you want an orange, you should not ask for a banana and hope someone will know you want an orange. In the same way, if I am communicating with you (actively listening), I will give you the banana you have asked for and not another fruit.* This chapter explores the role of communication in our lives and how to incorporate it when conveying decisions derived from critical thinking.

Section 1: Principles of Effective Communication

Communication is the art of exchanging information. But why do people do it? Reasons vary, but they come down to the following instances:

- **Making a request**, e.g., asking people to help you move to a new house.
- **Protesting something**, e.g., telling a stranger you do not want them to come into your home.
- **Connecting with others socially,** e.g., talking to your friends about your vacation plans.
- **When sharing information**, e.g., presenting a logical argument to your colleagues at work.

Communication helps us convey our needs, express our opinions, forge good relationships with others, and achieve our goals. In the same way, it helps us understand what other people need, think, and feel. But for this to happen, it has to be effective. What can prevent this?

Barriers to effective communication.

In an ideal world, you would share an opinion, and the recipient would agree with it or offer an alternative. But that's not always the case. Obstacles often get in the way of communication, and for you to be a good communicator, you need to understand them as follows:

a. **Physical barriers:** Background noises, time differences, invading someone's personal space, and general discomfort can interfere with a conversation. For example, *the noise can affect your audibility if you're trying to have an intimate conversation in a loud bar.*

b. **Perceptual barriers**: Attitudes, preferences, stereotypes, cognitive biases, and assumptions can affect communication skills and result in misunderstandings. *For example, if you expect someone to lie, you might not believe them even if they are telling the truth because you already have this negative perception of them.*

c. **Emotional barriers:** Negative states of mind like anxiety, pride, and anger can prevent you from listening to someone. For example, *if a friend has made you angry, you might oppose their ideas just to get back at them.*

d. **Cultural barriers:** Language, belief, and nonverbal cue differences can result in communication barriers. *Take the example of gestures. While pointing may be okay in most countries, it is seen as impolite in many European nations.*

Can you eliminate all barriers? Not quite. However, you can reduce their occurrence by considering if you are in the right space (physically and mentally) to embark on a conversation and if you have enough knowledge about the possible cultural barriers.

For example, if you're discussing parenting choices with someone from another country, you should broach the conversation carefully to avoid being offensive. However, cultural barriers will likely not affect your discussion with a friend who shares your values.

Let's consider how some principles can boost your communication skills.

Principles of Effective Communication

The key to a productive conversation is ensuring you convey your thoughts and allow others to do the same so you can understand each other. But how do you do this?

a. **Clear and concise messaging:** To ensure people understand your message, you must lead with a purpose (what you want) and ensure it is clear to everyone. Also, instead of using many sentences, summarize your idea in a short and direct way. Consider the following examples:

Clear: *Can you walk my dog tomorrow?*

Unclear: *I am so stressed that I can barely do anything. My dog hasn't been out all week, and my daughter hasn't been to the park in days. I am just overwhelmed.*

Visual aids can be helpful when presenting data. For example, a pie chart can explain why expanding the business to a new town is a good idea.

b. **Avoid Jargon and Slang:** Assume the doctor tells you that you risk getting a myocardial infarction. Would you understand that this was the medical term for a heart attack? Jargon is professional slang that works for people in the same profession but does not aid effective communication outside these circles. Slang, aka informal language, is often more common but does not always equate to effective communication. Consider these examples:

Slang: *Mark is salty about the new HOA rules.*

No slang: *Mark is unhappy with the new HOA rules.*

In the first instance, someone who does not use this slang will not understand what you mean. As such, if the recipient is unfamiliar with the slang or jargon you wish to use, avoid it to ensure the message is clear.

c. **Be coherent:** A message may have a clear purpose but lacks credibility or coherence, making it hard to understand. Let's use an example.

Coherent: *The PTA meeting has been rescheduled to 2 pm tomorrow due to unexpected heavy rains.*

Incoherent: *Stay indoors. Nobody is coming to the meeting.*

The second message would leave people wondering why and would likely result in questions. Chapter 5 sheds more light on constructing logical arguments by backing them with facts and avoiding generalizations.

d. Be respectful: People respond well to positive energy. Here is how you can create such an environment:

- *Address people by their names.*

- *Maintain good eye contact with your recipient.*

- *Relax your body and face your recipient.*

- *Avoid too many hand gestures and instead use your voice to convey the message.*

- *Use a tone that matches the topic, e.g., serious for more urgent issues.*

- *Do not raise your voice when asked to clarify your message or when faced with opposition.*

- *Use the proper facial cues per the subject. For example, smiling at jokes is okay, but you cannot smile as someone talks abou*t a sad topic.

e. Challenge your barriers: Identify the barriers to communication. For example, if noise is getting in the way, you can solve this by moving to a quieter room. Where the barriers are cultural, it's best to learn more about norms to understand different perspectives better.

f. Actively listen to others: Communication is two-way. Once you have conveyed your message, the recipient should get the chance to respond. What you hear and what they *actually* say can be very different if you are not listening to them. So, how can you ensure you understand their messaging?

- Let go of biases towards them and instead be open-minded and ready to hear things from their perspective. **Exercise 10** shows you how to step into someone else's shoes and view an issue from their angle.

- Listen to the whole message before responding. It's important not to judge people based on their beliefs or ideas, as this could bar you from paying attention to their message. Where you need clarification, ask for it rather than making assumptions.

- Give people time to respond to your message, and do not interrupt them mid-sentence. If you have questions, wait for an opening and pose them. It's also advisable to phrase your questions as gateways to longer conversations, e.g., *"Tell me more about that gym."*

- Pay attention to what they say and how they act. People communicate through words and actions. For example, a pained look on someone's face can show just how much they care about a subject. In the same way, fidgeting may signal nervousness. Or eyes begin to wander, signaling boredom. By watching out for such cues, you can know how to respond. For example, if someone is in pain about losing a job, now might not be the best time to question them about their long-term financial plans.

Effective communication requires you to understand your position, consider the other person's point of view (check out Exercise 10), convey your points respectfully, listen to the other person, identify and address barriers to communication, and respond in a way that matches their response and the general setting.

Section 2: Clear and Concise Writing

Harry enjoys eating his family and his cat.

Harry enjoys eating, his family, and his cat.

Punctuation makes a huge difference in your writing and the message the recipient receives. Whether sending a text to your friend group or writing an email, how can you ensure you convey what you intended? The principles are similar to those discussed in Section 1. However, you should also pay attention to the following:

1. **Ensure you use the correct grammar**: Errors such as incorrect punctuation and the wrong use of words can result in a misunderstanding. For example, a sentence can quickly change from *"Let's eat, dad"* to *"Let's eat dad."* To avoid such errors, review your work and consider using online grammar checkers.

2. **Stick to concise messaging**: Being clear helps you underpin your core message and saves time for everyone. You can do this by highlighting the goal and backing it with related information while avoiding unrelated topics. Here's an example of a concise message: *"I will leave work at 7:00 pm as I have a meeting from 5:00 pm till 6:45 pm. Please buy dinner for the kids."*

Backing your message with data is also a good idea in professional settings. For example, if you're sending an email regarding the success of a recent project, including the statistics can support your message.

Section 3: Negotiation and Conflict Resolution

No matter how great you communicate, you will hit bumps in the road. Sometimes, people will misunderstand you. At others, you will misunderstand them. And in many others, you will understand each other but not agree. So, how can you resolve such issues?

1. **Communicate with the other person:** While it may feel uncomfortable, addressing the elephant in the room is the first step to resolving conflicts. Here is how you do this:

   - *Let them know you'd like to discuss the conflict and ask them to suggest a good time and place.*

   - *Point out where you agree with them and the points you disagree with, and respect their views. For example, instead of saying, "**You don't understand the market conditions,**" you can say, "**Current market trends suggest this approach.**"*

   - *Allow the other person to share their views. Use the tips in Section 1 of this chapter to ensure you understand what they are saying and are not jumping to conclusions or dismissing their beliefs.*

2. **Highlight the differing opinions:** Being on different sides does not mean one of you is wrong. So, how can you come to a consensus?

   a. ***Determine the core differing opinions and focus more on them.*** *Let's use the example of organizing a child's birthday party. Possible areas of focus can be:*

      - *Choosing a theme for the party - essential.*

      - *Contracting a reliable caterer - essential.*

      - *Sending invites - essential.*

      - *Choosing fun, child-friendly activities - essential.*

      - *Packing party favors for the guests - optional.*

      - *Hiring a clown - optional.*

      - *Entertaining adults - optional.*

      Based on these areas, you can determine the ones that have the most priority. For example, choosing a theme is much more important than packing party favors for the guests. So, if you can all agree on the main aspects, e.g., theme, food, and invites, the party can still be a success even if you have differences in the less important elements.

   b. ***Support your opinions with logical arguments*** *and allow the other person to do the same. Now is an excellent time to seek clarity from the other person by asking questions about their stance. You also need to answer questions respectfully.*

   c. ***Talk through the differences and try to arrive at a compromise.*** *For example, a pink theme can work if you want a red theme and the other person wants a purple one.*

3. **Manage your emotions:** Negotiations can get heated, especially when the issue being discussed is important to everyone involved. In such cases, staying on top of your emotions and taking a break when you feel overwhelmed is best. Allow the other person to do the same. Where parties cannot agree to a respectful approach, it's best to consider involving a neutral third party, pausing the negotiations, or doing away with the talks altogether.

PS: You don't need to agree on everything at once. Sometimes, one stride in the right direction is enough.

Section 4: Persuasive Communication

Persuasion is an art that encompasses the principles of effective communication. To become persuasive, you must pay attention to yourself (the communicator), the message, how you convey the message, and the audience. Let's consider how you can use these elements of persuasive communication to your advantage:

1. **You (The Communicator):** Several studies have shown that the messenger is essential in communication. So, consider the following:

   - *Are you a credible source?* Reports by Xie & Liu (2022) and Kumkale et al. (2010) highlighted the effect of credibility on message acceptance, showing that people are more likely to embrace a message if they trust its source. For example, a doctor is seen as a good source of medical information. What qualifications or experiences make you a good candidate for the message? It's best to point them out when communicating. For example, *"In my years of law practice, I have encountered hundreds of such cases."*

   - *Are you likable?* Do you know why influencers sell so many products? - They are likable! A Wallace et al. (2020) study gives insights into how non-verbal cues such as appearances and demeanors affect how the recipient views the message. For example, if you are well-dressed and respectful, you will be more likable than someone who shows up in a foul mood. Dress to impress and communicate positively with your body to encourage your recipients to view you favorably.

   Here's an interesting tip: *Mimicking people's body language has been shown to increase credibility. For example, if someone has crossed their legs, doing the same thing could influence them to like you more!*

2. **The recipient:** The content of the message should reflect the audience. Consider these aspects:

- *Reasoning*: Rational people prefer analytical arguments, while other recipients care more about the emotional side. So, when posing a message to a rational person, you'd need to back it with facts. But when talking to an impulsive person, you can benefit more from leaning on the emotional side, e.g., how supplements companies promise to change people's lives in a week!

- *Mood*: As stated in Section 1, emotions play a part in effective communication. You can use this to your advantage by communicating with people in a good mood, as they will respond better to your ideas. Interestingly, you can also set the mood. *For example, showering your spouse with attention and good food can pave the way for discussing family planning.* A study by Forgas (1999) also points out that your mood can adversely affect how you communicate; e.g., happy moods can result in impoliteness, which can annoy the recipient. It is thus valuable to manage positive and negative moods to achieve a balance that helps you be more persuasive in your messaging.

- *Age*: As explained in Chapter 6, older generations tend to have more biases. Thus, convincing them of different ideas may require more effort than broaching the same subject with younger generations. You need to acknowledge such differences when preparing your messaging.

What about objections? A great way to avoid resistance is to convey your message clearly and ensure your recipients are not distracted. It's also necessary to make them feel responsible for evaluating the message, which indicates you have nothing to hide. While you can also use distractions (like in TV ads) to get your way, this is unethical as it distracts people from the messaging and robs them of the chance to think critically. As such, the best way to handle opposition is to allow your recipient to ask questions so you can clarify what they have missed and double down on your persuasion.

Key Chapter Takeaways

✓ Communication is the art of exchanging information. People do this when making requests, protesting against something, connecting socially, or sharing ideas and opinions.

✓ Obstacles in communication, including physical, perceptual, emotional, and cultural barriers, can result in misunderstandings. It's critical to recognize and remove these barriers.

✓ To be an effective communicator, you must use clear messaging, avoid jargon or slang, be coherent, maintain respect, address communication barriers, and actively listen to others.

✓ Conflicts can occur even during effective communication. You can resolve them by addressing the other person, noting areas where you agree, and finding solutions to differing opinions.

✓ Persuasive communication enables you to win people over to your side. You can achieve this by establishing your credibility and using non-verbal cues to be likable. You must also tweak the messaging to reflect the audience's reasoning, age, and mood.

Chapter 11:
Critical Thinking In The Digital Age

"In this age of information abundance and overload, those who get ahead will be the folks who figure out what to leave out, so they can concentrate on what they need to know."

- AUSTIN KLEON.

We live in a world where information is available at the tap of a button. But should you believe everything you see or read? Well, just because there is smoke does not mean there is a fire. Consider this: *In 2018, a teenager in Florida, Emma Gonzalez, survived a shooting in which 17 of her schoolmates died, and she started campaigning for gun control. Soon afterward, images of her tearing up a copy of the US Constitution surfaced online, prompting people to question her patriotism. But it turns out that these images were nothing short of photo manipulation geared at distracting people from Emma's campaigns and painting her in a bad light.* Imagine that!

Emma's story is not an outlier. Since anyone can spread information online (whether true, half-baked, or otherwise), it's becoming increasingly difficult to spot fake news, which challenges critical thinkers to stop, assess the source, verify the information, and determine if what's before their eyes is as obvious as it seems.

This chapter explores why fake news has become so common and how you can consume information without jumping on the bandwagon and instead embrace an ethical approach.

Section 1: Understanding Information Overload

The school phoned me today and said, "Your son's been telling lies."

I replied, "Well, tell him he's really good - I haven't got any kids!"

When I was a child, my father often told me that lies traveled so fast that the truth barely had time to put on its shoes before lies became headlines. This cannot be truer on social media, where people often get one side of a story, prompting them to think they have the facts when they barely know what's happening. *Think of the COVID misinformation era. Or see a photo of something and believe it to be an accurate picture when it's really AI.*

This bias is not by chance. Social media platforms rely on engagement to remain sustainable. After all, the more time people spend on social media, the more ads that social media platforms can run and the more revenue they can generate. To keep this ecosystem working, they use algorithms that learn your preferences and determine what you see and when you see it. *Say, for example, that you search for gym shorts on Instagram or Facebook. Soon enough, you notice that your feed changes and starts showing you more workout wear ads and accounts, prompting you to click on those accounts and learn more.*

But the algorithms don't just link you to purchasing decisions. They also influence the kind of news you see by presenting information in a way that tugs at your impulses, sparking moral outrage and compelling you to spend more time on the social media platform, which results in the following concepts:

a. **Echo chambers**: When you continuously search for specific perspectives, algorithms suggest data aligning with the main ideology. *For example, if you love vegan products and follow vegans on social media, you may realize that the information you encounter online revolves around veganism.* On the upside, getting information becomes easy. On the downside, the lack of different perspectives paves the way for misinformation, which can affect how you perceive the world, resulting in biases and logical fallacies that reinforce your current beliefs.

b. **Filter Bubbles:** Algorithms keep track of the accounts you engage with, and they use this information to predict what you may like and present it to you. *For example, if you often look up animal rights associations, you will find that your page will increasingly show accounts that relate to this topic.* The more you engage with the content, the more similar accounts you will see until you are finally in a filter bubble. Like with the echo chamber, this allows you to see information specific to your interests. But it also has the downside of isolating you from dissenting opinions. For example, the algorithm may only present one side of a story, leaving you out of the whole picture.

Filter bubble versus echo chamber: *In a filter bubble, the algorithm limits your access to contradicting information. But in an echo chamber, you limit your access by only accessing accounts that match your ideologies.*

Have you (or the algorithm) isolated yourself from the world? Here's how you can tell you're not getting the whole picture.

- *The sources will only have one perspective.*
- *The viewpoints will have incomplete evidence or none at all.*
- *The viewpoints will ignore data that conflicts with them.*

c. **Polarization**: The longer you spend in an echo chamber or filter bubble, the more removed you become from the rest of the world. Take the example of political elections. People in echo chambers and filter bubbles receive updates that reinforce their thinking, e.g., if you support a candidate, you will see news that highlights them in a good way. But if you don't like a candidate, you might not see them on your feed, or the information may paint them in a bad light. You thus develop strong feelings about a candidate based on this and may support or oppose them per your assessment. But that's not all. This increased exposure to one side of a story results in an "us versus them" mentality, as evidenced by a Shapiro et al. (2022) report. Thanks to this mentality, people view those who don't agree with them as opponents rather than accepting that people can have different views and that complex issues are often nuanced. A good example is the HAES (Health at Every Size) movement, as discussed by Räty et al. (2022). This movement argues that people can be healthy at all sizes. On social media, the lines in the sand are clear, with supporters and opposers going at each other based on their echo chambers and filter bubbles. Of course, there is a middle ground for people who consider both viewpoints but this population is much smaller compared to the polarized groups that dominate the discussions. Most people find themselves picking a side based on the information they have, reinforcing the moral outrage that exists on social platforms.

Combine echo chambers, filter bubbles, and polarization, and it's easy to see why more people offer half-baked theories and think of them as true. Unfortunately, algorithms follow social media users wherever they go. The minute you go online, these automated systems start learning your behaviors and curating information to suit your preferences, thus locking you out even when you do not intend to see just one side of the equation. So, how can you get the bigger picture? As discussed in the section below, you must use your critical thinking skills to evaluate the credibility and reliability of what you read. Moreover, you must continuously seek varying opinions to get out of your echo chamber or filter bubble and avoid polarization.

Section 2: Adapting Critical Thinking Strategies for the Digital Realm

A man saw an epitaph in a cemetery that read: 'Here lies an honest man and politician.'

"Shame," he cried, "two people in the same grave!"

Fake news spreads so well because it hinges on biases and logical fallacies. For example, an IPSOS (2023) study involving 1,000 British adults showed that only 9% trusted what politicians said. Thus, anyone aware of this bias can release information that paints politicians in a bad light, knowing that some people will accept whatever is in the fine print. Add echo chambers, filter bubbles, and polarization to this mix, and you will have the power to turn people against a politician they already think is bad news.

However, fake news is not always so evident in the digital context, which is why even well-meaning social media users sometimes miss the red flags. Consider these examples:

a. **Disneyland lowers drinking age to 18:** When @mousetrapnews wrote this piece and posted a similar video on TikTok, they did so satirically, as evidenced by Liles (2023). After all, their entire page is about misinforming people about Disney, and this is clear in their site bio. But people, without due diligence, took the story and ran with it, circulating it to millions of viewers. It wasn't until ABC 10 news and Snopes fact-checked it that it became clear the story was a hoax!

b. **85% of people who wear masks get COVID-19**: When Donald Trump stated this during an NBC town hall broadcast, he misquoted a CDC (2020) study. The study had established that wearing masks was not enough and that people had to practice other prevention measures for mask-wearing to be effective. Per the study, 85% of the people who had contracted the virus had reported wearing masks. However, the way Trump posed the statistics skewed this data. To make matters even more complicated, people on the far right of the political spectrum picked up the story, which only aided the spread of this skewed statistic.

These are but a few instances where fake news has spread like wildfire. While these got squashed because of the high public interest, many other stories go unchecked and become normalized in digital spaces, e.g., *when people thought COVID-19 vaccines were a gateway to help the government implant microchips in people.* So, how can you ensure you're not being swayed one way or the other through misinformation? First, you must be skeptical of everything you see, even if a verified social media account has posted it. Only then can you take the steps below:

1. **Understand what constitutes fake news:** Chapter 2 of this book breaks down the different kinds of fake news you will encounter online and in real life. Having these basics helps you categorize news pieces as you come across them.

2. **Check the source:** A story may look compelling, but it's only as credible as its source. Consider the following

   - *Is the source a legitimate site? If you don't know the site, read its "About" section to learn more about its work. You might find that it's a satirical site.*

   - *Is the author trustworthy? Are they cracking jokes, or are they serious about the subject matter? For example, many sites post jokes on April Fools Day, which you might think are facts.*

3. **Consider other sources**: To avoid bias, review whether other credible sources have reported the same news. *Do the facts align? Are there figures to support the data?* International editorial websites usually use exhaustive fact-checking processes to maintain their integrity, and these are often great for comparison.

4. **Review the whole story:** Even if several sources have reported the story, it may still have gaps. Consider the following:

   - *How old is the story?* Reposted stories may not always be relevant. For example, if a blog posts about a theft in your neighborhood from five years ago, that may not reflect the area's safety today.

   - *What does the source claim?*

   - *Are there facts to back the story?*

   - *How credible are the facts?* A good way to fact-check is to use a credible fact-checking website such as BBC Reality Check or Snopes.

   - *What is the aim behind the story?* Sometimes, stories try to elicit emotions, get you to buy something, or push you to embrace or ignore someone. You need to consider the cause behind the story. Does it feel legitimate, or is it clickbait?

5. **Consider your biases:** How you respond to a story comes down to your beliefs, which previous experiences can shape. *For example, if a story reports that a CEO was in the wrong and you have authority bias, you may fail to believe the facts because they do not align with your biases.* Use Chapter 6 and Exercise 6 to uncover your cognitive biases to help you push through beliefs that may skew your decision-making.

By taking these steps (which you can practice using **Exercise 11**), you will be better positioned to assess the stories you encounter and decide if they are worth sharing with other people. To help you with this, consider the next section.

Section 3: Ethical Considerations in the Digital World

Fake news not only hurts the person it paints in a bad light but also adversely affects other people by planting seeds of doubt and discord. But social media platforms don't spread the news—people do! As such, organizations and governments can only do so much to protect people. For example, social media platforms should protect people's data, ensure fairness in online communities by developing reasonable community guidelines, and only obtain people's data with consent. Governments can help by holding social media platforms accountable and requiring them to toe the line. But at the end of the day, these platforms have been created to help people connect, which comes with the risk of discourse and fake news.

As a critical thinker, it's thus important to engage in ethical digital behavior to ensure you're not actively pushing false agendas or harassing other people in the name of dialogue. How can you do this?

1. **Always fact-check stories:** Use the strategies in Section 2 to gauge the validity of any information you see. If you can back it with unbiased data, you can share it. But if you don't have enough data to back it, do not share it.

2. **Respect other people**: Being on different sides of a story does not equal a fight. It's important to recognize that people have different values and biases, especially those who have been polarized. The answer is not to ridicule or fight them over what they say. Instead, it lies in creating an inclusive environment where everyone can share their opinions. Of course, if someone has resorted to harassment or bullying, you can always restrict your interactions with them.

3. **Understand intellectual property rights:** Social media allows people to stitch other people's videos, repost their content, or even repurpose it. While this is all good and fair in the eyes

of social media, you cannot do so without crediting the original creator, as this constitutes intellectual property rights infringements. Ensure you abide by this to avoid legal woes.

4. **Be critical in your discussions:** Digital spaces allow people to hide behind their keyboards and share even the most extreme sides of a story. As a critical thinker, you must be more rational in your approach, as follows:

- *Follow community guidelines in the platforms you use.*

- *Don't share sensitive details on social media, which can undermine your safety.*

- *Engage with others with an open mind and use positive language even when you disagree with someone's point of view.*

- *Consider the impact of what you share and determine if this is a good decision using the strategies discussed in Chapter 9.*

5. **Protect your peace:** Echo chambers might isolate you from the real world, but they can also be positive for social media users. Following accounts that post positive stories is a great way to protect your mental health so that your online experiences can be fruitful and not fuel your anxiety. After all, constant exposure to negative stories has been proven to harm people's mental health.

6. **Take breaks**: Social media can be addictive. The more time you spend on it, the more exposure you get to curated stories that spark your moral outrage. Thus, scheduling social media time and taking frequent breaks is important.

Fake news comes in many forms and can be hard to spot, especially if you live in an echo chamber. Make the habit of questioning information based on the credibility of its source, author, and data, and you will have an easier time being an ethical digital citizen.

Key Chapter Takeaways

✓ As described in Chapter 2 of this book, fake news takes many forms. It spreads misinformation, especially in the digital era, where sharing information has become easy.

✓ Social media algorithms contribute significantly to echo chambers, filter bubbles, and polarization, which expose people to one side of the story and aid in the spread of fake news.

✓ Critical thinkers can avoid getting on the fake news bandwagon by understanding what it entails, addressing their cognitive biases, and learning how to review stories based on their sources, authors, and the credibility of their facts.

✓ Besides reviewing information, critical thinkers should also be ethical digital citizens who respect other social media users, understand intellectual property rights, approach discussions with integrity, and know when to take a break from online discussions.

PART 3:
PRACTICAL EXERCISES FOR CRITICAL THINKING

Practical Exercises For Critical Thinking

Are you ready to practice critical thinking skills? This exercise section has activities that relate to the chapters in this book, allowing you to polish your skills using practical examples you will encounter in real life.

Points to Note

- You can complete most of these exercises in just **under 15 minutes**, making them ideal for daily practice, whether on your way to work or as you unwind from a long day.

- All the exercises tackle **different critical thinking skills** and thus suit different goals. You don't have to do all the exercises and can instead choose the ones that match your needs the most!

Let's start practicing!

EXERCISE 1: Elements in Action
Duration: 45 minutes

This exercise helps you practice the thought processes above by challenging your problem-solving skills. You can use it whenever faced with a challenge.

→ *Identify a real-life problem or challenge you're facing.*

→ *Practice breaking down each problem into smaller components.*

→ *Set a timer for 10 minutes and brainstorm as many potential solutions as possible without censoring or evaluating ideas.*

→ *After the brainstorming session, review the list of solutions and select the most promising ones to explore further.*

→ *Challenge conventional assumptions and consider unconventional solutions.*

→ *Generate at least three alternative approaches to solving the problem.*

You know what comes next - it's time to review credible information and make inferences!

EXERCISE 2: Becoming a Better Skeptic

Here is a 5-minute exercise you can do to improve your ability to identify false claims.

→ *Watch the news and pick out a story that does not add up.*

→ *Pick out the claims you think do not hold water.*

→ *Evaluate the news source - is it trustworthy? Why?*

→ *Are the claims credible? What supports your answer?*

→ *Do you have a bias?*

→ *Does the story hold up after this assessment?*

You can practice this at least once each week to make this a habit.

EXERCISE 3: Daily Reflection and Goal Setting

Duration: 10 minutes daily

This exercise ties in with Chapter 3, which emphasizes the need for SMART goals in developing critical thinking skills. Here is how you do it:

→ *Set aside time each day for reflection on your critical thinking, problem-solving, and decision-making processes.*

→ *Review your accomplishments, challenges, and areas for improvement.*

→ *Set specific, actionable goals for enhancing your cognitive skills and commit to implementing them daily.*

You can even do this on your commute!

EXERCISE 4: Challenge Your Assumptions

Duration: 10 minutes

Think of one assumption you have, e.g., for a safe and reliable car, you should get a Toyota Corolla.

→ *Analyze the assumption by figuring out the supporting reason.*

→ *Question this reason - what makes you think that? What do studies show? Can you find contradicting information?*

→ *Assess the strength of your argument and determine if the assumption is credible or if you need to eliminate it from your thinking.*

You can do this once every week.

EXERCISE 5: Logical Fallacy Detective

Duration: 15 minutes

This exercise helps you learn how to spot flawed reasoning in everyday discussions. It helps you develop your skepticism and critical evaluation skills, as discussed in **Chapter 1**. As such, it can help you be more discerning when consuming information.

Steps

→ *Choose an article, advertisement, or conversation where arguments are presented. Read or listen to the content carefully.*

→ *Analyze the content to identify any logical fallacies present. Use a reference guide or online resources to familiarize yourself with different types of logical fallacies.*

→ *Identify instances where the arguments contain flawed reasoning or logical inconsistencies.*

→ *Focus on recognizing common fallacies such as ad hominem, straw man, or burden of proof.*

→ *Note down the specific fallacies you find and explain why they are fallacious.*

→ *You can even do this in social discussions, noting where people use fallacies in their arguments.*

EXERCISE 6: Cognitive Bias Bingo

Duration: Ongoing (5-10 minutes daily)

Did you know you can have fun while challenging your biases? Here is a fun game you can play.

Steps

→ *Create a bingo card with common cognitive biases, e.g., confirmation bias, pessimism bias, action bias, etc.*

→ *Throughout the day, mark off instances where you recognize these biases in yourself or others.*

→ *Reflect on how these biases impact decision-making and problem-solving.*

Soon enough, you'll be able to identify and challenge biases on the spot.

EXERCISE 7: Practicing the 5 Whys Technique

Duration: 20 minutes

Get to the root cause of a problem and define it using this simple exercise.

Steps

→ *Identify a problem or challenge you're facing and ask yourself "why" it occurred.*

→ *Continue asking "why" for each subsequent answer, probing deeper into the root causes of the issue.*

→ *Use the insights gained from this exercise to develop targeted solutions addressing the underlying issues.*

You can refer to Chapter 7 to determine what to do after you have identified the problem.

EXERCISE 8: The Pareto Analysis

Duration: 10 - 15 minutes.

Scoring your problems helps you identify the ones with the highest priority. Practice doing this to focus your energy on what has the most impact on your life.

Steps

→ *Identify a problem you're facing, e.g., not doing well in school.*

→ *Use the root cause analysis method from Chapter 8 to figure out the causes behind the problem, e.g., lack of access to study materials, limited study time, etc.*

→ *Assess the impact of each problem and assign each with a score based on its significance.*

→ *Do this for all the problems, ranking similar problems in the same group.*

→ *Calculate the total scores in each category to figure out the one that needs the most attention.*

→ *Evaluate the best ways to address the problem using the strategies in Chapters 8 and 10.*

Move through your list, eliminating each problem until you feel the main problem is no longer getting in the way of your life.

EXERCISE 9: Mind Mapping

Duration: 20 minutes

Remember the decision tree from Chapter 9? This technique works the same way by enabling you to organize thoughts and ideas related to a key decision.

Steps

→ *Choose a complex problem or project you're working on.*

→ *Write down the central theme or problem in the center of a blank sheet of paper or a digital mind-mapping tool.*

→ *Brainstorm related ideas and concepts, branching out from the central theme.*

→ *Connect related ideas with lines or arrows to illustrate relationships.*

→ *Continue expanding the mind map with more detailed subtopics and connections.*

Doing this helps you explore different aspects and subtopics, which helps you understand complex information for planning, problem-solving, and decision-making.

EXERCISE 10: Devil's Advocate

Duration: 15 minutes

Being a good communicator requires you to identify weaknesses or blind spots in your own reasoning, which allows you to evaluate arguments from multiple perspectives. Here is how you do this when presenting an argument:

Steps

→ *Choose a decision or position you've taken and articulate it.*

→ *Consider counterarguments and evidence that might contradict your viewpoint.*

→ *Generate arguments against your position, focusing on potential flaws or weaknesses.*

→ *Evaluate the strength of your original position in light of the opposing arguments.*

→ *Challenge your assumptions and consider alternative perspectives.*

This exercise enables you to consider different opinions and is key to developing intellectual humility.

EXERCISE 11: Compare News Sources

Duration: 10 minutes

→ *Select six national news sites. Three should be sites you would read, and three should be sites you usually avoid because they do not match your beliefs.*

→ *Look for a common story on all the sites.*

→ *Review the similarities and differences in how different authors have portrayed the story.*

→ *How different are the approaches? Are the differences significant? What are the authors communicating?*

→ *Fact-check the story using credible sites like Snopes or Politifact.*

Doing this helps you understand how news sources can present the same information differently for varying motivations.

EXERCISE 12: Role Reversal

Duration: 20 minutes

Seeing things from other people's perspectives can be challenging. But to be a critical thinker, you must be able to step out of your echo chamber and consider other people's reasoning. Here is how you do this:

Steps

Choose a situation or conflict involving another person.

> → *Put yourself in the other person's shoes and consider their perspective.*
>
> → *Consider the background, experiences, and priorities that may influence their behavior.*
>
> → *Imagine how you would feel and act if you were in their position.*
>
> → *Reflect on how understanding their perspective can lead to better communication and resolution of the conflict.*

This exercise can help you be more empathetic, allowing easier collaboration and conflict resolution.

EXERCISE 13: Let's Get Critical.

As a bonus, this exercise includes two parts to help you be more analytical when you encounter information online or in print media.

Part 1: Analyzing Product Reviews

Duration: 15 minutes

Steps

> → *Read a few product reviews for a popular item on an e-commerce website.*
>
> → *Evaluate the credibility of the reviews and identify potential biases or conflicts of interest.*
>
> → *Use critical thinking skills to determine whether the product is worth purchasing based on the information provided.*

Part 2: Analyzing Advertising Strategies

Duration: 20 minutes

Steps

→ *Watch a few television commercials or browse advertisements online, e.g., on YouTube.*

→ *Analyze the marketing techniques used and consider their effectiveness.*

→ *Reflect on how advertisers appeal to emotions, logic, and social influence to persuade consumers.*

EXERCISE 14: Analyzing Arguments in Debates or Discussions

Duration: Variable

Are you logical in your reasoning, or are fallacies or biases getting in the way? Here is an easy way to find out!

Steps

→ *Participate in debates or discussions on topics of interest to you.*

→ *Practice critically analyzing arguments presented by yourself and others, focusing on the validity of premises and the strength of reasoning.*

→ *Seek feedback from peers or mentors on your analytical skills and areas for improvement.*

You can also do this with your children to help them get better at analyzing premises.

EXERCISE 15: The Ladder of Inference

Duration: 15-20 minutes (can be done during commuting).

Are you making rational decisions? Review your decision-making to assess whether cognitive biases or logical fallacies have affected your thought processes.

Steps

→ *Reflect on a recent decision or action you took.*

→ *Trace back through the steps of the ladder of inference to identify your thought process.*

→ *Examine how your assumptions, beliefs, and experiences influenced your conclusions.*

ADDITIONAL RESOURCES
FOR YOUR CRITICAL THINKING PRACTICE

I hope you're finding the exercises and insights in this book valuable. To further enrich your learning experience, I've created some exclusive bonuses that complement the content of this book. These resources are designed to provide additional tools and strategies to enhance your critical thinking skills.

1. How to Teach Kids Critical Thinking

   • Discover effective methods to nurture critical thinking in children, complete with a bonus exercise tailored for young minds.

2. Applying Critical Thinking Skills in Everyday Life

   • Learn how to apply critical thinking techniques to everyday situations, improving your problem-solving and decision-making skills.

3. History of Critical Thinking

   • Dive into the fascinating history of critical thinking and learn from the great thinkers of the past. Includes a Socratic questioning exercise.

4. The Resilience Handbook

   • Gain insights from Stoicism and Emotional Intelligence to build resilience and emotional strength.

To access these free bonuses, simply scan the QR code or visit the link provided.

https://personalgrowthpages.com/winston-free-gift

PART 4:
LAST BUT NOT LEAST

Chapter 12:

Eat, Sleep, Think Critical, Repeat

"Most people do not have a problem with you thinking for yourself, as long as your conclusions are the same as or at least compatible with their beliefs."

- MOKOKOMA MOKHONOANA.

Critical thinking can be scary. After all, once you start questioning your beliefs and logical fallacies, the questions never end. *Are you pursuing the right career? Are you parenting your children right? Should you be supporting that politician? Are you playing your part in environmental conservation? Are you part of the problem on social media?* It gets even more complicated once you start looking for answers. The more information you have, the more responsibility you take on, e.g., *if you know you have biases and work in HR, you will need to take extra measures to ensure you are objective in your hiring and disciplinary actions.* But while these changes, doubts, and responsibilities may feel challenging, it's important to think about the light at the end of the tunnel. Being a critical thinker not only benefits your life but also the lives of people around you, directly and indirectly. Let's consider how you can push through when change feels scary or overwhelming.

Section 1: Embracing a Mindset of Lifelong Learning

"Critical thinking is not something you do once with an issue and then drop it. It requires that we update our knowledge as new information comes in. Time spent evaluating claims is not just time well spent. It should be considered part of an implicit bargain we've all made."

- DANIEL LEVITIN

How great would it be if you could read this book and learn everything about critical thinking by the time you flip the last page? Ah, the dream! However, critical thinking is not theoretical. Instead, it is a practical way of living that you need to embed into your daily life. Here are ways you can practice this new mindset:

1. **Practice curiosity, exploration, and intellectual humility:** *Aristotle believed that moving objects would gradually stop because this was their nature. It wasn't until Galileo and Newton looked into this theory that they brought up the impact of gravity, which slowed object movement, eventually halting the movement!* Imagine if people had accepted Aristotle's theory and stuck with it. Who knows where scientific developments would be today? Critical thinking is a process of unlearning and learning. What you know today could change instantly, and you must keep revisiting your beliefs and assessing them in light of new and credible data. Chapters 1 and 9 have more on curiosity and analytical thinking.

2. **Remain open-minded:** To learn, you must be open to new information. *For example, many marketers have been leveraging social media to increase engagement. But those who have ignored these current trends and insisted on previous marketing approaches have missed out on growing their engagement and, thus their brands.* Such mistakes are common as it is human to use shortcuts, as discussed in Chapter 6. Here are ways you can get ahead of biases and logical fallacies:

   - **Stay informed:** *What you know now will not be the standard tomorrow. For example, Pluto was once the ninth planet in our solar system before it became reclassified as a dwarf planet. Don't get caught up in establishing beliefs so much that you ignore hard facts as they arise.*

   - **Consider other perspectives:** *Feeling strongly about certain subjects is human nature. Take the issue of political elections as an example - these are often emotionally charged. But no matter your vested interests, listening to other opinions is important. You can get these from different sources, as discussed in Chapter 8, enabling you to get the bigger picture.*

   - **Challenge your assumptions:** *Are you reasoning based on your cognitive biases? Are you relying on logical fallacies to support your arguments? Make a habit of taking a step back when* *formulating opinions—this helps you challenge your position by addressing loopholes in your thinking. For example, you may find that you are only voting for your friend as head of the HOA because she will agree to your suggestions even if she is not the best person for the job.*

3. **Be critical:** Open-mindedness comes with the caveat of getting sucked into echo chambers and filter bubbles. You must thus keep analyzing the information you get and gauging its credibility, as discussed in Chapter 11. **Exercise 12**, which builds on Chapter 8, includes exercises you can use to keep your analytical skills sharp.

Continuous learning enables you to be more rational in your actions, which makes you a better friend, partner, neighbor, colleague, employee, boss, and citizen. Critical thinkers are often more successful in their personal and professional lives thanks to their ability to look at situations from all sides of the coin. E.g., they are better friends because they can empathize and avoid making assumptions without communicating with their friends.

Section 2: Cultivating Habits of Critical Inquiry

"Responsibility to yourself means refusing to let others do your thinking, talking, and naming for you; it means learning to respect and use your own brains and instincts; hence, grappling with hard work."

- ADRIENNE RICH.

Critical thinking is not only for more than just big decisions involving complex issues like climate change. Instead, it is a way of thinking that helps you get better results from your daily routine. So, how can you make it part of your life?

1. **Embrace mindfulness:** Awareness of your thought patterns is essential in critical thinking. You can achieve this in two ways:

   - *Pay attention to your surroundings: Are you listening to people when they talk to you? Do you take note of people's non-verbal cues? Are you missing details because you're too focused on what's next rather than the present? By slowing down and being in the now, you can be more mindful of how you approach decisions. For instance, deep breathing can help you calm down during a heated argument so you can listen to what others are saying without getting defensive.*

   - *Take note of your thoughts: Journaling is a great way to explore your thoughts and feelings. For example, if you have argued with a friend, you can write your thoughts about it. Doing this helps you explore the part you may have played and the best way to seek a resolution.*

- *Find healthy outlets: What can you do when you feel angry? How about devastation? These feelings are natural and will not disappear because you are a critical thinker. The best way to handle them is to figure out how to deal with them as they present. Examples of healthy outlets include taking a walk, doing light yoga, talking to someone you trust, and eating a meal you enjoy. Therapy is also a great way to deal with limiting beliefs that feed your cognitive biases and logical fallacies, as these can stall your critical thinking journey.*

2. **Set critical thinking goals:** Conduct a SWOT analysis (see this in Chapter 8) and review your critical thinking skills. Use this knowledge to set goals. E.g., if you need more practice with decision-making, prioritize this. By tackling one element of thought at a time, you can learn how they interact to help you be more critical in your thinking.

3. **Manage your time effectively:** How much time do you spend scrolling social media or sitting in traffic? While you don't always have to be productive, you can use these windows to enhance your critical thinking. For example, you can assess your day - *what could you have done differently? In what instances did your emotions take the lead?* The exercises in part 3, which are easy to follow, enable you to sharpen your skills whenever you have free time. By productively using these openings, you will find that you have less time to get sucked into unproductive conversations, e.g., *rumors about new colleagues.*

4. **Be selective in what you consume:** While being open to new perspectives is important, it's also advisable to determine the things that deserve your time. This selection ranges from the people you hang out with, the books you read, the social media accounts you follow, and the mentors you have. For example, if a news site is known for unbiased political coverage, you can use it as your baseline for evaluating news stories. It will be much easier to check the stories using reputable sites for credibility. It will reduce your chances of being in an echo chamber or filter bubble. Do the same for social media and all other places where you often seek knowledge and eliminate sources that diminish critical thinking.

So, what does this look like in real life? Let's use an example of a common problem we all face - road rage in traffic. A critical thinker will understand that others are not to blame for the traffic and will not be honking and yelling at other drivers. They will know not to take things personally if another driver cuts them off or acts rudely. While it might annoy them, the critical thinker will maintain their calm, e.g., by deep breathing. If the critical thinker responds negatively to the situation, they will reflect on their behavior (e.g., through journaling) and try to figure out why they did that. In doing this, they might realize they were taking out their work frustrations on strangers on the road. They will find healthy ways to deal with these frustrations to be better road users in the future. See? It's not about perfection - it's about unlearning conditioned actions and thought patterns and replacing them with rational approaches. **Exercise 15** explores the ladder of inference, which helps you understand your thought processes and challenge them based on the beliefs and assumptions that informed them.

Section 3: Building a Community of Critical Thinkers

"Change will not come if we wait for some other person or some other time. We are the ones we've been waiting for. We are the change that we seek."

- President Barack Obama

Being a critical thinker can be isolating. Take the example of social settings. You might feel alienated if many people jump on a trend you do not find rational. So, what should you do? Should you bite the bullet and reject critical thinking to be part of the group? Should you lead a solitary life and oppose people who do not think rationally? Well, there is a balance that you will love - you can pass on your skills to others and help them embrace critical thinking. Let's discuss how you can have your cake and eat it:

1. **Nurture critical thinking in others:** Many people are unaware of their cognitive biases and logical fallacies and often rely on them when making decisions. You can help them unlearn these ways of thinking by imparting critical thinking skills to them. *For example, your friend who wants to join a gym may think that all fitness trainers require clients to work out five days a week. On further inquiry, you may realize he has **an anchoring bias** based on the first trainer he met who had such requirements. You can then point out the value of reviewing different training plans before he decides what to do.*

   Here are some pointers to help you navigate cognitive biases and logical fallacies in other people.

   - *Ask open-ended questions regarding someone's thinking or decisions.*
   - *Use the Devil's Advocate exercise in **Exercise 10** to see things from a different point of view.*
   - *Highlight strengths and weaknesses in someone's argument and communicate them using **effective communication techniques,** as explained in Chapter 10.*

2. **Foster constructive dialogue:** Nobody knows everything. Even as you become a critical thinker, there will still be gaps left in your reasoning. These can result from insufficient information

or biases. An excellent way to get ahead of these barriers to sound reasoning is to employ the strategies below:

- *Be open to other people's perspectives.*

- *Take the time to actively listen to what other people say.*

- *Be respectful in debates even if things do not work out your way.*

- *Share valuable information in conversations and back it with credible sources.*

For example, you and your friends might be part of a trivia. Everyone insists there are nine planets in the solar system, but you know there are eight. Rather than go with groupthink, you can listen to their arguments and present your opinion, allowing everyone to consider different perspectives. In some cases, you will learn new things; in others, you will teach people something. Nobody has all the answers - work with others to find solutions. A good way to do this is by engaging in debates, as highlighted in **Exercise 14**.

Critical thinking skills are essential when interacting with others, be it at work, home, or other settings. By modeling them, you can promote the importance of analytical approaches in social, economic, political, environmental, technological, and legal issues. For example, during community workshops, you can be the voice of reason by pointing out that all voices matter and everyone should have a chance to air their opinion. Only by working together with other people can we highlight how critical thinking can be part of a thriving society. To sum this up, I leave you with this quote:

"Never doubt that a small group of thoughtful, committed citizens can change the world: indeed, it's the only thing that ever has."

- MARGARET MEAD.

Key Chapter Takeaways

✓ Critical thinking comes with challenges, including self-doubt, huge life changes, and more responsibilities. On the bright side, it paves the way for personal growth, career development, and healthier relationships. Moreover, it is a catalyst for positive political, economic, environmental, legal, social, and technological changes.

✓ To navigate these challenges and embrace the opportunities, critical thinkers must be ready to embark on a journey of lifelong learning. In this path, they must remain curious, explore different ideas, practice intellectual humility, and remain critical.

✓ Since critical thinking is not something you do once and is a part of your life, practicing mindfulness, getting serious with your goals, using your time productively, and assessing where you spend your energy and time is essential.

✓ It's also important for critical thinkers to integrate themselves into the community, where they can set the ball rolling for positive changes. To do this, you must be open to nurturing critical thinking skills in others and fostering constructive dialogue in community settings. These actions will have a positive ripple effect, resulting in more people being curious about how they, too, can approach issues without biases.

Conclusion

An engineer, a scientist, a mathematician, and a philosopher are on a hike when they come across one black sheep in a field. The engineer says, "What do you know, it looks like the sheep around here are black!" The scientist looks at him skeptically and replies, "Well, at least some of them are." The mathematician considers this momentarily and replies, "Well, at least one of them is." Then the philosopher turns to them and says, "Well, at least on one side!"

Our lives are full of nuances, and things are not always as obvious as they seem. Take the examples of animal testing, artificial intelligence, dairy consumption, political agendas, social media, zoos, and other global debates that attract different viewpoints. Can one honestly say that there is one way to address these concerns? While most of these debates feature polarization, the opposing groups often have data to back their claims, which makes it hard to decide on the best approach.

Away from the worldwide scene, we encounter nuances in our daily lives, ranging from dealing with noisy neighbors, pursuing promotions, handling arguments in our relationships, or whether we should try social media trends. Many people approach these issues with cognitive biases and fallacies. *For example, if everyone in your family thinks that Andy is a bad person, you might find it much easier to accept this thinking rather than explore the reasons behind it.* The same is the case in global debates where people often side with the majority or the side their loved ones pick. But why do they do this?

The Flaws In Our Thinking

One core reason behind irrational decisions is conditioning - from the time we are young, we are taught how to fit into society. For many schools of thought, this requires children to strive to be part of the community by following the social norms - *go to school, get a degree, get married, have children, go on a few vacations, and retire happily.* People who question this thinking often end up shunned and are frequently categorized as black sheep. For fear of standing out, many people avoid the path less traveled and trudge along the path set out for them by their parents, teachers, and peers. *I was also on a similar path before I discovered the benefits of breaking away and embracing individuality in my life.*

The other reason people are unwilling to dig deep is our mental shortcuts. Your brain makes more than 30,000 decisions a day. Over time, it categorizes information to make decision-making easier. *For example, if you once had a bad experience with a PR manager, you might classify all people in this profession as one and treat them all like they have wronged you.* The brain does this to protect you and ease its decision-making processes. However, these biases also result in irrational thinking, making it harder for you to make sound decisions. *For example, someone may have an excellent business idea that aligns with your goals. But you might reject it just because you do not think they are smart enough to have a good idea!*

Is It Time To Get Critical?

While conditioned thinking and mental shortcuts are easy and fun, they come with caveats as they limit our thinking. Take the example of someone with a pessimistic bias - they are unlikely to tap into their potential as they already think their efforts will fall flat on their face. Critical thinking helps you break away from these shortcuts and instead embrace the elements of thought that require you to:

- *Be clear about what you want to achieve, e.g., address a problem at work.*

- *Review other people's perspectives and how these may compare to ours.*

- *Challenge your cognitive biases and logical fallacies.*

- *Ask the tough questions about the topic.*

- *Seek credible sources of information and collect enough data.*

- *Analyze the data using proven concepts.*

- *Consider different approaches to addressing the problem.*

- *Communicate your findings with affected people.*

- *Select and implement the best approach.*

- *Review outcomes and determine the best course of action.*

But why would anyone go through all these steps when they can take the shortcut as many people do? **Critical thinking enables you to make better and evidence-based decisions that enhance the** *quality of your life, help you build better relationships, and propel your career growth.* Take the example of the workplace. Critical thinkers are known for their refined research skills and rational decisions and are thus favored for better positions. So, by taking the long road, you can actually speed up your personal and professional growth!

Embracing The Unknown

Critical thinking requires you to unlearn your current ways of thinking and instead approach new information free of biases and logical fallacies. To do this, you must embrace intellectual humility, open your mind to new perspectives, challenge your beliefs, critique sources of information, and be mindful. The truth is that the journey ahead will be rocky. You will not master critical thinking in a week or a month. Instead, you must continuously work on yourself to impart these critical skills into your daily life. The more you think critically, the more it becomes like second nature, e.g., if your response during an argument is usually to raise your voice, you can embrace healthier emotional outlets and instead use effective communication strategies to reason with people when things go south. Critical thinking also requires you to weigh the situations that deserve your energy - you don't have to convince everyone of the importance of reason. But where an opportunity presents itself, e.g., nurturing critical thinking in your children or fostering curiosity in your friends, go for it! In the end, your efforts will go a long way in changing people's mindsets for the betterment of the community.

The Way Forward

Are you ready for the journey ahead? This book is a practical life guide that you can use to reinforce your critical thinking skills at any point. Whenever you need to refine your skills, read through the chapters and complete the exercises in Part 3. The more you practice, the more you will change your thinking and become more self-aware. So, take the time to reflect on what you have learned so it can become ingrained in your thinking, paving the way for positive changes in your life. There is no hard deadline for this process, and there is no need to rush through it. Like Confucius once said, *"It does not matter how slowly you go as long as you do not stop."*

Thank you!

I want to express my deepest gratitude to you for choosing to read my book. It brings me immense joy and satisfaction to know that my work has reached your hands. I hope it has provided you with valuable insights and knowledge.

As a small independent author, knowing that my words inspire and resonate with readers like you is always gratifying. Your support and enthusiasm for my book mean a lot to me.

I have a small favor to ask you: Would you be willing to help me if it only took less than 1 minute of your time?

If so, fantastic! All I need is for you to leave an honest review on Amazon for this book. Even though it takes less than a minute, your review can make a huge difference.

Your feedback may help another person unlock their critical thinking potential, improve their decision-making skills, or conquer logical fallacies. It could transform someone's approach to problem-solving and positively impact their life. To keep it quick and easy, follow the link below or scan a QR code with your phone's camera and follow the link that pops up to go directly to your Amazon review page:

https://www.amazon.com/review/create-review?&asin=B0D4YVWHPW

If you prefer not to use the links, you can go to your Amazon orders page, find this book, scroll down to the reviews section, and click the "Write a review" option.

Thank you from the bottom of my heart for your time. Your support means the world to me.

References

1. Augustus, M. (2006). *Meditations.* (Hammond, M., Trans.). Penguin Classics. (Original title unknown, probably untitled, written between 170-180 AD).

2. Carus, P. (1894). *The gospel of Buddha.* (Self-published)

3. Centers for Disease Control and Prevention. (n.d.). *Physical activity: adults.* https://www.cdc.gov/physicalactivity/basics/adults/index.htm#:~

4. Epictetus. (2008). *Discourses and selected writings* (Dobbin, R., Trans.). Penguin Classics. (Originally work published in the 2nd century).

5. *King James Bible.* (2017). King James Bible Online. https://www.kingjamesbibleonline.org/ (Original work published 1769)

6. Laërtius, D. (2022). *The lives and opinions of eminent philosophers* (Yonge, C. D., Trans.). (Originally work published in the early 3rd century).

7. McRaven, W. H. (2014). *Commencement address for the University of Texas* [video]. YouTube. https://www.youtube.com/watch?v=pxBQLFLei70&ab_channel=TexasExes

8. Roosevelt, T. (1910, April 23). *The man in the arena* [Transcript]. World Future Fund. https://www.worldfuturefund.org/Documents/maninarena.htm

9. Sidgwick, H. (1874). *The methods of ethics.* Self-published.

10. Seneca. (2004). *Letters from a stoic: Epistulae morales ad lucilium* (Campbell, R., Trans.). Penguin Classics. (Originally work published 65 AD).

11. Seneca. (2017). *Medea & Thyestes* (Miller, F., Trans.). LRP. (Originally work published 50 AD and 62 AD, respectively).

12.   Seneca. (2011). *Phaedra* (Smith, R. S., Trans.). Penguin Classics. (Originally work published 54 AD).

13.   Wong, Y. J., Owen, J., Gabana, N. T., Brown, J. W., McInnis, S., Toth, P. & Gilman, L. (2018). Does gratitude writing improve the mental health of psychotherapy clients? Evidence from a randomized controlled trial. *Psychotherapy Research, 28*(2), 192-202.

14.   Ackerman, C. (2019, February 4). *13 emotional intelligence activities, excercises & PDFs*. PositivePsychology. https://positivepsychology.com/emotional-intelligence-exercises/

15.   Ackerman, C. E. (2018, November 4). *What is emotional intelligence? +23 ways to improve it*. PositivePsychology. https://positivepsychology.com/emotional-intelligence-eq/

16.   Allo Health. (2023, June 7). *7 relationship exercises to strengthen your bond*. AlloHealth. https://www.allohealth.care/healthfeed/sex-education/relationship-exercises

17.   Anthony, S. (n.d.). *Why is emotional intelligence important?* Skills You Need. https://www.skillsyouneed.com/rhubarb/emotional-intelligence-important.html

18.   Wann, Benjamin. (2023, July 12). *Empathy and compassion: 40 leadership quotes on the power of emotional intelligence*. Benjamin Wann. https://benjaminwann.com/blog/empathy-and-compassion-40-leadership-quotes-on-the-power-of-emotional-intelligenc

19.   Bettino, K. (2021, June 21). *Tips to soothe your worries of what others think of you*. Psych Central. https://psychcentral.com/blog/mental-shifts-to-stop-caring-what-people-think-of-you

20.   Bisignano, A. (2018, June 1). *Making love last: The importance of emotional intelligence*. GoodTherapy. https://www.goodtherapy.org/blog/making-love-last-importance-of-emotional-intelligence-0601184

21.   Britton, G. (2023, February 21). *12 communication-based team building activities to improve relationships*. Poppulo. https://www.poppulo.com/blog/12-communication-based-team-building-activities-to-improve-relationships

22.   Cassata, C. (2021, September 27). *The benefits of emotional intelligence (EQ) at work*. Psychcentral. https://psychcentral.com/blog/the-benefits-of-emotional-intelligence

23.   Cherry, K. (2022, December 7). *IQ vs. EQ: Which one is more important?* Verywell Mind. https://www.verywellmind.com/iq-or-eq-which-one-is-more-important-2795287

24.   Cherry, K. (2023, May 2). *Emotional intelligence: How we perceive, evaluate, express, and control emotions*. Verywell Mind. https://www.verywellmind.com/what-is-emotional-intelligence-2795423

25.   Connolly, S. (2013, March 4). *5 habits of emotionally intelligent families*. MentalHelp.net. https://www.mentalhelp.net/blogs/5-habits-of-emotionally-intelligent-families/

26.   Continu Team. (2022, April 14). *15 powerful benefits of emotional intelligence training*. Continu. https://www.continu.com/blog/15-benefits-of-emotional-intelligence-training

27. Drigas, A., & Papoutsi, C. (2018). A new layered model on emotional intelligence. *Behavioral Sciences, 8*(5), 45. NCBI. https://doi.org/10.3390/bs8050045

28. Goleman, D., & Boyatzis, R. (2017, February 6). *Emotional intelligence has 12 elements. Which do you need to work on?* Harvard Business Review. https://hbr.org/2017/02/emotional-intelligence-has-12-elements-which-do-you-need-to-work-on

29. Harvard Professional Development. (2019, August 26). *How to improve your emotional intelligence.* Harvard DCE. https://professional.dce.harvard.edu/blog/how-to-improve-your-emotional-intelligence/

30. Houston, E. (2019, February 6). *The importance of emotional intelligence (Incl. quotes).* PositivePsychology. https://positivepsychology.com/importance-of-emotional-intelligence/

31. Iacono, V. L. (2022, June 16). *10 emotional intelligence training activities.* Linkedin. https://www.linkedin.com/pulse/10-emotional-intelligence-training-activities-dr-valeria-lo-iacono/

32. Emeritus. (2023, May 22). *Why emotional intelligence is important in leadership.* Emeritus. https://emeritus.org/in/learn/why-emotional-intelligence-is-important-in-leadership/

33. Kazemitabar, M., Lajoie, S. P., & Doleck, T. (2022). A process model of team emotion regulation: An expansion of gross' individual ER model. *Learning, Culture and Social Interaction, 33,* 100612. https://doi.org/10.1016/j.lcsi.2022.100612

34. Knight, R. (2019, April 29). *How to manage your perfectionism.* Harvard Business Review. https://hbr.org/2019/04/how-to-manage-your-perfectionism

35. Landry, L. (2019, April 3). *Why emotional intelligence is important in leadership.* Harvard Business School Online. https://online.hbs.edu/blog/post/emotional-intelligence-in-leadership

36. Lebow, H. I. (2021, June 7). *What is emotional intelligence (EQ)?* Psych Central. https://psychcentral.com/lib/what-is-emotional-intelligence-eq

37. Lynn, S. (2020, November 8). *How to teach emotional intelligence to children: 30 powerful activites.* Bettering Youth. https://betteringyouth.co.uk/blog/emotional-literacy-30-activities

38. Miller, K. (2020, March 13). *How to increase self-awareness: 16 activities & tools (+PDF).* PositivePsychology. https://positivepsychology.com/building-self-awareness-activities/

39. Moore, C. (2019, June 2). *How to practice self-compassion: 8 techniques and tips.* Positive Psychology. https://positive-psychology.com/how-to-practice-self-compassion/

40. Nash, J. (2018, January 5). *How to set healthy boundaries and build positive relationships.* PositivePsychology. https://positivepsychology.com/great-self-care-setting-healthy-boundaries/

41. OU Online. (2020, October 15). *Why emotional intelligence is important in the workplace.* Ottawa. https://www.ottawa.edu/online-and-evening/blog/october-2020/the-importance-of-emotional-intelligence-in-the-wo

42.   Ox and Barn. (2023, April 2). *The role of emotional intelligence in healthy family relationships.* Ox & Barn. https://oxandbarn.com/blogs/news/the-role-of-emotional-intelligence-in-healthy-family-relationships

43.   Pattemore, C. (2021, June 3). *10 ways to build and preserve better boundaries.* Psych Central. https://psychcentral.com/lib/10-way-to-build-and-preserve-better-boundaries

44.   Paul H. Brookes Publishing. (2021, December 7). *8 activities to boost students' emotional intelligence.* Brookes Blog. https://blog.brookespublishing.com/8-activities-to-boost-students-emotional-intelligence/

45.   Prodigy. (2023, February 15). *25 social emotional learning activities & how they promote student well-being.* Prodigy Game. https://www.prodigygame.com/main-en/blog/social-emotional-learning-activities/

46.   Psychology Today Staff. (2019). *Emotional intelligence.* Psychology Today. https://www.psychologytoday.com/us/basics/emotional-intelligence

47.   Ramanathan, M. (2018, October 15). *Hormones and chemicals linked with our emotion.* Amrita. https://www.amrita.edu/news/hormones-and-chemicals-linked-with-our-emotion/

48.   Riopel, L. (2019, September 14). *17 self-awareness activities and exercises (+ test).* Positive Psychology. https://positive-psychology.com/self-awareness-exercises-activities-test/

49.   Robertson, C. (2022, May 25). *25 emotional intelligence activities for happy and productive teams.* SessionLab. https://www.sessionlab.com/blog/emotional-intelligence-activities/

50.   Sander, V. (2022, May 20). *How to not care what people think (with clear examples).* SocialSelf. https://socialself.com/blog/stop-caring-what-others-think/

51.   Saunders, E. G. (2022, February 22). *To reach your goals, embrace self-compassion.* Harvard Business Review. https://hbr.org/2022/02/to-reach-your-goals-embrace-self-compassion

52.   Segal, J., Smith, M., Robinson, L., & Shubin, J. (2023, February 28). *Improving emotional intelligence (EQ).* Help-Guide. https://www.helpguide.org/articles/mental-health/emotional-intelligence-eq.htm

53.   Smith, J. T. (2019, March 19). *Emotional intelligence in relationships (+ activities for couples).* PositivePsychology. https://positivepsychology.com/emotional-intelligence-relationships/

54.   Symonds, P. (2020, November 5). *8 steps for improving social awareness classroom training activity.* Symonds Research Training Course Materials. https://symondsresearch.com/social-awareness/

55.   Taylor, M. (2019, January 6). *Emotional intelligence activities for kids.* Imagination Soup. https://imaginationsoup.net/emotional-intelligence-activities-kids/

56.   Very Special Tales. (2023, January 30). *28 fun emotional intelligence activities for kids.* Very Special Tales. https://veryspecialtales.com/emotional-intelligence-activities-for-kids/

57. Waterford. (2018, December 18). *15 activities for teaching CASEL core competencies*. Waterford.org. https://www.waterford.org/education/15-activities-for-teaching-casel-core-competencies/

58. Whitener, S. (2022, December 30). *Council post: Why is emotional intelligence important?* Forbes. https://www.forbes.com/sites/forbescoachescouncil/2022/12/30/why-is-emotional-intelligence-important/?sh=7c0ef2163289   Quantifying gender biases to accelerate equality for women and girls. World Bank Blogs. (2023). https://blogs.worldbank.org/opendata/quantifying-gender-biases-accelerate-equality-women-and-girls

59. American Psychological Association. (2022). By the numbers: Older adults report high levels of ageism. https://www.apa.org/monitor/2022/09/older-adults-ageism

60. Associates, H. (2013). *IT TAKES MORE THAN A MAJOR: Employer Priorities for College Learning and Student Success*. https://dgmg81phhvh63.cloudfront.net/content/user-photos/Research/PDFs/2013_EmployerSurvey.pdf

61. Henley, J. (2020, January 29). How Finland starts its fight against fake news in primary schools. *The Guardian*. https://www.theguardian.com/world/2020/jan/28/fact-from-fiction-finlands-new-lessons-in-combating-fake-news

62. University of Louisville. (2010). *Paul-Elder Critical Thinking Framework — University of Louisville Ideas To Action*. Louisville.edu. https://louisville.edu/ideastoaction/about/criticalthinking/framework

63. Miller, W. E., & J Merrill Shanks. (1997). *WQ VOL21 W 1997 Research*. http://archive.wilsonquarterly.com/sites/default/files/articles/WQ_VOL21_W_1997_Research.pdf

64. Uteuova, A. (2024, February 14). Nearly 15% of Americans don't believe climate change is real, study finds. *The Guardian*. https://www.theguardian.com/us-news/2024/feb/14/americans-believe-climate-change-study

65. Guttman, J. (2019, June 27). *The Relationship With Yourself | Psychology Today*. https://www.psychologytoday.com/us/blog/sustainable-life-satisfaction/201906/the-relationship-yourself

66. Paul, R. (2019). *The State of Critical Thinking Today*. Criticalthinking.org. https://www.criticalthinking.org/pages/the-state-of-critical-thinking-today/523

67. Sharma, A. (2023, October 24). *Importance Of Critical Thinking In The Workplace* [Review of *Importance Of Critical Thinking In The Workplace*]. Adaface. https://www.adaface.com/blog/importance-of-critical-thinking-in-workplace/

68. Nauert, R. (2017, February 15). *Herd Mentality Explained*. Psych Central. https://psychcentral.com/news/2017/02/15/herd-mentality-explained#1

69. Prychitko, D. *Marxism*. Econlib. https://www.econlib.org/library/Enc/Marxism.html

70. Baker-Smith, D. (2014). *Thomas More (Stanford Encyclopedia of Philosophy)*. Stanford.edu. https://plato.stanford.edu/entries/thomas-more/

71.   Paul, R. W., Elder, L., & Bartell, T. (1997). California Teacher Preparation for Instruction in Critical Thinking: Research Findings and Policy Recommendations.https://eric.ed.gov/?q=California+Teacher+Preparation+for+Instruction+in+Critical+Thinking%3a+Research+Findings+and+Policy+Recommendations&ft=on&id=ED437379

72.   Kriegel, U. *Sketch for a Theory of the History of Philosophy*. Retrieved March 25, 2024, from https://philpapers.org/archive/KRISFA-4.pdf

73.   De Zoysa, Harini. (2015). A Conceptual Analysis and Historical Overview of Philosophy. 'SANTHATHI 2015' Journal of Social Sciences Academic Magazine University of Kelaniya. 7th. 305.

74.   *The State of Critical Thinking in 2020 | REBOOT FOUNDATION*. (2020, October 27). Reboot-Foundation.org. https://reboot-foundation.org/the-state-of-critical-thinking-2020/#:~:text=Among%20teachers%2C%2041%20percent%20think

75.   *Road Rage Statistics 2023 | ConsumerAffairs®*. (2023, October 6). https://www.consumeraffairs.com/automotive/road-rage-statistics.html

76.   Yuan, R., & Liao, W. (2023). Critical thinking in teacher education: where do we stand and where can we go? *Teachers and Teaching: Theory and Practice*, *29*(6), 543–552. https://doi.org/10.1080/13540602.2023.2252688

77.   Wang, Y., Nakamura, T., & Sanefuji, W. (2020). The influence of parental rearing styles on university students' critical thinking dispositions: The mediating role of self-esteem. *Thinking Skills and Creativity*, *37*, 100679. https://doi.org/10.1016/j.tsc.2020.100679

78.   Huang, L., Wang, Z., Yao, Y., Shan, C., Wang, H., Zhu, M., Lu, Y., Sun, P., & Zhao, X. (2015). Exploring the association between parental rearing styles and medical students' critical thinking disposition in China. *BMC Medical Education*, *15*. https://doi.org/10.1186/s12909-015-0367-5

79.   Mcleod, S. (2023, November 14). *Stanley Milgram Shock Experiment: Summary, Results, & Ethics*. Simply Psychology; Simply Psychology. https://www.simplypsychology.org/milgram.html

80.   Ericsson, K. A., Prietula, M. J., & Cokely, E. T. (2014, August 1). *The making of an expert*. Harvard Business Review. https://hbr.org/2007/07/the-making-of-an-expert

81.   Allen, A. (2014, October 22). *Chess Grandmastery: Nature, Gender, and the Genius of Judit Polgár*. JSTOR Daily. https://daily.jstor.org/chess-grandmastery-nature-gender-genius-judit-polgar/

82.   Cavaliere, G., & Fletcher, J. R. (2021). Age-discriminated IVF access and evidence-based ageism: Is there a better way? *Science, Technology, & Human Values*, *47*(5), 986–1010. https://doi.org/10.1177/01622439211021914

83.   Kim, J. Y. (2020). Optimal Diet Strategies for Weight Loss and Weight Loss Maintenance. *Journal of Obesity & Metabolic Syndrome*, *30*(1), 20–31. https://doi.org/10.7570/jomes20065

84. Murata, Atsuo & Yoshimura, Haruka. (2015). Statistics of a Variety of Cognitive Biases in Decision Making in Crucial Accident Analyses. Procedia Manufacturing. 3. 3898-3905. 10.1016/j.promfg.2015.07.907.

85. Berthet, V. (2022). The Impact of Cognitive Biases on Professionals' Decision-Making: A Review of Four Occupational Areas. *Frontiers in Psychology, 12*(802439). https://doi.org/10.3389/fpsyg.2021.802439

86. Friedman, Hershey. (2023). Cognitive Biases and Their Influence on Critical Thinking and Scientific Reasoning: A Practical Guide for Students and Teachers. SSRN Electronic Journal. 10.2139/ssrn.2958800.

87. Reill, A. (2023, December 5). *A Simple Way to Make Better Decisions*. Harvard Business Review. https://hbr.org/2023/12/a-simple-way-to-make-better-decisions#:~:text=Why%20You%20Should%20Make%20Journaling

88. Snowden, D., & Boone, M. (2007, November). *A Leader's Framework for Decision Making*. Harvard Business Review. https://hbr.org/2007/11/a-leaders-framework-for-decision-making

89. *Chapter 3. Assessing Community Needs and Resources | Section 14. SWOT Analysis: Strengths, Weaknesses, Opportunities, and Threats | Main Section | Community Tool Box*. (n.d.). https://ctb.ku.edu/en/table-of-contents/assessment/assessing-community-needs-and-resources/swot-analysis/main

90. Milosavljevic, M., Koch, C., & Rangel, A. (2023, January 1). *Consumers can make decisions in as little as a third of a second: Judgment and decision making*. Cambridge Core. https://www.cambridge.org/core/journals/judgment-and-decision-making/article/consumers-can-make-decisions-in-as-little-as-a-third-of-a-second/9711447249D813E954260FDCA39E3C70

91. Grabmeier, J. (2022, February 4). People are fast and accurate when making high-value decisions. https://news.osu.edu/people-are-fast-and-accurate-when-making-high-value-decisions/

92. Räty, S., Chen, B., & Kavuluru, R. (2022). Tracking sentiments toward fat acceptance over a decade on Twitter. *Health Informatics Journal, 28*(1), 146045822110657. https://doi.org/10.1177/14604582211065702

93. Xie, J., & Liu, L. (2022b, April 22). *Identifying features of source and message that influence the retweeting of health information on social media during the COVID-19 pandemic - BMC public health*. BioMed Central. https://bmcpublichealth.biomedcentral.com/articles/10.1186/s12889-022-13213-w#Sec18

94. Kumkale, G. T., Albarracín, D., & Seignourel, P. J. (2010). The Effects of Source Credibility in the Presence or Absence of Prior Attitudes: Implications for the Design of Persuasive Communication Campaigns. *Journal of Applied Social Psychology, 40*(6), 1325. https://doi.org/10.1111/j.1559-1816.2010.00620.x

95. Wallace, L. E., Simon, K. A., & Wegener, D. T. (2020, October 1). *Lay concepts of source likeability, trustworthiness, expertise, and power: A prototype analysis - behavior research methods*. SpringerLink. https://link.springer.com/article/10.3758/s13428-020-01478-1#Sec10

96. Forgas, Joseph. (1999). Feeling and Speaking: Mood Effects on Verbal Communication Strategies. Personality and Social Psychology Bulletin. 25. 850-863. 10.1177/0146167299025007007.

97. IPSOS. (2023, December 14). *Trust in politicians reaches its lowest score in 40 years.* https://www.ipsos.com/en-uk/ipsos-trust-in-professions-veracity-index-2023

98. Shapiro, A., Levitt, M., & Intagliata, C. (2022, September 9). *How the polarizing effect of social media is speeding up.* NPR. https://www.npr.org/2022/09/09/1121295499/facebook-twitter-youtube-instagram-tiktok-social-media

99. Liles, J. (2023, May 23). *Is Disney World lowering the drinking age to 18?.* Snopes. https://www.snopes.com/fact-check/disney-world-drinking-age/

100. Centers for Disease Control and Prevention. (2020). *Community and close contact exposures associated with covid-19 among symptomatic adults ≥18 years in 11 outpatient health care facilities - United States, July 2020.* Centers for Disease Control and Prevention. https://www.cdc.gov/mmwr/volumes/69/wr/mm6936a5.htm#contribAff

101. Aghdaei, Roxana & Tabrizi, Aryan. (2021). A Review Study of How and Why People Are Different. Journal of Social Sciences and Humanities. 9. 1-11.

102. DeTurk, C. (2022, May 16). *Critical thinking is an essential workplace skill, research shows.* Dale Carnegie Franchise. https://dalecarnegiefranchise.com/blog/critical-thinking-is-an-essential-workplace-skill-research-shows/

103. Jusienė, R., Urbonas, V., Laurinaitytė, I., Rakickienė, L., Breidokienė, R., Kuzminskaitė, M., & Praninskienė, R. (2019). Screen Use During Meals Among Young Children: Exploration of Associated Variables. *Medicina*, *55*(10). https://doi.org/10.3390/medicina55100688

104. Deringöl, Y. (2019, July 7). *THE RELATIONSHIP BETWEEN REFLECTIVE THINKING SKILLS AND ACADEMIC SUCCESS IN MATHEMATICS IN FOURTH-GRADE PRIMARY SCHOOL STUDENTS.* https://iojet.org/index.php/IOJET/article/view/532

105. Fwu, B. J., Chen, S. W., Wei, C. F., & Wang, H. H. (2018, December 1). *I believe; therefore, I work harder: The significance of reflective thinking on effort-making in academic failure in a Confucian-heritage cultural context.* Thinking Skills and Creativity. https://doi.org/10.1016/j.tsc.2018.01.004

Made in the USA
Columbia, SC
28 December 2024